SOLDIERS, REBELS, AND DRIFTERS

SOLDIERS, REBELS, AND DRIFTERS
Gay Representation in Israeli Cinema

Nir Cohen

Wayne State University Press Detroit

© 2012 by Wayne State University Press, Detroit, Michigan 48201. All rights reserved. No part of this book may be reproduced without formal permission. Manufactured in the United States of America.

16 15 14 13 12   5 4 3 2 1

Library of Congress Cataloging-in-Publication Data

Cohen, Nir, 1976–
Soldiers, rebels, and drifters : gay representation in Israeli cinema / Nir Cohen.
     p. cm.
Includes bibliographical references and index.
ISBN 978-0-8143-3478-2 (pbk. : alk. paper)
1. Homosexuality in motion pictures. 2. Gays in motion pictures. 3. Motion pictures—Israel. I. Title.
PN1995.9.H55C63 2011
791.43086'64—dc22

2011016089

Typeset by Alpha Design & Composition
Composed in Warnock Pro and Meta

In memory of my grandparents, Zipora and Haim Dov Cohen
and Kalman and Rachel Even-Tov

Contents

	Acknowledgments	ix
	Introduction: Zionism, Homosexuality, and Film	1
1	An Imagined City for an Imagined Community: Tel Aviv and Gay Identity on the Israeli Screen	25
2	Melodrama, Decadence, and Death in Amos Guttman's Cinema	57
3	Gay Men and the Establishment in the Films of Eytan Fox	89
4	Real Lives: New Israeli Nonfiction Gay Cinema	129
5	Recent Developments and Future Directions: Some Concluding Notes	183
	Notes	201
	Filmography	217
	Bibliography	221
	Index	235

Acknowledgments

This book is based on my doctoral dissertation completed in 2006 at University College London. I am deeply grateful to my supervisors, David Forgacs and Tsila Ratner, for their invaluable insight, unconditional support, and stimulating advice. Their intellectual rigor and commitment have been crucial to the development of this project.

I am indebted to my PhD examiners, Paul Julian Smith and Hanna Naveh, whose continuing support has encouraged me to turn my dissertation into a book.

I am also grateful to the following institutions for their financial support: University College London for various scholarships, the Anglo-Jewish Association for the Ian Karten Scholarship, the Arts and Humanities Research Council for the Fieldwork Grant, and Hanadiv Charitable Foundation and the Posen Foundation for my postdoctoral fellowships.

I would like to express my very special gratitude to the following people, who, apart from their friendship, offered much of their time and effort: to Michael Berkowitz for encouraging me to turn my dissertation into a book and giving precious advice; to Ross Forman for continually supporting me in the researching and writing process and for reading drafts and papers; to Nathan Abrams for offering me important advice on how to write an effective book proposal, and for publishing one of my first pieces; to Yosefa Loshitzky for reading early versions of this manuscript and making important comments; to Shimshi Ben-Ron, Inbal Keidar, and Tali Silver for their useful suggestions; to Raz Yosef for sharing his knowledge with me; and to Pedro Castelo, Selina Packard, and Ofer Rog for spending long hours selecting images, editing, proofreading, and making significant comments.

I also thank the people at the Sam Spiegel Film School in Jerusalem and the Tel Aviv Cinémathèque library as well as the following filmmakers for providing me with films, written materials, and images: David Deri,

Elle Flanders, Ayal Goldberg, Tomer Heymann, Yair Hochner, Ran Kotzer, Yair Lev, Nir Ne'eman, Ruthie Shatz, Haim Tabakman, and Sigal Yehuda. I would also like to express my gratitude to all the people at Wayne State University Press, and especially Kathryn Wildfong, for their warm encouragement and extreme care, and for making the work on this book an incredibly rewarding and enjoyable process.

I would like to take this opportunity to thank my friends for sustaining me through the often challenging times of researching and writing: Yason Banal, Daphna Baram, Nimrod Ben-Cnaan, Peter Bergamin, Geoff Brumfiel, Eleanor Chiari, Eyal Cohen, Hagi Cohen, Mark Doran, Limor Flanter, Yael Friedman, Naomi Fry, Roi Giladi, Aeyal Gross, Kim Hoch, Marcus Kleinfeld, Tamar Kutner Shirley, Ori Lahat, Alex Mankowitz Ben-Yehuda, Cristina Massaccesi, Amit Merla, Adi Mester, Amiya Moshovitz, Nikos Panayiotou, Natasha Romanova, Adi Schneider, Michal Shapira, and Itamar Zohar.

Finally, this book is for my parents, Miri and Menachem Cohen; my brother, Shai Cohen; and my partner, Andrew Bevan; for all the love, support, and pride I could ever ask for.

Introduction

Zionism, Homosexuality, and Film

Soldiers, Rebels, and Drifters: Gay Representation in Israeli Cinema studies the role of cinema in portraying gay identities, environments, and lifestyles in Israel over the past three decades, particularly in the wake of a series of legal battles for gay rights in the 1980s and 1990s. Alongside literature, journalism, and popular music, cinema has contributed to the shift of gay men and lesbians from the margins of Israeli society into its mainstream. Despite the canonical status of the written word as the main vehicle for forging the Zionist-Israeli national narrative as well as its subversive derivatives, the emergence of gay consciousness in the mid-1970s relied more on cinematic representations than literary ones. Films have also reached wider overseas audiences and have emphasized gay men and lesbians' role in representing "liberal" Israel to the world.

This book is a work of cultural history that aims to understand self-proclaimed gay cinema in Israel in relation to a particular, and distinctively Israeli, ideological trajectory—Zionism/Muscle Jew/ruralism/militarism—to be reconstructed later in this introduction. The book attempts to explore the ways in which cinema, as a primary source of gay cultural production in Israel, has defined gay identity since the late 1970s. As Jeffrey Weeks has argued, following the writings of Michel Foucault and Karl Marx, "Identity is not inborn, pregiven, or 'natural.' It is striven for, contested, negotiated, and achieved, often in struggles of the subordinated against the dominant. Moreover, it is not achieved just by an individual act of will, or discovered hidden in the recesses of the soul. It is put together in circumstances bequeathed by history, in collective experiences as much as by individual destiny" ("Against Nature" 207).

This research also brings together two different objects of study: Israeli society—in particular the gay community, its history, and the incorporation of gay men and lesbians into the Israeli public sphere—and Israeli cinema—film texts in particular but also production and distribution apparatuses. In the latter context the focus is on representations of gay life on the screen along the axes of ethnicity; gender; nation and religion; the reception of the films both in Israel and abroad; and matters of censorship, both self-imposed by writers/directors and external. I am especially interested in the way in which gay concerns have enriched Israeli films both visually and thematically. Of course it could be argued that this influence is mutual, as cinema has also contributed to the promotion of gay causes in Israel and helped shape a movement, but although I believe such a study should be undertaken, it is beyond the scope of this book.

From its very early stages, my project has corresponded to a remarkable revival of Israeli cinema in international markets. The worldwide success of numerous recent films, a few of which are gay films, and the ever-growing interest in the work of young filmmakers on the international film festival circuit (the majority of the films analyzed in chapter 4 have been shown in festivals around the world), prove that Israel can be a source of cultural interest beyond its contentious politics.[1] The expanding discussion of Israeli cinema in general, demonstrated also by a growing number of books on the subject published in the past decade, suggests that the medium might now serve alongside Hebrew literature as a major expressive tool of a torn and polarized society.

My work is indebted to the increasing scholarly interest in Israeli cinema in the past two decades. Ella Shohat's now canonical *Israeli Cinema: East/West and the Politics of Representation* (1989), a revised version of which came out in 2010, marked the beginning of this scholarship. A series of essays and books published in the 1990s and 2000s have widened and elaborated on Shohat's seminal project. These include Judd Ne'eman's "The Empty Tomb in the Postmodern Pyramid: Israeli Cinema in the 1980s and 1990s" (1995), Nurith Gertz, Orly Lubin, and Judd Ne'eman's edited volume *Fictive Looks: On Israeli Cinema* (in Hebrew, 1998), Yosefa Loshitzky's *Identity Politics on the Israeli Screen* (2001), Raz Yosef's *Beyond*

Flesh: Queer Masculinities and Nationalism in Israeli Cinema (2004), and Nurith Gertz's *Holocaust Survivors, Aliens and Others in Israeli Cinema and Literature* (in Hebrew, 2004). These works have critically explored the ways in which Israeli cinema has redefined alternatives to the artificially unified Israeli collective identity.

As the first scholar to offer a comprehensive study of Israeli filmmaking and its role in constructing Israeli nationality, Ella Shohat had to map a whole new field of study. Her book was a groundbreaking piece of work, and some of the fundamental arguments in it are treated almost as axiomatic today. For example, the inherent inequality of Mizrahi Jews (or Mizrahim, a term referring to Jews of the Middle East, North Africa, and the Caucasus) in Israeli society and the Zionist movement as an extension of European colonialism are well-rehearsed concepts. However, the array of voices in contemporary Israeli culture, reflecting a fragmented society, requires further investigation and specification. Shohat's followers have been encouraged to look more closely at specific aspects of Israeli cinema. Of the many books and articles published on Israeli cinema in the past decade, Yosef's *Beyond Flesh* is perhaps the closest to my object of study. At the same time, there are some fundamental differences between my project and Yosef's, namely my focus on gay cinema rather than representations of masculinities in all areas of Israeli society.

Drawing on Yosefa Loshitzky's discussion of racism and sexuality in Israeli culture (*Identity Politics*), Raz Yosef identifies an unexplored aspect of Israeli cinema: its role in the construction of masculinity and queerness in a militaristic, heterosexist society that was founded on the myth of the Sabra, the new "Muscle Jew" of Palestine. Rather than focusing on the booming gay Israeli cinema of the past decade, Yosef's work provides a subversive textual reading that aims to liberate the "repressed queer" Jew in what are generally regarded as canonical or at least mainstream cinematic texts, culled from different genres and eras. In his research he encompasses propagandistic pre-state Zionist films, military films of the 1970s and 1980s, and "queer films" of the 1990s. Although the last chapter of his book deals with the work of self-proclaimed gay directors, it is by no means the book's main concern. As Yosef describes his study in the introduction, in most of the films he analyzes, "there are no ostensibly gay characters," and "the word 'gay' is not even mentioned in any form or context" (*Beyond Flesh* 5).

I have chosen to begin this study where Yosef ends his, namely the emergence of proclaimed cinematic representations of gayness. Unlike previous projects, this book focuses on films that seek, mostly, to undermine Israeli-dominant national-masculine discourse in order to allow diverse sexual codes and practices to reveal themselves. Unlike Yosef's discussion of the films, mine looks predominantly at the text rather than the subtext (an exception is made in chapter 1, to which I shall return later). I seek to take apart the texts of gay cinema in order to look at their different components. I intend to do that by tracing the historical and sociocultural conditions that were involved in the films' conception and production and the different political agendas that they choose to embrace. In other words, I am interested in the way the films are linked to an explicit social project of coming out, of giving gay desire a name and a recognizable identity.

My research has combined close analysis of individual film texts with theoretical discussions drawing on feminism and postcolonial theory to analyze issues concerning marginality and its subversion, and on queer theory to discuss the ongoing destabilization inherent in gay identity politics. In my textual analyses I have aimed to draw attention to the interplay between the overt thematic level of the films (story, plot, character, motivation, etc.) and their various formal elements (mise-en-scène, lighting, music, and costume). I have also sought to relate the films to the cultural and political history of Israel since the late 1970s. Beyond textual analysis, the discussion reaches toward the institutional apparatuses involved in the cinema industry, which includes the political decision making concerning allocation of funding, censorship, and television broadcasting.

This book revolves around thematic principles in order to provide a coherent picture of the various phases that Israeli gay cinema, and gay culture, has gone through since the late 1970s. Although the study of these phases implies the tracing of a historical development, the book is not a comprehensive chronicle of gay cinema in Israel. Although I have endeavored to include as many films as possible, I have not taken account of every Israeli film in which there is a gay or a homosexual reference. Rather, I have chosen films that are either symptomatic or initiators of certain advances, trajectories, and discursive practices in Israeli gay society and cultural production. My approach is intertextual in that it is interested in the relation between different cinematic (and at times, literary or journalistic) texts, whether they are Israeli or foreign.

By studying the role of film in the rise of the gay movement in Israel, I aim to offer a possible definition of gay cinema. This vexed term does not designate a specific genre. As this study demonstrates, a gay film can be a fiction or a nonfiction film. It can be a drama, a comedy, or a thriller. Or it can be none of the above. It can adhere to a strict set of generic conventions or defy them. It can be made by a self-proclaimed gay director or by a heterosexual one. For the purpose of this particular project, a gay film does not necessarily have to be gay themed at all: a few of the films that are discussed in the following chapters do not directly address gay concerns, but they were made by publicly open gay filmmakers whose well-known sexual preference and lifestyle call for, or at least enable, a gay reading of their ostensibly nongay films, as in the case of Eytan Fox's *Song of the Siren* (*Shirat HaSirena*, 1994), which is analyzed in chapter 1. Furthermore, at least two films—*Tel Aviv Stories* (*Sipurei Tel Aviv*, Nirit Yaron and Ayelet Menahemi, 1992) and *Life According to Agfa* (*HaChayim Al Pi Agfa*, Assi Dayan, 1992), also discussed in chapter 1—are neither gay themed nor made by openly gay filmmakers. I have chosen to include *Tel Aviv Stories*, however, as I believe it played an important role in expanding the boundaries of Israeli discourse around wider matters of sexuality and gender at the time of its release, thus contributing, indirectly, to the burgeoning Israeli gay discourse in the early 1990s. I have chosen to include *Life According to Agfa* because it illustrates a central point that I make in the chapter, namely the emphasis on Tel Aviv as a site where normative identifications with the state are contested. In so doing, the film responded at the time of its release to shifts within Israeli society, which had influenced, like *Tel Aviv Stories*, the Israeli gay discourse.

The concept of a gay community, to which I refer in several instances in the text, is probably as difficult to circumscribe as the term "gay cinema." It has been noted that the Israeli gay and lesbian community is an "amorphous entity" (Walzer x). One of the main objectives of this project is to point to the diversity of gay, lesbian, transgender, and queer experiences and practices in Israel that has inevitably raised different perceptions of who exactly is represented by the "community" and, more crucially, what constitutes a community in the first place. The assumption that a gay community can be formed based solely on a shared sexuality may "leave unexplored any 'internal' contradictions which undermine the coherence we desire from the imagined certainty of an unassailable commonality or of incontestable sexuality" (Cohen 72).

Rather than suggesting that there is a single Israeli gay community, I aim to show the complexity of this idea. The films I have chosen to include in this study demonstrate well cases in which the different branches of the imagined gay community (borrowing the term from Benedict Anderson's *Imagined Communities*) come together, as well as cases in which they split and, at times, even clash. For the most part, the use of the term "community" in the context of gay life in Israel implies an aspiration for a unified community or an image of one, propelled by the media, and especially by a few prominent figures, highly visible gay men and lesbians who have become unofficial spokespersons on gay issues. In some cases it refers to public institutions that were founded to represent gay men and lesbians. One such institution is Aguda ("society" or "association" in Hebrew). Aguda was established as the Society for the Protection of Personal Rights (SPPR) in 1975 by a group of men in order to provide a support network for gay men and lesbians (Kama, "From *Terra Incognita* to *Terra Firma*" 142). As Amir Sumaka'i Fink and Jacob Press show (369), the organization's agenda has shifted and changed since its establishment, reflecting the shifting boundaries of inclusion or perhaps corresponding to changes in awareness. Alterations of its title have illustrated these ideological and political shifts. In 1988, after Israel's dormant antisodomy law was repealed, it added the phrase "for Gay Men, Lesbians, and Bisexuals in Israel" to its title. The title was changed yet again in 1995 to the Association of Gay Men, Lesbians, and Bisexuals in Israel; in 1999 "Transgendered People" was also added. The organization is simply called Aguda by gay men, lesbians, and transsexuals.

Some of the films I discuss in the book make a point of exploring and questioning the cultural, social, and geographical boundaries of the Israeli gay community—that is, the ideal of a unified community, envisioned by Aguda—by portraying the life of those who cross them, among them Mizrahim, Palestinian-Israeli gay men, lesbians, those who live outside urban centers, and those who work in the sex industry.

One last linguistic note on the words "gay," "homosexual," and "queer," which some writers use interchangeably, adding to the confusion they may create. I have used the term "gay" to refer to self-professed male or female gay people and to films that have been marketed or introduced to the public as gay-themed films. The word "homosexual" is often used in place of "gay." However, following Eve Kosofsky Sedgwick's observation, I have chosen to use the term "gay" "since it is the explicit choice of a large number of the people to whom it refers" (16). As Sedgwick points out, the word "homosexual" risks anachronism and sounds "diagnostic" (16).

Whereas the term homosexuality has been in use since the nineteenth century,[2] modern gay identity as it is known and practiced today is a relatively modern invention and a Western concept. Unlike "homosexual," "gay" implies the formation of identity (and subsequently culture) that, although based on sexual preference, is constructed as a much more complex weave of human traits. This can be limiting but also empowering: it is through the construction of a gay identity and society that oppressive practices in the area of sexuality and sexual choice can be challenged, and political objectives can be developed.

I have used the term "queer" throughout the book to refer to people and films that take a defiant stance regarding the culturally constructed straight-gay dichotomy. Queer culture attempts to embrace notions of fluidity and flexibility in order to negate the fixed and seemingly stable categories of sexual identities. Queer ideology defies an essentialist approach to sexualities and claims that they are in a constant state of being formed and deconstructed. It refuses any possibility of regularity and provokes and repudiates any attempt at rigid conceptualization. Lee Edelman argues that "queerness can never define an identity; it can only ever disturb one" (*No Future* 17). Similarly, Sara Ahmed asserts that deviation from what she terms "compulsory heterosexuality" (94) alone will not necessarily produce a queer effect because "if the compulsion to deviate from the straight line was to become 'a line' in queer politics, then this itself could have a straightening effect" (174–75). A queer commitment, therefore, "would be a commitment not to presume that lives have to follow certain lines in order to count as lives, rather than being a commitment to a line of deviation" (178). In applying queer approaches to cultural production, Mark W. Turner has argued that they "seek less to define a specific and agreed upon historical narrative than to offer possible, contingent ways of reading the past in order to engage with the present in ways that do not rely on normative ideas and behaviours" (45–46).

At the same time, as Leo Bersani has argued, queerness may prevent the formation of a solid gay identity and community, both of which have been highly significant for homosexuals in their battle for rights and recognition. Referring to the gay movement in America, Bersani writes, "It would be foolish and unjust to deny that the quality of life for gay men and women in America has markedly improved precisely because a politicized gay and lesbian community does exist" (*Homos* 52–53). For Bersani, queerness is no more than a new discursive category, but one that denies its unique (homo)sexual referent.

Influenced by Bersani, other scholars of gay and lesbian studies have pointed to the flaws of "queer." Eric Savoy, for instance, argues that "it is precisely this ease of appropriation, combined with the queer project's destabilizations of 'coherence' and the refusal of the term itself to settle definitively, that has occasioned so much uneasiness for lesbian- and gay-centered scholarship and the consequent dialogics of reproach" (154). In discussing either "queer" or "gay" approaches in relation to certain films, filmmakers, and movements, I hope to have shed some light on the different political, social, and cultural agendas they stand for.

In the first section of the introduction, I aim to offer a succinct overview of the Israeli gay movement and representations of homosexuality (mainly male homosexuality) in Israeli films before the release of Amos Guttman's first feature film *Drifting* in 1983. For reasons I shall explain below and more extensively in chapter 2, I see Guttman's cinema as the first comprehensive cultural attempt to define gay identity in Israel. Guttman envisaged his films as links in a bigger project whose main objective was to create a cultural space in which new identities would appear.

The second part of the introduction will offer a brief history of the Zionist concept of the new Jew of Palestine (or the Muscle Jew), which was the blueprint for Israeli masculinity after 1948. Serving as the model against which most gay men have had to define themselves either through resistance or assimilation, and a focal point of reference in almost all of the films discussed in the book, it is important to understand the social and cultural reasons that have brought it about. I am indebted to scholars Daniel Boyarin, George L. Mosse, Sander L. Gilman, David Biale, and Michael Gluzman, among others, whose seminal work on the complex relation between Judaism and sexuality has inspired my own interest in the subject.

In the third and last part of the introduction, I will delineate the structure of the book, introduce each of the five chapters that follow it, and point to the connections that I believe may be made between them. Throughout the introduction I hope to situate the project within the various scholarly fields on which it draws.

The Emergence of the Israeli Gay Movement and Its Representations on the Screen

The gay movement in Israel has gone through dramatic changes over the years. It has moved from a militant, uncompromising position to become a significant social, cultural, and political player in the public arena. However, recent years have seen the gay movement, and indeed filmmaking, returning to its belligerent roots, bringing to the fore problematic topics that had previously been avoided, such as the occupation and its impact on interracial gay couples, the relation between gayness and institutional religion, and male prostitution.

As in other countries the gay revolution in Israel was inspired and shaped by the gay rights movement in the United States, ignited in the 1960s as part of the broader civil rights movement. However, the prominence of gay identity is no longer unique to the United States. These ideas have now long been exported around the globe to non-Western, as well as Western, cultures. Dennis Altman has argued that what was first considered a local phenomenon in the United States has turned out to be, since the late 1960s, an international movement that encompasses people of different national, racial, and religious backgrounds, who see themselves as part of a global community. This tendency, obviously, is not without its risks, as Altman observes: "American 'queer theory' remains as relentlessly Atlantic-centric in its view of the world as the mainstream culture it critiques" (3).

In the first decades of the state, homosexual life in Israel was clandestine: it was a long time before Israeli society saw its own visible gay rights movement take shape.[3] As Altman claims, the gay movement of North America had a more widespread, immediate influence on similar movements in Europe and Australia, where "the largely American symbols could be made relevant to local conditions" (Altman 3).[4] Despite the widespread aspiration of Israeli society to follow European-Western societies, the prominence of the military and related heteronormative values blocked the chance for the emergence of gay identity and community at an earlier stage and in tandem with the American civil rights movement. According to Sami Shalom Chetrit, while the civil rights movement in the United States and the 1968 student riots in Paris were taking place, Israel was still in a euphoric state following its victory in the 1967 Six Day War (137). The opposition to the Vietnam War in the United States was replaced in Israel with a celebration and corroboration of its heteronormative and militaristic character.

The early 1970s saw the beginning of social rebellion. Feminism, the Israeli Black Panthers movement—which fought state discrimination against the Mizrahi community—and the rise of gay consciousness all took place around that time and were influenced by similar trends in the United States and the West.[5] In the case of the Black Panthers, the members of the movement went as far as adopting the name of the American black organization that inspired them.[6] These new movements came both to threaten the hegemony of the ruling political elites and to confirm Israel's "liberal" and "Westernized" disposition. To date, the emergence of a self-defined gay community is directly linked to Israeli society's effort to assimilate itself to Western values.

Although late to arrive, gay consciousness has been on the rise since the mid-1970s, gradually lifting the legal restrictions that the state had imposed on its gay citizens for many years. The changing representations of gay men and lesbians in the media and the frequent references to them in popular culture led to a legal revolution, which took place mostly between 1988 and 1993 (starting with the decriminalization of sodomy), and secured gay men and women an almost equal standing in society.[7] Following these far-reaching changes the 1990s were, in the words of Aeyal M. Gross, "Israel's 'gay decade'" (391).

Introduction

Even though, at first, the gay movement had certain elements of queer resistance by opposing the heterosexist, militaristic values Israeli society was based on, they gradually vanished from its agenda.[8] Instead, members of the gay community have internalized these heterosexist norms, hoping for social acceptance rather than social change, and allied themselves with the fading Ashkenazi (a term referring to Jews of Central or Eastern European origins) elite that stood behind them. The establishment's acceptance of the gay community resulted from an understanding that, in the current state of affairs, a minor sexual "deviation" was less threatening than the danger presented by other minority groups that have gradually gained political power over the past couple of decades, among them Orthodox Jews.

The community's "integrationist" approach (Walzer 250), discussed in chapter 1, has helped dispel fears that other minorities often evoke, for example, Russian immigrants (who have established their own education and media networks) and the ultra-Orthodox community, which is often seen as trying to impose its beliefs on the rest of the Israeli population. For the most part, unlike the common perception of other "separatist" groups in Israel, the gay community has wished to be seen as part of "the rest of the nation" rather than to impose "its way."

In terms of visibility and legalization, the gay movement has acquired a stable place in hegemonic Israel. However, some of the oppressive practices in Israeli mainstream society have been endorsed by the gay community as part of its quest to produce a clean-cut, wholesome picture of homosexual life. Thus, most of the representations of gay men focus on a limited gay experience, namely that of a middle-class, Ashkenazi (read in Israel as "white"), urban man. Ignoring lesbians, transsexuals, and Mizrahi gay men, and turning its back on burning issues like the AIDS epidemic, the gay community has created a homogenized, exclusionist model of gay life.

References to homosexuality and gay culture had been part of Israeli films long before the first acclaimed gay filmmaker Amos Guttman completed his first feature film *Drifting* in 1983. The first overt mentions of homosexuality can be found in Israeli films of the early 1970s. Most of these films are popular comedies that offer a grotesque portrayal of homosexuality. Homosexuality in these films is mostly used as a narrative ornamentation, a device for extorting laughs, and has very little role, if any, in moving the plot forward.

One of the first films to feature a gay character was George Ovadia's *They Call Me Shmil* (*Kor'im Li Shmil*, 1973), a riotous comedy in which homosexuality is portrayed in a stereotypical manner by a marginal character in very few scenes. In Assi Dayan's *Fine Trouble* (*Eize Yofi Shel Tsarot*,

1976), a film that resembles Ovadia's film not only in its use of certain generic formulas but also in the director's choice of cast, one of the characters is an Italian hairdresser (Moshe Ish Kassit), who does not speak Hebrew. Made in the mid-1970s, the filmmakers suggest that homosexuality, hinted at in the character's feminine gestures and in his overt interest in male customers, cannot be contained within the boundaries of the Israeli discourse. The film also features Ze'ev Revach, a famous actor and comedian of Mizrahi origin, as the owner of the beauty salon where the Italian hairdresser works. The proclaimed heterosexuality of Revach's flamboyant character is merely suggested, never proven. Practicing exaggerated feminine gestures, and dressed in brightly colored clothes (in one of the scenes he appears in full drag, following the lead of a similar drag scene in *Snuker* [*Hagiga BaSnoker,* Boaz Davidson, 1975]), Revach's character embodies what was considered a demonstration of sexual otherness in 1970s Israel. Throughout the film he is seen trying to avoid the sexual favors his wealthy female clients try to confer on him. He eventually falls in love with Ofra (Yona Elian), the female protagonist, but their subsequent wedding is only discussed, not shown. The fact that his heterosexuality is never practiced suggests he is actually a homosexual in disguise.

The late 1970s see another gay character in Avi Nesher's *The Troupe* (*HaLahaka,* 1978), which instantly became a huge commercial and critical success. The film depicts the behind-the-scenes activities of an army troupe, traveling the country after the 1967 war. Benny, the gay member (Menachem Einy), confesses his homosexuality during a game of Truth or Dare. The alleged liberal stance of the film is undermined by the fact that the gay soldier is the least developed character in the script. Very little is said about or by him, and unlike his heterosexual counterparts, who are fully engaged in complex romantic relationships, he seems to lack a personal life (a gay relationship is hinted at in the film but is never seen or spoken of in detail).

Ze'ev Revach's portrayal of a pseudohomosexual character in *Fine Trouble* is further developed in *The Hairdresser* (*Sapar Nashim,* 1984), which he also cowrote and directed.[9] Following the tradition of the "comedy of errors" (in films such as *He Who Steals from a Thief Is Not Guilty* [*Gonev MiGanav Patur,* Ze'ev Revach, 1977], *Kuni Lemel in Tel Aviv* [Yoel Zilberg, 1978], and *The Aunt from Argentina* [*HaDoda MeArgentina,* George Ovadia, 1983]), Revach plays the dual role of estranged twin brothers: Michel is a successful, wealthy gay hairdresser whereas Victor is a poor cleaner, married, and a father of seven. Having stolen money from the safe at his workplace, Victor contacts his brother, who suggests they switch roles: Michel

Outside the Israeli discourse: the Italian hairdresser (Moshe Ish Kassit) in Assi Dayan's *Fine Trouble* (1976).

will pass as a married heterosexual man, and Victor will pretend to be a gay man, so that the police will not be able to match the fingerprints left on the safe with those of Victor.

As in previous films, by employing exaggerated body language and effeminate gestures, Revach's Michel represents the stereotypical image of gay men. At the same time, Michel is portrayed as a successful, savvy professional, whose bright idea saves his brother from imprisonment. Furthermore, his lavish lifestyle is a source of envy for his heterosexual brother. Indeed, it is Victor and his wife who join Michel's business at the end of the film. Victor, who had rejected his gay brother to the point of denial (his wife and children did not even know he had a brother), now embraces both him and his desirable life. The film offers a subversive view of gayness by resisting the heterosexual-homosexual dichotomy and demonstrating how the two constantly overlap: Michel is Victor, Victor is Michel, and the two are Ze'ev Revach. In the film, Revach is constantly being made and remade according to circumstances, his identity becoming increasingly unstable and dependent on semantic confusion.

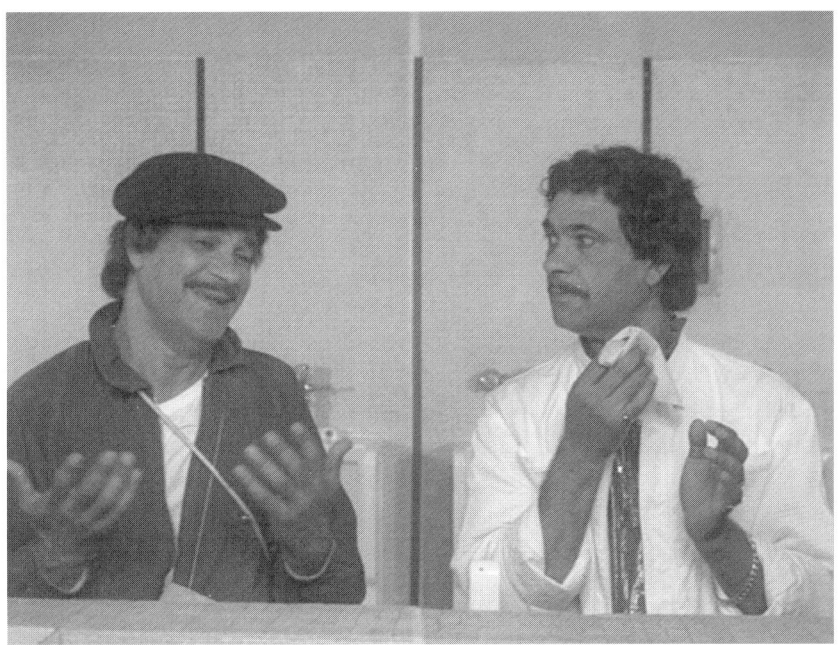

Resisting the heterosexual-homosexual dichotomy: twin brothers Victor and Michel (both played by Ze'ev Revach) switch roles in Revach's "comedy of errors" *The Hairdresser* (1984).

It is interesting to note that these early representations of different types of masculinity are located in the context of Jewish Mizrahi rather than Ashkenazi masculinity. *Fine Trouble* and *Snooker*, for example, were released shortly after Uri Zohar's *Peeping Toms* (*Metzitzim*, 1972) and *Big Eyes* (*Einayim G'dolot*, 1974), which celebrated the antics of sex-crazed heterosexual Ashkenazi men. One of the Zionist movement's main objectives was to create a new, virile Jewish man. The idea was to transform the old Jew of the European Diaspora into a "Muscle Jew" and a native of Palestine. Mizrahi men could never fully become part of this project because of their different ethnic origin. Their difference was marked by hegemonic (Ashkenazi) culture, not only in relation to their different "racial" attributes but also in relation to their sexuality: Mizrahi men were suspected either of hypersexuality and overreproduction or of homosexuality (Yosef, *Beyond Flesh* 87–89). In order to expose the artificially constructed ideal of the Zionist body, Mizrahi men embraced the discriminative approaches practiced against them. They were the first to transgress the rigid boundaries of Zionist-Israeli masculinity and cultural categories in general on the screen and beyond.[10]

Introduction

The grotesque portrayal of gay men offered by Ze'ev Revach forms part of the quest to explore ways to undermine the foundations of hegemonic Ashkenazi masculinity. Stereotypical as they were, Revach's performances in his 1970s and 1980s films took homosexuality and the need for creating a gay space and identity more seriously than other, allegedly more respectable, cinematic attempts to do so in films such as *The Troupe,* Dan Wolman's *Hide and Seek* (*Machbo'im,* 1980), and Shimon Dotan's *Repeat Dive* (*Tslila Hozeret,* 1982). *Hide and Seek* takes place in 1946 Jerusalem during the British Mandate. It was the first dramatic film to make a direct reference to a male-male relationship. In the film, Balaban (Doron Tavori), the young schoolteacher protagonist, is caught by members of the Haganah—one of the pre-state armed Jewish underground organizations—having an affair with an Arab man. This is seen as an act of treason, for which he and his lover are punished. Although homosexuality is a key dramatic element in *Hide and Seek,* it is not discussed in itself: the viewers find out about the protagonist's love affair, and indeed homosexuality, only toward the end of the film and the Arab lover remains nameless. Rather, it is an expression of a "sexual entanglement with the Arab enemy" (Yosef, *Beyond Flesh* 133).

The theme of biracial sexual entanglement is developed further in Daniel Wachsmann's 1982 film *Hamsin.* The homoerotic feelings hinted at between Gedalia (Shlomo Tarshish), the Jewish protagonist, and Khaled (Yassin Shoaf), his Arab employee and friend, and the complex feelings of envy and anxiety evoked in him by the sexual relationship between the Arab man and his (the Jewish protagonist's) sister Hava (Hemda Levi) lead to a fatal ending. By killing the Arab man, the Jewish protagonist attempts to both disrupt the forbidden (heterosexual) biracial relationship and cleanse himself of his homosexual desire.

Homosexual desire is suggested but never consummated in *Repeat Dive.* The protagonist, Yoav (Doron Nesher) is a diver in the Israeli navy commando. His best friend Yochi dies in a military operation. When a fellow soldier notes after the funeral that Yochi spent more time with Yoav than with his wife, Mira (Liron Nirgad), Yoav replies, "Yes, but we don't date anymore." This emphasizes the close relationship the two men had. In his will, Yochi "leaves" Mira to Yoav. Mira then becomes a "mediating" object between the two men. The death of Yochi and the subsequent wedding of Yoav and Mira imply that homosexuality can only exist in the realm of fantasy. It is not surprising that some unequivocal homoerotic gestures, like a kiss between Yoav and one of the soldiers, occur during a party they have in a pub after the funeral of Yochi. Only when drunk, that is when they step outside the realm of rationality, can these manly, brave soldiers express their most hidden desires.

The 1980s saw the first earnest attempts to produce films that did not merely mention homosexuality or use it as a motif in the narrative but rather presented it as their focal theme. These films, in so doing, contributed to the construction of an Israeli gay identity. One such film is the short drama *A Different Shadow* (*Tsel Acher*, 1983). The film, directed by then unknown filmmaker Ron Asulin, tells the story of a young gay man (Danny Rot) who falls in and out of love with another man (Daniel Amar). He comes out to his family, who react badly to their son's news. The broadcast of the film, which was commissioned by the state TV channel, was eventually banned because of its subject matter.

Like *A Different Shadow*, Amos Guttman's first short film *Drifting* (*Nagua*, 1976) was banned by Israeli TV. Whereas Asulin has not made another gay film,[11] Guttman dedicated most of his cinematic career to addressing this theme until his death of AIDS-related illness in 1993. In 1983 he completed the feature version of *Drifting*, a film that has since become a landmark for gay cultural production in Israel. In Guttman's cinema, homosexuality and gay identity are finally foregrounded as a major theme. In a series of shorts and feature films, Guttman has captured the marginality of people who live and die outside the boundaries of the Zionist-Israeli discourse. Guttman has earned his pioneering status not only for his films' thematic shift from committed and nationalist topics to socially challenging ones but also for their innovative hyperrealistic aesthetics. The films' stylistic excesses reveal the ideological fissures that other "nationalist" films seek to conceal.

The late 1970s and 1980s were also the years in which the first overt lesbian references were made in Israeli films. In *Weekend Circles* (*Ma'agalim Shel Shishi-Shabat*, Idit Shechori, 1980), for instance, Lior (Galit Roitman-Gil), one of the four protagonists, is openly lesbian, and the subject is brought up and discussed by the four throughout the film. They do so while exploring the bustling nightlife of Tel Aviv during one long weekend, moving from a rock concert to a party to a late-night swim in the sea, consuming alcohol and drugs. Their surroundings, it is implied, encourage their sexual liberation and openness to same-sex experiences. It is important to note, though, that *Weekend Circles* is an exception. Apart from suggestive scenes in a few films produced before and after it, Shechori's film remained an isolated attempt to portray lesbianism on the Israeli screen until a decade ago. The majority of the new lesbian films are documentaries.

Brief references to lesbianism are included in films such as *Dizengof 99* (Avi Nesher, 1979), *Big Girl* (*Yalda G'dola*, Nirit Yaron, 1987), *The Last Winter* (*HaChoref HaAcharon*, Riki Shelach Nissimoff, 1983), and *Moments*

(*Rega'im,* Michal Bat-Adam, 1979). In both *Dizengof 99* and *Moments,* the interfemale intimacy occurs only in the presence of another man as part of an orgy. Orly Lubin has argued that *Moments* "does not offer any (lesbian) alternatives—the ultimate connection between the two women is achieved by means of the male organ: the movement of the phallus from one woman to the other. Only the phallus, we are being told, has the power to constitute female and interfemale sexuality" ("The Woman as Other" 301). Similarly, intimacy between the two heterosexual female protagonists, Israeli Maya (Yona Elian) and American Joyce (Kathleen Quinlan), in *The Last Winter* is mediated through men and only made possible by their absence. The two women meet at the information center for families of Israeli POWs during the 1973 war. In the course of several weeks, while waiting for information regarding their husbands' fate, they get closer, and even physically intimate. Toward the end of the film, Joyce reunites with her husband, Eddie (Stephen Macht), whereas Maya finds out that her spouse is dead. By suggesting that her husband will have sexual intercourse with her widowed friend, Joyce establishes a contact, physical and emotional, with Maya, a contact she could not have made otherwise. Shortly after Joyce and her family return to America, Maya writes a letter to Joyce in which she expresses her love and longing for her.

The 1990s were the years in which a significant progress in the legal and social status of gay men and lesbians was finally achieved. It was also the decade in which certain sectors of the gay community became closer than ever to the Ashkenazi hegemonic elite. This rapprochement and the wish for total integration into mainstream Israeli culture are encouraged and celebrated in the films of established gay filmmaker Eytan Fox. His recent mainstream films *Yossi and Jagger* (2002), *Walk on Water* (*Lalechet Al HaMayim,* 2004), and *The Bubble* (*HaBuah,* 2006) avoid posing difficult questions but rather aim at the status quo. Unlike Guttman's, Fox's films manifest the current social status the gay community has achieved for itself: gayness is perceived as a legitimate way of life, and even desirable, as long as it does not transgress the rigid boundaries of Israeli hegemonic culture. Emphasizing the sameness of the community's members and everybody else, the meaning of gay identity in contemporary Israel, as depicted in those films, has been reduced to a mere different sexual orientation. Fox's films are more about men who happen to be homosexuals than about men who lead a *gay* life, which is, by definition, a deviation from the norm.

However, a few of the new, less established filmmakers who have emerged in the past few years have a different vision to Fox's. Their films, mostly documentaries and autobiographical films, attempt to expand the boundaries of gay discourse and to find a broader, more flexible definition of what it means to be gay in Israel today. Drawing on the cinema of Guttman, but at the same time riding on the back of the wide commercial and critical acclaim received by Fox's films, these filmmakers continue to examine previously unexplored aspects of gay life in Israel. Moving on from Guttman's isolation and from Fox's embrace of Israeli core values, these filmmakers push the boundaries of the discourse further and search for new means of representation. Trying to define nonheteronormative identities, some of these films blur boundaries, mix genres, and create, in turn, new "hybrid" modes of filmmaking. The blurring or crossing of boundaries, including that between documentary and fiction, reflects and reenacts the blurring of identities such as lesbian, gay, and queer.

Heterosexuality as a Zionist Imperative

I started this project aiming to be as inclusive as possible: my wish was to produce a text that dealt with films about gay men *and* lesbians, as well as bisexuals and transsexuals. My intention was to discuss, equally, the cinematic representations of all the subgroups that constitute the Israeli gay population. However, I gradually realized that this objective would be difficult to fulfill. Gay male experience, unlike women's experience, is what I felt personally competent to write about. Furthermore, I have been interested in tracing a particular ideological trajectory that involves gay men more than it does lesbians, namely the development of a strongly normative set of links in Israel between Israeli nationalism/Zionism, the muscular male body and heterosexuality, and the fact that gay cinema in Israel has always had to situate itself somehow in relation to that trajectory, from the early *Bourekas* films[12] to recent fiction and nonfiction work. Nonetheless, this is not a systematic exclusion: some lesbian-themed films are discussed or briefly mentioned in this book, in relevance to a particular argument or as part of a larger group of films (*Almost There,* for example, is discussed in the context of the rise of gay and lesbian autobiographical films).

Indeed, although the ideological configuration I describe (Muscle Jew, Zionism, heterosexuality) centers on men, it must involve women too, albeit indirectly. If masculinity needs the binary opposite femininity in order to be defined, then the Zionist discourse must also involve a construction of the feminine in relation to the masculine and thus of women in relation to men (as mothers, wives, sexual partners, working comrades on the kibbutz). It is, of course, important to explore the place of lesbians within this configuration, and their possible exclusion from this discourse (because

Introduction

they may not fit into those approved categories of women) is significant in itself, as is the exclusion of the Jewish "effeminate" man. I deliberately chose, however, not to engage with lesbian filmmaking in Israel, as it is, or should be, a separate object for study. It deserves its own comprehensive research, which I hope will be conducted in the future.

It is important to note that there are very few films made by or about lesbians, and hardly any made about transsexuals.[13] This is one manifestation of the dominance of the male experience in Israel, epitomized in the image of the heroic warrior, and the relatively marginal status given to women. Ironically, it is the marginalization of women that has allowed lesbian experiences to go unnoticed, or at least to be seen as less of a threat than male homosexual experiences. Gay men, on the other hand, have had to respond to scorn from male-dominated and militaristic Israeli society. Consequently, they have had a greater need to create their own cultural and social circles from which they could reimagine themselves and their community. However, since at the same time they have enjoyed the privilege of belonging to the dominant male group, they have had better means to achieve that.

The roots of Israel's male-dominant culture can be found in the Zionist quest to create a new society in Palestine (*Eretz Yisrael*), which would be based on the image of the new Jew. The story of homosexuality and gayness in Israel cannot be understood without considering the desire of the Zionist movement and, later, Israeli hegemonic culture, to transform the nature of European Jewish masculinity and create a new type of a Jew and an Israeli man. The transformation of Jewish masculinity was based on the universalistic premise that the unmarked norm is masculine and therefore it is masculinity that needs to be modified (unlike femininity, which is already marked as different from the norm). Zionism, like most political narratives, used sex and gender for ideological and propagandistic ends. According to David Biale, the Zionist movement presented itself as an erotic revolution, which allowed young Jews to overcome centuries of sexual repression (183, 189). Heterosexuality and values such as procreation—even though not encouraged explicitly but presented as a by-product of Zionism's celebrated secularism and nation-building aspiration—were an important part of the new Jewish code.

Gay men and lesbians have been excluded from the public sphere in most societies throughout the years. The dominant heterosexual and familial culture employed heterosexual patriarchy as the "normal" condition, considering homosexuality as "unnatural." This perception derived from the belief that "men can only continue to rule the world, if they are prepared to live their lives in accordance with their real natures, their essential heterosexuality" (Brittan 65). The Zionist movement was no different, and the public sphere in the new state, ruled by Ashkenazi immigrants, was based on the same notions of masculinity and power. One of Zionism's primary goals was to create, or rather recreate, a "muscular" Jew, a concept with which it strove to overcome and reverse the dominant stereotype in Christian Europe of Diasporic Jewish men as feminine.

"Judaism is saturated with femininity," declared Otto Weininger in his book *Sex and Character* (1906; qtd. in Garber 224) in which he attempted to prove that all Jews are inherently women "insofar as they lack any essence and can only imitate the true masculine" (Golomb-Hoffman 38). Weininger was not the only one to argue this: it had been a common belief in the years before he wrote. Daniel Boyarin maintains that the common description of women in Victorian culture—"enduringly, incorruptibly, good; instinctively, infallibly wise," as suggested by John Ruskin (*Unheroic Conduct* 3)—can be easily applied to traditional rabbis. According to Boyarin, the male Jew was often represented as a sort of woman who gave "a set of performances that are culturally read as non-male within a given historical culture" ("Homotopia" 43). The most visible sign of Jewish feminization was the religious act of circumcision, which was associated in the late nineteenth century with "the act of castration, the unmanning, the feminizing of the Jew in the act of making him a Jew" (Gilman, *Sexuality* 265).

Right from its conception Zionism was linked with heterosexuality and manhood as a reaction to the imagery of the effeminate, supposedly homosexual Jew of the Diaspora. In Max Nordau's view, the redemption of Jews could not be reached solely by their settling in Palestine. It also required a transformation of the Jewish body and mind from the victimized European Diaspora Jews, portrayed as weak and feminine, into their masculine image as heroic warriors, a transformation that would reinstate the link with their glorious pre-Diaspora past.[14] Summarizing a central argument of Nordau's book *Degeneration* (1892), George L. Mosse writes, "The Jew must acquire solid stomachs and hard muscles, not just to overcome his stereotype—though this was important for Nordau—but also to compete, to find his place in the world" (*Confronting* 164).

In Zionist thought, the two goals, that of recreating the Jew as muscular and heterosexual and of settling in Palestine, could not be separated. As Joseph Massad maintains, "The objective of the Zionist movement was not simply to transplant European Jews into a new geographic area but also to transform the very nature of European Jewish society and identity as it had existed in the Diaspora until then. The locus of this transformation was the

European Jew's body" (325). According to Biale, Zionist political ideology "was not only based on the body as metaphor; it sought, in addition, to transform the Jewish body itself, and especially the sexual body" (176).

The negation of the Diaspora and the development of the image of the "Muscle Jew," as Anne Golomb-Hoffman notes, suggests the internalization of the image of the feminized Jewish male (39), an image that marked Jews' inferiority and otherness in Christian Europe, similar to the way in which the inferiority of homosexuals was marked.[15] Like homosexuals, Jews were seen as biological deviations from the norm. It is not surprising the two were connected and presented as the evil "others" in Christian Europe (Garber 226). The Jews' alleged feminized nature was often ascribed to the essential difference inherent in them rather than to a social reaction to their stigmatization and was believed to put them at risk of becoming homosexuals (Gilman, *Freud* 162). The danger of becoming a sexual pervert, a homosexual in particular, was considered one of the biggest threats in European bourgeois societies.[16] It is this feminized Jewish male that the new Jew of Palestine tries to repress. The male Zionist embodies the eternal connection of the warrior, muscle, and heterosexual Jew to his ancient land.

The concept of a new, "Muscle Jew" was the blueprint for the heterosexual and militaristic society Israel has turned out to be, a tendency that became even stronger due to the growing dependency of Israeli society on the army, a male-dominated institution. As was the case in many other times and places, gay men in Israel were excluded, if they were acknowledged at all, from the Zionist dream. They were perceived not only as disrupting the gender-oriented new society but also as damaging the security of the state, one of the most sacred values in Israel (hence, the restrictions imposed on recruiting gay men to certain positions in the army—in combat units, for instance—up until recent times). Eventually, a local gay movement emerged in Israel in order to change the legal and social status of gay men and lesbians. This happened, however, long after similar movements had formed in other Western countries. In the late 1960s, after Israel's sweeping victory in the 1967 Six Day War, Israeli society's mobilized and militaristic nature was still very much celebrated. It was not until the 1970s that these sacred values could be challenged, and this critical tendency became even more pronounced in the 1980s and 1990s.

Israeli cinema has been instrumental in promoting certain representations of Israeli manhood. This has been achieved through various cinematic genres such as the documentary and pre-state Zionist narrative cinema, the heroic-nationalist genre (a term coined by Ella Shohat), Israeli "New Wave" cinema (known also as "personal" or "modernist" cinema) and the

Bourekas films. Even though these models varied in style and content, they all reinforced (or at least did not undermine) a representation of male heterosexual identity, the perfect antithesis to the stereotyped latently homosexual Jew of the Diaspora.

However, as Raz Yosef claims (using the term "queer," where I would use "gay"), the relationship between the new Jew and the queer Jew should be read "not in terms of dichotomies, but rather in terms of ambivalence, displacement, and disidentification [. . .] the queer Jew is not the 'other' of the new Zionist 'self,' but rather a structural element of it" (*Beyond Flesh* 2–3). It is through a dialectical process that Israeli hegemony has defined itself and its outsiders.

Similarly, Alisa Solomon traces opposing forces that shaped the nature of Zionist, and later Israeli, society. According to Solomon, Zionism was not based solely on "masculine" attributes but on "feminine" ones as well. Solomon sees gayness and the culturally "feminine" signifiers that are attributed to it as integral to the construction of Zionist-Israeli identity: the positive value ascribed by Zionism to the soft Sabra and the state's reliance on its vulnerability to achieve international sympathy are signifiers that are as important as the hypermasculine nature of the army (158).

As I stated above, this book focuses on films that were made at a time when the taboo on explicit gay themes had already been lifted. Unlike many of the films that Yosef examines, those included here were produced in, and thus reflect, a reality in which the basic acknowledgment of the Israeli gay population and culture had already been attained.

The Chapters

My arguments are presented in five chapters. Each of the first four chapters is devoted to one particular group of films, united by a shared theme, filmmaker, or generic classification, whereas chapter 5 explores recent trends as well as possible future directions in Israeli gay film production. In my discussion of the films, I consider both the films' narratives as well as their formal and visual features. The latter are discussed mainly, but not exclusively, in relation to Guttman's films and a few of the nonfiction films included in chapter 4, in which I explore how the visual dimension of the films is used either to corroborate, or at times to contradict, the films' narrative dimension or overt themes.

Chapter 1 traces the distinctive characteristics of the imagined Israeli gay community back to its urban setting. It examines the mutual dependency of two interlinked projects: the construction of a gay community and identity and the reimagining of the city of Tel Aviv as a cosmopolitan metropolis, influenced by global trends and dissociated from, or in contrast to, the rest of Israeli reality. Some of the films emphasize the role of Tel Aviv as an alternative to Zionist-Israeli ideology, or, in the words of Nurith Gertz, "a geographical representation *par excellence* of the personal narrative" (*Myths* 163). The chapter stresses the interdependence of these two projects: in order to allow the gay community to flourish, it was necessary to imagine Tel Aviv as a major cultural urban center. In order for Tel Aviv to become a major cultural urban center, it was necessary to have a visible gay community in the city. Many of the Tel Aviv films made in the 1980s depict the way in which these two phenomena interact.

The chapter discusses, among other films, two by Amos Guttman and Eytan Fox, whose respective bodies of work as directors are analyzed in depth in the next two chapters. The fact that the book is structured thematically rather than chronologically means that overlaps are, at times, inevitable. As the two most influential Israeli gay filmmakers, Guttman and Fox set the templates for gay filmmaking in Israel, in relation to which most contemporary gay films have been made since. Their films represent the two extremes of the gay social and cultural spectrum in Israel, namely dissociation from Israeli mainstream culture, in the case of Guttman, and a strong wish for total inclusion, in the case of Fox. Guttman and Fox's cinema and their contribution to gay culture in Israel deserve a comprehensive discussion, which is offered in chapters 2 and 3. At the same time, some of their films can be placed within other groupings as well. By including a brief discussion of Guttman's *Amazing Grace* (*Hessed Mufla*, 1992) and of Fox's *Song of the Siren* in chapter 1, I offer the reader a brief introduction to their work, which is then examined more comprehensively later in the book.

Chapter 2 explores the ways in which the films of Guttman contributed to the evolution of a gay identity in 1980s Israel. As the first director to develop alternative national and sexual narratives to those offered by the dominant culture, Guttman marked the beginning of a much more critical and socially committed cinema in Israel. Heavily influenced by 1950s Hollywood melodrama and its appropriation by Rainer Werner Fassbinder, Guttman's films positioned themselves outside the traditional realism that dominated Israeli cinema at the time. The influence of melodrama is also powerfully present at the visual level in the films, which is at times in tension with the overt narrative level. As I shall argue, this tension is an important aspect of Guttman's cinema.

Guttman rejected not only the mainstream ideology but also the prevalent politics of the gay community, which aspired to fit into the master Zionist-Israeli narrative. By including, for example, a sex scene in *Drifting* (1983), in which the white Jewish protagonist renounces his alleged mastery to a nameless Arab, Guttman undermined both the national-Zionist discourse and the demands of the gay community for "positive" self images of themselves. Although most of Guttman's films have unmistakably clear gay themes (based on his own experiences), the influence they have had on the ever-changing sociocultural climate in Israel is much broader. Situating the films in the wider nexus of minority discourse and identity politics raises further questions regarding the possibility of challenging nationalist and normalizing narratives through subversive practices.

Chapter 3 focuses on the work of Eytan Fox, probably the most prolific gay Israeli director since the death of Guttman. Fox's films are the antithesis of Guttman's. They usually adopt, uncritically and unconditionally, Zionist-Israeli values and shift them from their "natural" context (a heterosexist environment such as a military base, heterosexual couples, and family life) to a gay narrative. Fox's films celebrate the revival of the Sabra—the heroic, Ashkenazi soldier who, as the myth goes, would be willing to die for his land—only that in Fox's vision, as opposed to previous Israeli films, the protagonists are gay. It is no wonder that at least two of Fox's films, *Time Off* (*After,* 1990) and *Yossi and Jagger* (2002), deal with questions of sexual otherness through the prism of army, and particularly combat, experience. This is part of an inevitable dialogue gay men have with the heterosexual hegemony, a dialogue that indicates the impossibility for gay men in Israel to be completely separated from the hegemonic Zionist narrative.

As much as there is a subversive element to Fox's films they still surrender to prevalent and oppressive heteronormative, even colonial, values. In his films there is a strong link between the protagonists' "clean-cut" lifestyle (despite their sexuality) and their Ashkenazi ethnic origin. Fox's films are an example of the alliance between the old liberal-Left elite and the gay community, revealing homophobic feelings toward certain groups within the gay minority itself (Mizrahi Jews, for example) and negating a diversity of gay voices and experiences.

Chapter 4 focuses on nonfiction gay filmmaking in Israel, namely documentaries and self-authored films. The latter serve to constitute a national, religious, and sexual identity for those who made them. They also offer an interesting insight into practices of exclusion and inclusion within the imagined Israeli gay community, whose awareness of the politics of otherness has not always been reflected in its practices. In their subjective, personal outlook on the families and cultures within which their protagonists/makers operate, the films, like all autobiographical documentaries, offer, in the words of Keith Beattie, "a significant revision of an objective, externalizing, documentary practice" (107). The chapter links the films' political content to their formal aspects and examines, among other things, the purpose of the blurring of distinctions between fiction and nonfiction and what it might serve. The chapter shows how the films construct selfhood, in particular gay/queer selfhood, vis-à-vis the call for collective identity, both from mainstream society and the gay community in Israel.

Chapter 5 offers brief concluding remarks on the current state of gay filmmaking in Israel. My intention is to look at some of the new directions that recent films have taken, one of which is an increasing interest in the experience of gay men and lesbians who come from religious communities. As in the previous chapter, many of the directors discussed in this final chapter are emerging talents who have made a deliberate point of expanding the scope of gay discourse in Israel.

This thematic division has enabled me to identify what, I argue, has become an important cultural phenomenon in the past three decades. At the same time it has also allowed me to discuss the inherent differences between these films, which represent the changing phases of the gay movement and cinema in Israel over the years. The array of voices explored in the book hints at the myriad possibilities that different Israeli gay groups, and filmmakers within these groups, can now choose from. Like Israeli society as a whole, the gay population in Israel keeps dividing along numerous axes and nodal points. This may take gay men and lesbians further away from the initial hope for a single, unified community, but it promises many more years of challenging filmmaking.

1

An Imagined City for an Imagined Community

Tel Aviv and Gay Identity on the Israeli Screen

The 1980s and 1990s saw the rise of two interlinked phenomena in Israel: the emergence of a visible urban gay community and the (re)invention of the city of Tel Aviv as the undisputed center for culture and new social movements. Both Tel Aviv and its gay community are, to different degrees, invented entities that have continuously fed on each other. In order for Tel Aviv to imagine itself as the Western metropolis it has aspired to be, it has needed the presence of a discernible gay community to mark it as such. Similarly, gay men and lesbians have needed the city of Tel Aviv as a site from which and in relation to which they could envision their "community."

These two phenomena overlap but are not coterminous: although certain aspects of the "reinvented" Tel Aviv intersect with gay identity and culture, neither the city nor gay culture is totally reducible to the other. Other cultural processes such as consumerism, Americanization, and the decline in traditional Zionist utopian ideals all played a major part in the reinvention of the city of Tel Aviv as well as in the construction of a local gay identity. In this chapter, I aim to explore these processes and their manifestations on screen. The importance of the films I discuss here lies in the contribution they made to the creation of a cultural climate of which the urban gay sensibility became an inseparable part. Sensibility, of course, is an elusive term[1] and should not be confused with gay presence. For this reason, the majority of the films are not actually gay themed or gay authored. Rather, the films capture, even if it was not part of the filmmakers' explicit agenda and was an indirect effect of the films themselves, a moment in the life of the city that enabled the rise of gay consciousness and cinema within it.

The dialectical relationship between the city and its gay community highlights the discursive nature of both. The city, as a culturally constructed concept, defies an essentialist approach to identities, sexual and other. Cities, like subjectivities, are made by people and changeable. Homosexuality may be experienced outside cities, but gayness, as a shared cultural attribute that unifies as well as defines a collective, rarely is. As David Forrest notes, "The emergence of the 'homosexual man'—someone able and willing to define himself as a distinct type of individual on the basis of his same-sex desires and behaviour—took place within a largely middle-class, metropolitan milieu" (100–01). Thus, the "urban migration story," namely the exploration of one's homosexuality in an urban environment, has become a prominent narrative in the category of gayness (Turner 45).

The promise of a progressive Jewish community in a modern, Hebrew city has attracted both ardent Zionist settlers and people from the margins of society since the foundation of Tel Aviv as "a garden suburb" of Jaffa in 1909.[2] The members of the gay community in Tel Aviv are internal migrants who came to the city to experience life in a way that is not possible elsewhere. The city has allowed them to embrace a gay identity and be absorbed into gay social circles. The city has changed their lives, and they have assisted in changing the life of the city. The gentrification of the aging center of Tel Aviv and the invention of the local press in the early 1980s reflected the new developments in the city and were linked to the establishment of the gay community at that time.

> The "real city" is never experienced simply as such, as separate from the "paper city." At the same time that the city is experienced as a physically factual built environment, it is also, in the perception of its inhabitants, a city in a novel, a film, a photograph, a television programme, a comic strip, and so on.
>
> Victor Burgin 175

The Tel Aviv Experience

Like all metropolises, Tel Aviv is at once real (objectively present) and shaped/defined by the human experience and use of it. The city was described by the late poet David Avidan as "a weird collage of parts of Manhattan, Los Angeles and Miami Beach" (18). In order to maintain this view of Tel Aviv, the city is constantly "produced" and reinvented in films, novels, and the local and national press.

Indeed, like most cities, Tel Aviv was built, to a certain extent, in people's imagination with words, images, sounds, and what Michel de Certeau has called "the practice of everyday life" (as he titled the 1984 English translation of his book). Roland Barthes has argued that "the city is a discourse and this discourse is truly a language: the city speaks to its inhabitants, we speak our city, the city where we are, simply by living in it, by wandering through it, by looking at it" (92). In praise of the "the chorus of idle footsteps," Certeau writes how "their intertwined paths give their shape to spaces. They weave places together" (97). Writing about modern urban novels, Hana Wirth-Nesher has argued that "fictional representation of cities intensifies [. . .] acts of invention and reconstruction that are endemic to metropolitan life" (10).

The discursive creation of cities depends on the ways cities are experienced and/or the function they are expected to fulfill. Avidan's insistence on seeing in Tel Aviv a miniature model of New York expresses his impression of both cities. Despite the immense difference between them, Tel Aviv for Avidan was just as exciting as the city he equated it with. Peter Preston and Paul Simpson-Housley have argued that "the city is an aggregation or accumulation, not just in demographic, economic or planning terms, but also in terms of feeling and emotion. Cities thus become more than their built environment, more than a set of class or economic relationships; they are also an experience to be lived, suffered, undergone" (1–2).

Yet Tel Aviv was not built on subjective feelings and inspirations alone but also with concrete and cement. Tel Aviv, like other cities, exists on the verge between the "real" and the "imaginary." It is an actual geographical site, but its buildings, roads, and squares are laden with symbolic, both historical and cultural, significance. The city's architectural legacy is only one example of the way in which the real and the imaginary intersect. The wish for Tel Aviv to represent progress, modernity, and secularism, as well as an affinity with the West, is well illustrated in the thousands of International Style buildings, designed by German Jews who arrived in Israel in the 1930s. Indeed, many of the films discussed in this chapter point to the constant tension between the "real" and the "imaginary" planes of the city and to the inevitable slippage between the two.

Referring to Edward Said's phrase "imaginative geography," Yosefa Loshitzky observes how the strikingly different perceptions of Israel's two largest cities have been created by their different landscapes: "The hilly and rocky Jerusalem produces the image of a closed, static and conservative city, whereas Tel Aviv, as a beach city, creates an image of an open, dynamic, and permissive metropolis" ("A Tale of Three Cities" 135). The difference in climate has also played a role: Tel Aviv's humidity may be associated with body fluids and more overt sexuality. Jerusalem, on the other hand, is famous for its dry climate and cold and snowy winters. Often perceived by Zionist pioneers as a place of "superstition, backwardness, and theocracy [. . .] national icons and religious relics" (Elon 238–39), Jerusalem has been discarded, first by secular Zionism and later by the gay and lesbian movement, in favor of Tel Aviv.[3] In films, Jerusalem is traditionally portrayed as a conservative and oppressive city, where nonnormative sexual practices are rendered inappropriate and so are scorned. In *Hide and Seek* (*Machbo'im,* Dan Wolman, 1980), for example, a film set in pre-state Jerusalem, the secretive homosexual affair that the protagonist is having with an Arab man is violently disrupted by underground Jewish fighters. Whereas Tel Aviv of the 1960s and 1970s already offered some kind of sexual liberty, as in Uri Zohar's films for example,[4] Jerusalem remained a place of tradition and conformism (see also my discussion of *Eyes Wide Open* [Haim Tabakman, 2009] in chapter 5).

Indeed, the city had offered refuge to those who did not fit in the heteronormative Zionist order even before the emergence of the gay movement.[5] However, this tendency has become more prevalent since the first gay-themed films by Amos Guttman of the late 1970s, and especially his feature films of the 1980s. Guttman's films, which represent the more militant wing of the gay movement in Israel (see chapter 2), portray Tel Aviv as a city that, in a striking contrast to the rest of Israel, can tolerate otherness. The majority of Guttman's films feature characters who leave their provincial town for what they see as a new life in the city.[6] Interestingly, the change in status of the gay community in Israel in recent years, reflected in Eytan Fox's films (see chapter 3), has also signaled the weakening of the status of Tel Aviv as the ultimate haven for gay men and lesbians. In these films, gay-themed plots move from the center outward to the periphery. This move indicates a growing, mainly male, gay presence in Israeli culture. In these films the "urban migration" narrative is no longer the only option available for young gay men. Rather, they attest to the ubiquity of gay culture in contemporary Israeli society, which can be read as a sign of successful integration.

The "integrationist" approach of the Israeli gay community may also explain the absence of an official, or at least a well-defined, gay district in Tel Aviv, unlike in most Western capitals. The establishment of separate gay districts is a fairly new phenomenon, linked to the emergence of a politically oriented, minority-modeled gay identity in the United States in the 1960s.

According to David Higgs, there has been "a quantum leap" in gay districts, or villages as they are sometimes called, since the 1970s (8). The existence of such demarcated areas helps to develop an economic infrastructure and allows cultural life to flourish. Gay districts are important because of the dual roles they play: they are both places to which young gay men and women from the hinterland move in order to come to terms with their sexuality and economic and political centers for the community (Knopp and Lauria 161). At the same time, gay districts are often seen as ghettos, serving as buffers between the community and the rest of society. In the case of Israel, the foundation of a separate gay district, either official or not, would contradict the movement's fundamental aspiration for total integration.

The task I undertake in this chapter is twofold: to trace the trajectories on the screen of two phenomena—the emergence of the gay movement and the reinvention of Tel Aviv since the 1980s—and to explore the influences they have had on one another. This chapter offers close textual analysis of films that present Tel Aviv as a generator and a symbol of social change. Not all the films included in this chapter fall into one of the conventional definitions of gay films. However, they have all had an important role to play in cementing the connection between the city of Tel Aviv and alternative modes of existence in contemporary Israel.

Some of the later films discussed in this chapter represent Tel Aviv as a postmodern dystopian alternative to Israeli hegemonic culture. In their harsh critique of state institutions, they open up a space in which new subjectivities and practices can be constituted. Although Tel Aviv has always been an inseparable part of the Zionist project, it has also formed a strong alternative to Zionist and Israeli core values. Responding to disturbing events that interrupted life in the city, such as the first Gulf War in 1991, these films emphasize the end of the Zionist-Israeli utopian vision of a new Jewish life as it has manifested itself in Tel Aviv. Other films expand the boundaries of the Israeli discourse around sexuality and gender and, consequently, undermine the forced heteronormative nature of middle Israel. All films share an imaginary vision of Tel Aviv as a city in which sexual, social, and cultural dispositions are being constantly reexamined and altered.

> It is to the city that the migrants, the minorities, the diasporic come to change the history of the nation [...] in the west, and increasingly elsewhere, it is the city which provides the space in which emergent identifications and new social movements of the people are played out. It is there that, in our time, the perplexity of the living is most acutely experienced.
>
> Homi K. Bhabha, "DissemiNation" 319–20

Tel Aviv and Gay Identity on the Israeli Screen

CROWS: THE CITY AS A SANCTUARY

Crows (*Orvim,* 1987), Ayelet Menahemi's short film, is an expressionistic fable about a group of Israeli runaways, mostly gay teenage boys, who live in a commune in Tel Aviv. Menahemi wrote and directed the film while still a student (she attended the Beit Tzvi film school in Ramat Gan, as did Amos Guttman, whose cinematic vision, it seems, greatly inspired Menahemi in the making of *Crows*). She claimed to have based the film on some of the actors' as well as her own personal experiences as outcasts on the margins of militaristic 1980s Israel.

Menahemi's depiction of Tel Aviv as a decadent metropolis alludes, whether deliberately or not, to the outlandish vision of New York City in Slava Tsukerman's *Liquid Sky* (USA, 1982). Akin to the latter's nihilistic attitude and expressionist visuals, Menahemi's film was based on a postmodern—in the Israeli context read also as post-Zionist—narrative, which aimed at abolishing hierarchies and boundaries, and hyperrealistic design. Menahemi's film is also similar to those of American filmmaker Susan Seidelman (who directed her debut feature film, *Smithereens,* in 1982, followed by the commercially successful *Desperately Seeking Susan* in 1985) in focusing on what Richard K. Ferncase has described as a "suburban refugee who becomes a city girl, caught up in the excitement and chaos of the urban environment" (50). This narrative is similar to the gay "urban migratory story" discussed by Mark W. Turner.

Whereas *Liquid Sky* was a sci-fi tale featuring aliens in search of a euphoria-inducing chemical produced by the human brain during orgasm, *Crows* introduces Tel Aviv to another kind of alien—although no less dangerous, in the eyes of the establishment—in the shape of a flamboyant group of homosexuals wearing bizarre costumes and hairdos. As Emanuel Levy has pointed out, *Liquid Sky,* directed by a Soviet émigré to the United States, portrays the city as a sanctuary for foreigners, be they immigrants, space aliens, or merely outsiders—spaced-out models, junkies, and performance artists (185–86).[7] *Liquid Sky* portrays the city as a site in which old conventions are demolished in favor of a new world order. As one of the characters claims when asked about her sexual identity, "Homosexual, heterosexual, bisexual, whether I like someone doesn't depend on the genitals as long as I find them attractive. I'm always curious why people have to make these sexual definitions."

Drawing on *Liquid Sky*'s nocturnal urban atmosphere and sexual and gender rebellion, *Crows* tries to emphasize the extravagant lifestyle of its characters, compared with the uniform lives led by most of their Israeli nongay counterparts. *Crows*, like Guttman's films of the same era, renders gay life as an exotic way of life, outside ordinary Israel. This tendency did not fit in with the respectable image and integrationist agenda the gay community aspired to at the time. Like Guttman, in his bold, unapologetic portrayal of gay sex and demonstrable anti-Zionist sentiments, Menahemi aims, first and foremost, to shock the audience. Her sympathetic representation of idle "freaks" living in a rundown apartment and scavenging for food mocks the values of the society that rejected them.

The story of the gay commune in *Crows* is told from the point of view of another misfit, Margalit (Gili Benousilio), a girl from a remote village who enters their lives. The film begins with her running away from home to Tel Aviv. In a voice-over narration she says, "In such a small country, if someone decides to run away it is always to Tel Aviv." Wandering the streets of the city she runs into Yuval (Boaz Turjeman)[8] and Eli (Doron Barbi), who take her to the commune they share with a group of eccentric homosexuals and transvestites. For Margalit, who introduces herself to the others as Maggie, this is a first encounter with gay men. In a voice-over she comments, "I never knew anything about homosexuals, but now it seems like the most logical thing in the world." During the time she spends with the group (as she informs the viewers in a voice-over, she had intended to leave the next day but somehow found herself staying), she reinvents herself with the help of the others.

Changing her name from Jewish-Israeli Margalit to Western Maggie is only the first step she takes in her efforts to erase her past, and her Israeli identity. With her shorn hair, shaved by one of the members of the group, and dressed in a man's suit, Maggie sports a new appearance that blurs her sexual identity and gender and echoes the androgynous Margaret, the main character in *Liquid Sky*, and her male alter ego, Jimmy (both played by Anne Carlisle). Maggie adopts a rootless existence, like that of the city of Tel Aviv. Tel Aviv, according to popular myth, was established "from the sands" and has been known as the city without a past ever since. It is synonymous with reinvention, progress, and liberal thinking (the word *Hol* in Hebrew, meaning "sand," also stands for "secular"). Maggie's reinvention encapsulates the idea of Tel Aviv as a city in constant transformation and, although known as the "first Hebrew city," cosmopolitan and pluralistic.[9]

The members of the group she joins gradually become her alternate family. Despite their frequent feuds, they give Maggie a sense of belonging that she has never had before. She decided to run away because ever since her mother, who had suffered from a mental illness, committed suicide, her father neglected her. As she is seen sneaking from her father's farm, she says in a voice-over, "My dad, he doesn't give a damn [. . .] all he can think of is my mum. I knew he wouldn't look for me." Maggie carries a picture of a beautiful woman whom she claims was her mother. Only later does she admit that her mother was nothing like the woman in the picture. In her endless attempts to make her life more bearable, the commune she finds herself in is the only place where she does not need to pretend.

Traumatized by her mother's death, Maggie is especially alarmed by the repeated suicide attempts of transvestite Daniel (Itzik Nini). It is his death at the end of the film that marks the disintegration of the group. Maggie then leaves for an unknown destination and an unknown future, an open ending that reflects the filmmaker's somber view on the readiness of 1980s Israeli society to accept those who are different from the norm. The open ending is quite ironic against the background of bildungsroman, or novel of formation, narratives, which Maggie's story seems to follow at first.[10] Maggie's experiences in Tel Aviv do not pave the way to successful integration in society, the outcome of the classic male bildungsroman; it is doubtful whether they lead to "the evolution of a coherent self" (Abel, Hirsch, and Langland 13), the objective of the classic female bildungsroman.

Menahemi depicted her protagonists' existence as the antithesis of the fundamental principles of Israeli society. Her characters live in the Israel of the early 1980s but create for themselves a parallel universe in which there is no trace of national symbols such as the Israel Defense Forces (IDF) or traumas such as the Lebanon War. Leading a nocturnal life, the characters in *Crows* do not take part in the life of productive, daytime Tel Aviv and hardly make contact with fellow Israelis. Their brief encounter with ultra-Orthodox Jews, whose ritual baths are located opposite their apartment, is one of very few instances in which people outside their coterie enter the frame. However, this encounter does not lead to dialogue: the only sign of communication between them is when Maggie and her friends play a trick on their Orthodox neighbors. Standing at two opposite poles of Israeli society, the chance meeting between Orthodox Jews and a group of young misfits represents the unbridgeable chasm in Israeli society. At the same time, it is important to note that although both groups are presented as each other's antithesis, ultra-Orthodox Jews are also traditionally perceived as great opponents of secular Zionism and liberal Israel. Their presence in the film, therefore, describes the clash between homosexuality and Judaism rather than homosexuality and Israeli mainstream society. Menahemi has chosen to show two marginal subgroups but to avoid representing dominant Israeli culture, a choice that emphasizes the uniqueness of Tel Aviv as a neutral space where one can escape oppressive hegemonic culture.

In contrast to the "integrationist" approach adopted by the gay community, and similar to the Orthodox Jews they come across, Menahemi's characters intentionally separate themselves from anything "Israeli." The outside world is not allowed in the realm of the apartment they share, not even its representations: the TV set is placed lopsided in a supermarket cart and shows nothing but "snow." As Maggie says in a voice-over, life in the commune does not start until nightfall, which is their cue to dress up and go out. They all divide their time between the apartment and the club where Yuval works as a dancer (there is also one scene that takes place backstage at a fashion show where Yuval works as a makeup artist).

They only step out of their small, demarcated world twice. In the first instance they are seen trying to hitch a ride back to Tel Aviv but are refused time and again because of their appearance. The industrial, deserted landscape of the power station in Hadera, a small town between Tel Aviv and Haifa, is behind them and lends an apocalyptic tone to the scene. Abandoned on the margins of a highway, their alienation from society is further emphasized. The second time is when they take a trip to Tel Baruch beach, an infamous center for prostitution on the northern edge of Tel Aviv. This trip ends with Daniel's death from an overdose and the subsequent disintegration of the group. The encounter with other parts of Israel, namely outside the borders of central Tel Aviv, proves to be deathly.

The viewer does not get to see the moshav (smallholders' cooperative settlement) that Maggie runs away from, apart from a short series of shots in the beginning of the film that serves as an exposition. However, the film does use the country-town binary to highlight the differences between Tel Aviv and the rest of Israel. Although urban settlers were initially considered a part of the Zionist project contributing to industry and commerce, they were never seen in the same light as their agrarian counterparts. The latter were the realization of the ideal of the New Jew and a product of the kibbutzim and moshavim. Turning away from the culture of the Diaspora, the new society in Palestine (and later Israel) adopted a new set of values, epitomized in the creation of those agriculture-based, socialist-inspired settlements. Yet shortly after the establishment of the state, Israel was already mostly urban. Its first master plan (also known as the Sharon plan, 1950) advocated an extensive network of metropolitan areas, regional cities, and development towns. The turn to a free-market economy in the 1980s effected further change in the power balance between urban and farm life. Israel rapidly became more urban than the world's most developed countries, and by 2003 91.8 percent of its population was living in cities.[11]

The urbanization of Israel reinforced the symbolic meaning that the moshavim and kibbutzim have had in Zionist and Israeli ideology. As Bruce King has stated, "Nationalism is an urban movement which identifies with the rural areas as a source of authenticity, finding in the 'folk' the attitudes, beliefs, customs and language to create a sense of national unity among people who have other loyalties. Nationalism aims at [. . .] rejection of cosmopolitan upper classes, intellectuals and others likely to be influenced by foreign ideas" (qtd. in Brennan 53). The implied contrast between the city and the village, as it is featured in *Crows,* animates the old Zionist debate about the role of the city in the new Jewish society. The film's portrayal of Tel Aviv confirms the view of the opponents of city life, who believe it is a nest of sexual deviants. In the first shot of Tel Aviv, right after Maggie arrives in the city, she is seen walking down a crowded street in the old central bus station with her back to a giant sex cinema sign, which heralds the loss of innocence the city inevitably brings with it.

The city, however, is where Maggie's life is saved. At one point in the film she opens up to Daniel and tells him about her mother's madness. Her mental state became worse, Maggie says, because of her life in the moshav. "I do not want to live my life like she did," Maggie exclaims, implying she would have ended the same way had she stayed. Whereas the city is traditionally perceived as an isolating place, Menahemi portrays it as the only place where people like Maggie and the members of the group she becomes part of are accepted. Paradoxically, in order to be accepted they have to form their own communal group, which is based on similar "socialist" notions to those of the kibbutz or the moshav.

The moshav and the Zionist mentality it symbolizes, on the other hand, is rendered dangerous, as it rejects those who do not fit in the dominant culture (the crows of the title) and pushes them to either suicide or escape. As Igal Bursztyn points out, although *Crows* makes use of symbols of a pastoral, village life such as a plowed field, a scarecrow, and cowsheds, they carry a dark, menacing meaning. Feelings of danger and threat are expressed by the dark skies, the bonfire in front of the warehouse, the village houses that look like black stains, and the grotesque scarecrow (Bursztyn, "Introduction" 15).

Running away from home after being abandoned by both her parents, Maggie experiences the city as her sanctuary. The city, the film suggests, can offer the security the moshav and Zionism cannot, even if only for a short while until the group disintegrates. The disintegration of the group, symbolizing the end of hope for the protagonists, also brings with it the end of the film. The future of the characters remains unknown but is partially unfolded in *Tel Aviv Stories* (1992), which Menahemi cowrote and codirected. *Tel Aviv Stories* allows its characters what *Crows* could not: its protagonists are no longer passive victims of an oppressive system, but rather characters who dare to try to change their given position in the world.

TEL AVIV STORIES: THE FICTIONALIZED CITY AND ITS "NEW BOHEMIANS"

Tel Aviv Stories (Nirit Yaron and Ayelet Menahemi, 1992), as its title suggests, was conceived as the Israeli version of *New York Stories* (Martin Scorsese, Francis Ford Coppola, Woody Allen, USA, 1989). Like the latter, *Tel Aviv Stories* comprises three different episodes that are meant to offer different points of view on life in the city. The title song suggests that Tel Aviv is not New York, and some of the critics agreed with this statement, arguing that the film, especially the two first episodes, surrenders to the image that the local press has created rather than reflecting the city's life as it "really" is.[12] Given that this is what films, and culture in general, do, namely construct meaning rather than reflect reality, I am interested in what kind of fictional construction *Tel Aviv Stories,* like the rest of the films examined in this chapter, offers.

The film can also be seen as a sequel to Judd Ne'eman's feature *The Dress* (*HaSimla,* 1969; made up of three episodes: "The Dress," "The Letter," and "The Return of Thomas"). Like Ne'eman's film, *Tel Aviv Stories* develops three stories that take place in the city. Both films focus on young people in their mid to late twenties and their complex love affairs, rather than on broader issues of national identity. Ella Shohat has argued that the three episodes of *The Dress* "revolve around attempts at communicating," and one of them in particular, "The Return of Thomas," echoes Truffaut's *Jules and Jim* in its triangular love affair of two men and a woman (198). Nitzan S. Ben-Shaul calls attention to *The Dress*'s "abstract European ambience" that supplants references to the specific society to which the protagonists belong (109).

Both films represent Tel Aviv as a vibrant city with its face to the West. The soundtrack of *The Dress* consists of jazz and rock music with English lyrics. The scene in the second episode, in which the protagonist is looking for his love interest in a club with a beat band performing in the background, is reminiscent of the Yardbirds' performance in Michelangelo Antonioni's *Blow Up* (1966), one of the key films that defined "Swinging London" in the mid-1960s. Ne'eman was one of the main members of the Israeli "New Wave" movement, which adopted a more improvised, impressionistic approach in order to break with the dominant realist tradition in Israeli cinema at the time. In *The Dress* he finds in Tel Aviv a resemblance to Paris. Similarly, Yaron and Menahemi portray the center of Tel Aviv as a bohemian, art-oriented district in a Western city. Even the last episode, clearly the most "Israeli" of all, takes place in Shalom Tower (Migdal Shalom), an architectural landmark that symbolized the beginning of Israel's rapid process of Americanization. It was built in 1961 on the site of the old Herzliya High School, the first public building in Tel Aviv and the first Hebrew high school. Shalom Tower was the first, and for many years the only, skyscraper in Tel Aviv, with a large American-style department store and wax museum, both of which feature in the episode.

The film epitomized the new, urban culture that the local press promoted during the 1980s. The first Tel Aviv local newspaper was *Ha'ir* ("The City"), first published in October 1980.[13] The weekly magazine was inspired by publications such as New York's *The Village Voice.* The publication of *mekomonim* (local newspapers) not only revolutionized the print media in Israel but also strengthened Tel Aviv's status as Israel's center for culture and the arts (even though the first local newspaper *Kol Ha'ir* in Israel appeared in Jerusalem in 1979).

The *mekomonim*'s "new journalism," which meant bringing the writer to the fore rather than the topic she or he was sent to cover, was part of a shift of emphasis from collective issues (endorsed by the ideological party-sponsored dailies, popular in the pre-state period and Israel's early decades) to the concerns of the individual. The emergence of a new, personal style of writing in Israeli journalism ("a direct import from the United States via writers who had spent time there" [Segev 68]) occurred in tandem with the strengthening of privatization and consumerism, processes Israeli society has undergone since the 1960s. This gave rise to both the breakdown of the kibbutzim and a dramatic change in sexual norms, of which the rise of a visible gay culture was a direct outcome. Journalist Tom Segev claims that Israel's new individualistic awareness "encouraged equality between the sexes and sexual permissiveness, and gave a measure of legitimacy to unconventional sexual orientations" (69).

The *mekomonim* first appeared at the beginning of a great internal migration from other parts of Israel to Tel Aviv, and they documented its influence on the new urban culture developed in those years. *Tel Aviv Magazine* dedicated a special issue in September 1992 to the "new Tel Aviv residents," in which native Tel Aviv residents and migrants to the city examined their different perceptions of it. In their writings about the city, the new migrants were mostly inspired by a fantasized concept of a cosmopolitan metropolis.[14]

The invention of the local newspapers was one way of reinforcing the image of Tel Aviv as an exciting urban center. Celebrating five years of *Ha'ir* in 1985, Israeli commentator Doron Rosenblum wrote that it had not been long before it became impossible to differentiate between writers' fiction and the reality of the city. Their words, he claimed, rebuilt the city, which was gradually becoming more vibrant, culturally diverse, democratic, and self-aware. In this way the *mekomonim* not only reflected cultural processes that took place in the city in the 1980s and 1990s but also contributed toward creating them. The *mekomonim* have been credited with the invention of a new Tel Aviv jargon and style of writing as well as setting a new agenda. Urgent national issues were pushed aside in favor of cultural and local events. The *mekomonim* created a cultural and social scene with a distinctive discourse, definite social codes, and local heroes. Like other cultural arenas at the time, such as Israeli rock music of the early 1980s, which adopted elements from the English and European postpunk music scenes (elements that can be traced in the set and costume designs in *Crows*), they aspired to imagine Tel Aviv as a bustling metropolis. The *mekomonim* emphasized the resemblance of Tel Aviv to New York and London as much as they blurred the link between Tel Aviv and the rest of Israel.

Putting a great emphasis on the construction of Tel Aviv as a subversive alternative to the rest of Israel, the local press perceived the nascent Israeli gay culture as an important and inseparable part of the city. Gay lifestyles, at least in the early and mid-1980s, despite the attempts of Aguda, represented an antiestablishment, antinormative attitude, which fitted in well with the agenda of the local press. Gay men and women helped expand Tel Aviv's urban infrastructure through their bars and clubs and added a sexualized, permissive dimension to the city with Independence Park, for example, functioning as a central, though unauthorized, cruising spot for gay men.

In the mid-1980s *Ha'ir* started publishing a weekly column called Moshe by an anonymous writer later revealed to be Gal Uchovsky, a journalist, scriptwriter, and TV personality. The column described the ordinary life of a gay couple in Tel Aviv and was seminal in its "matter-of-fact" approach to the subject, already very different from that of Amos Guttman's films, which were made only a few years earlier.[15] Uchovsky maintained this approach throughout his career. In his journalistic work (he became the chief editor of *Ha'ir* in the early 1990s before moving on to the national press),[16] his art and culture TV program, and the films he made with his partner, director Eytan Fox, he stressed the "normalcy" and "casualness" of gayness, to the extent that its uniqueness and subversive manners almost completely vanished in the wish for total integration.[17] Nonetheless, Uchovsky has played an important role in shifting the attitude toward homosexuality and gayness in Israeli society since he started publishing Moshe. He would not have been able to achieve that without establishing himself first in Tel Aviv.

Tel Aviv Stories was perceived by many as the cinematic version of the fictitious Tel Aviv of the local press. The film was even sponsored by *Tel Aviv Magazine,* one of the two leading local weeklies at the time. Most reviews argue that this construction of a fictitious city was a flaw in a film that otherwise could have been considered an impressive technical and artistic achievement.[18] The film, however, became a commercial success, and not only in Tel Aviv. It attracted more than 150,000 viewers (Bernheimer 42), 78 percent of whom watched it outside Tel Aviv. The success of the film attested to the spreading of what, in the 1980s, was considered an esoteric culture to the rest of Israel in the 1990s. Tel Aviv exported not only "its" cinema but also literature and music, which until then had been solely identified with a demarcated geographical space (Bernheimer 44).

The opening episode, *Sharona, Honey* (*Sharona, Motek*) tells the story of a young assistant art director (Yael Abecassis) and her four overly enthusiastic suitors. The episode includes a brief appearance by Amir Kaminer, a gay journalist who had become a well-known figure in Tel Aviv nightlife in those years, mainly due to his unique camp demeanor. By casting Kaminer as himself (he also appeared in Amos Guttman's *Amazing Grace* and Eytan Fox's *Song of the Siren*), Menahemi reaffirms the immanence of gay culture in the "new bohemian" scene of the city.

Of the three, this episode was seen as both the most aesthetically artificial and the least credible piece. The protagonist's career is not seen as "real" enough, let alone important. At one point in the episode one of Sharona's lovers tries to convince her to go to Los Angeles with him where working with sets, props, and costumes is "a real profession." The lives the characters lead seem to be out of touch with Israeli national concerns. The cosmopolitan nature of Tel Aviv seems to be more fantasized than authentic. The filmmakers admitted to having modified certain visual elements in order to give a more appealing look to the city. Yaron said, "I sweated in order to make Tel Aviv look as pretty and reasonably visual as possible. I 'made up' locations. A whole building was wrapped with yellow paper, so it would not be seen in the frame." Menahemi said, "There is the real Tel Aviv and the Tel Aviv that you dream about. [. . .] You bring it closer to the cinematic world you build up in your imagination" (Shaked 74).

The second episode, *A Cat Operation* (*Mivtsa Chatul*), tells the story of Tsofit (Ruthie Goldberg), a local newspaper journalist who, in the midst of a series of personal crises (her husband leaves her for his lover and she is about to lose her job) and suicide attempts, tries to save the life of a kitten trapped in a sewage tunnel. With scenes that sarcastically depict the inflated local art scene (echoing Martin Scorsese's *Life Lessons*, the first episode in *New York Stories*), the second episode, like the first, is a tongue-in-cheek portrayal of a group of urban people, most of whom work either in the media or in the arts and who are all equally disconnected from the national Israeli agenda.

Only the third episode, *Divorce* (*Get*), decidedly exceeds the limits of imaginary urban experience and touches on wider issues concerning modern Israeli reality. The episode tells the story of a policewoman (Anat Waxman), a deserted wife who spots her husband while patrolling in Shalom Tower. Determined to force him to give her a *get* (according to Jewish rabbinic law, the woman is not considered divorced until her husband agrees to divorce her), she takes hostage her superior officer and other passersby, including a rabbi. When her husband, an escaped criminal, offers her the long-awaited *get* on condition that she not hand him over to the police, she refuses. In her search for revenge, Tikva (Hope in Hebrew) is willing to risk all that she has: her job, children, and freedom.

The three films differ from each other in set design, characterization, and the stance they take toward Tel Aviv life. Each episode depicts a different side of the city, although they all take place in the same geographical area, the central-southern part of the city as opposed to the newer, more bourgeois northern part. Whereas the first episode tries to capture glamorous bohemian life—the protagonist moves from one chic apartment to another, stops at a fashion shoot, and ends up in a trendy bar—the last episode explores the life of a wretched policewoman, a single mother whose conservative lifestyle prevents her from getting involved with men. Whereas Sharona cheats on her boyfriend with at least one lover and flirts simultaneously with two others, Tsofit and Tikva react in a different way to their complicated love affairs: Tsofit tries to commit suicide because her husband abandoned her, and Tikva confesses to her hostages that she has been celibate since her husband left her five years ago.

However, the similarities between the episodes cannot be overlooked. Not only did the same two women writer-directors collaborate on them[19]; they also deal with female protagonists who defy a male chauvinistic and discriminating system. Sharona struggles with her men and their demands, Tsofit tries to avoid her male editor and former husband while fighting with male municipality clerks who do all they can to make her cat rescue operation impossible, and Tikva loses control when she realizes

Fighting male dominance: Tikva (Anat Waxman) and her hostages in Nirit Yaron and Ayelet Menahemi's *Tel Aviv Stories* (1992).

her husband has managed to escape once again. She then has to fight her male commander who comes to arrest her. In one scene she throws fireworks at the police force, declaring, "This is my independence day." She celebrates her independence not only from her husband but also from the male-dominated state organization she works for. The viewers are reminded throughout the episode that Tikva's promotion was denied because she had refused to have sex with her chief commander. It is therefore symbolic that her struggle for independence takes place inside a skyscraper, seen metaphorically as a phallic architectural symbol, one that represents might and masculinity.[20]

The three episodes come to explore the psyche of the city and they all do so from a female perspective, an unusual angle in Israeli cinema before the early 1990s. This interconnection between the exploration of women's lives and the life of the city is not accidental. The film, as a whole, produces a statement regarding the role of Tel Aviv as a site in which the old, sexist values of Israeli society should be reexamined and changed. As in Guttman's cinema and Menahemi's *Crows,* the city in *Tel Aviv Stories* is not merely a background but a generating factor: its landmarks, cultural scenes, and people have a direct influence on both the events and the actions of the protagonists seen on the screen.

The identification of the women protagonists with the city is unequivocal. At the end of *Sharona, Motek,* Sharona is seen chasing a garbage truck and she sits on it, looking from afar on her four confused suitors. The workers clear the streets of the heaps of garbage that were piled up during their long strike. The end of the strike, which brings the cleanup of the city, signals the beginning of Sharona's own cleansing process. Instead of adjusting to her lovers' wishes and plans—two of them want to have a child with her—she leaves them behind, reclaiming her freedom. Even before that Sharona is seen smashing binoculars that the four men used to spy on her from the balcony of an apartment across the street, and by doing so she demolishes their penetrative gaze.

As Orly Lubin points out ("The Woman as Other" 313–15), the first two episodes of *Tel Aviv Stories* focus on the formation of a female sexuality and an autonomous female subject, who is no longer dependent on the masculine world and is able to fulfill her own wishes and needs. In Tikva's case, Lubin argues, her claim to independence and freedom is more complicated, as she cannot give up her wish for the hegemonic masculine authority's approval (represented by the religious rabbinic system, the police, and the prison to which she is likely to be sent). Unlike Tsofit and Sharona, she cannot settle for an optional "alternative" feminine order, namely moving on with her life while ignoring the restrictions the system has set up for her. It is implied in the film that Tikva's poor socioeconomic background and conservatism, suggesting a Mizrahi ethnicity (although this is not made clear in the episode), may explain her difficulty in resisting the institutional restrictions imposed on her. Moreover, of the three characters, Tikva is the only one who has children—representing a more normative way of life— and whose place of residence is unknown. Tikva works in the city, but it is not clear if this is also where she lives. Thus Tikva's identification with the city and its alleged feminist, challenging values, as elaborated in the first two episodes, is at best partial and ambiguous.

The intersection of a feminist perspective and the city in *Tel Aviv Stories* brings up questions regarding the role of the city as facilitating an alternative sexual and gendered space. The resistance shown by the female characters in the three episodes and their determination, especially in the first two episodes, to live their lives in accordance with their own wishes echoes the struggle that gay men and, even more so lesbians and transsexuals, are faced with. The similarities between the four groups—gay men, straight women, lesbians, and transsexuals—are numerous. Of all four groups it seems that gay men have achieved a far better life than the rest. As stated before, Israeli society might have overcome, to a certain extent, its homophobic sentiments, but it still discriminates against women, be they "natural born" women, straight or gay, or men-turned-into-women. As Alisa Solomon has stated, "Zionism's masculinizing project has been harder to crack than its imperative to male heterosexuality" (160).

It is probably their more fragile standing that has allowed women to produce a queer, in the broad sense of the word, critique of the Israeli establishment, in the shape of Dana International[21]; the activities of women's groups such as Bat Shalom (one of the most active groups in the propeace, antioccupation movement) and Four Mothers (a group that called for Israel's unilateral withdrawal from its self-declared security zone in Southern Lebanon); and, indeed, filmmaking. It is not surprising that *Tel Aviv Stories* was directed by women filmmakers: their film aims to build a different narrative from the dominant Israeli one, an effort not easily detected in many recent (male) gay films. In this sense *Tel Aviv Stories,* although not dealing directly with gay subjectivity, offers a subversive outlook on Israeli life, one that encourages nonnormative sexual identities.

> Queer city histories attract a readership because gay men are intensely urban. Few live by choice in the country on a permanent basis since they usually feel that cities offer a much greater variety of ways in which to enjoy one's life.
>
> DAVID HIGGS 2

Song of the Siren: Gay Sensibility and the Culture of Consumerism

Song of the Siren, Eytan Fox's first feature film, gained unprecedented media attention long before its release in 1994. The film is based on Irit Linur's bestselling novel of the same title, first published in 1991. The novel, set in an advertising agency in Tel Aviv, not only has sold more than 50,000 copies in Israel but also has been perceived as a landmark in contemporary Hebrew culture, marking the rise of popular "lowbrow" literature as a legitimate cultural phenomenon. It also depicted a more individualistic and less politically committed society. The film was highly anticipated by audience and critics alike. The result, it seems, disappointed both: the reviews, in most cases, accused Fox of creating a pale imitation of the novel, and the audience reception was relatively poor. Although the film by no means failed commercially—it attracted more than 140,000 viewers—it did not live up to early expectations (Perchak). The film was also ignored in the Israeli Film Academy Awards of that year (Yosha 39). Nevertheless, the film has a special importance in reflecting cultural and social processes in Israeli society at the time, which had a direct link to evolving gay life in Tel Aviv.

Fox, fresh from directing his debut gay-themed short film *Time Off* (*After,* 1990) hoped to approach the novel from a gay perspective. His attempt to write a gay character into the film, however, was blocked by Linur, who also wrote the script. In an interview Fox gave three years after the release of the film, in November 1997, he claimed it was unrealistic to assume there were not any gay men working in an advertising agency based in Tel Aviv (Negev 39).

Despite the absence of gay characters in the film, Fox managed to produce a film that is characterized by a gay sensibility. This comes across in two instances: one is the portrayal of Talila (Dalit Kahn), the main female protagonist, as a single, career-driven, high-spending character. The other is Fox's emphasis on design in the excessive mise-en-scène and on consumption at the narrative level. Fox made use of his auteur status in order to undermine the authorship of Linur, the writer. It is interesting to explore the dissonance in the film between the ostensibly heterosexual story and the hints at a different, gay meaning. Fox's public homosexuality can be assumed to have altered not only his own agenda but also viewers' perception of the film, especially gay viewers who, having seen *Time Off* and read the interviews with Fox in which he discussed his sexuality, were ready to decode the film's gay symbols. The reading of texts from the margins, Orly Lubin argues, may expose and identify hegemonic norms that are positioned in the center as constructed and artificial (*Women Reading Women* 75). In the case of *Song of the Siren,* the film does not offer an alternative, that is, an overtly gay, narrative, but the reading of the film from a gay perspective enables the consumption of the text without surrendering to its overt system of values. Such a reading, or "act of refusal" as Lubin refers to it (*Women Reading Women* 75), allows a distance from the explicit stance of the film, thus guarding against internalizing its normative values.

Song of the Siren celebrates growing consumer affluence and escapist universalism in Tel Aviv, a tendency that was propelled, in part, by the heightened profile and social mobility of a certain group of urban gay men within the Israeli gay community in the years before the release of the book as well as the expansion of Western trends in Israeli society. The process of privatization and the rise of both consumerism and an urban, high-spending gay community are, as Alisa Solomon shows, well connected. Solomon identifies what she calls a "free-market mania" as a principal factor in the emergence of gay consciousness (155).

Throughout his career, Fox has attempted to create crowd-pleasing films by adapting popular Hollywood genres for the Israeli screen. His film *Walk on Water* (2004), for example, is a psychological thriller featuring a Mossad secret agent, whose job justifies some high-octane action scenes, whereas his debut feature film was a light romantic comedy. Unlike Guttman's dark, expressionistic melodramas, *Song of the Siren* reads as an uncritical adaptation of Hollywood conventions. In an interview with *The Jerusalem Post* ("Twentieth Century Fox" 13), Fox said, "I wanted it to feel like a musical. I wanted it to have a 'studio' look, very colorful, very playful. A romantic comedy that is beautiful, pleasant and has an unabashedly romantic ending" (13). Whereas most Israeli filmmakers choose to deal with "national" themes, mainly the Israeli-Palestinian conflict or the deprivation of Mizrahi Jews, or at least refer to them, Fox opted in this case for an allegedly apolitical, nonartistic, genre film.

Fox's attempt to follow a Hollywood model in conflict-ridden Israel, a state that lacks a long tradition of filmmaking, is, of course, a political statement in itself.[22] His attempt to create a "standard" romantic comedy reflecting a "normal" society, without having the infrastructure required for that, was not received well by critics. It is important to note that Fox was not the first Israeli filmmaker who tried to exceed the limits that the local film industry and culture had set him. A group of directors who created "New Wave" cinema in Israel in the 1960s and 1970s (see also chapter 2) had set a precedent. In her analysis of the Israeli film industry, published in 1989, Ella Shohat argues,

> The situation of cinema in Israel is comparable to that of countries such as Algeria, not only in terms of the challenge of developing ex nihilo a cinematic infrastructure and wresting control of the domestic market from foreign domination, but also in terms of the overall historical evolution of the films themselves, moving from a somewhat idealizing nation-building "mythic" cinema into a more diversified "normal" kind of industry. Yet Israeli filmmakers and critics almost invariably speak, and make films, as if the natural points of reference were to countries with long-developed infrastructures. [. . .] They rarely refer to Third World films or directors, or to the intense debates [. . .] that have animated Third World film discourse. [. . .] Third World debates linking production strategies, aesthetics, and politics within the search for a dealienating, non-Hollywood mode of filmic discourse have unfortunately had little or no resonance in Israel. (4–5)

However, it is this aspiration that makes *Song of the Siren* an important cultural document. Fox's cinematic vision is part of a broader tendency to create an alternative to the highly politicized Israeli reality by adopting a "Western" way of life, mainly in Tel Aviv. By the time Irit Linur published her book in 1991, the *mekomonim* had already instilled a whole new local culture, which was more interested in global culture than national politics. *Song of the Siren*, the novel, published three years before the release of the film, was an attempt to canonize this culture, to establish it as a valid alternative.

The story takes place at the time of the missile attacks on Israel during the Gulf War in 1991. A traumatic event in Israeli cultural memory is described in the novel as a surreal background to the romantic actions and caprices of the characters. Talila, the heroine, a cynical advertising agent who lives in Tel Aviv, reveals an incredible ignorance about the war and refuses to believe that Scud missiles will ever land on the city. Even after being proven wrong, she still cannot take the threat as seriously as one might expect her to. Through her eyes the war seems to be no more than material for a comic gag, a perception that undermines the serious state of alertness Israel was in at the time. Distracted by her love life, the protagonist refuses to let the national agenda interfere with her private life. In so doing, she defies the hitherto prevalent tendency to give "national," "militaristic," and "security" causes top priority. This should be read as a broader critique of Israel's tendency to push aside civil issues in the name of state security.

In the course of the war Talila falls in love with Noah (Boaz Gur-Lavi), a food engineer who lives in Mazkeret Batya, a small, pastoral, village-like community. They lead dramatically different lives: Talila represents a post-feminist, confident, and financially independent woman who lives in the city and enjoys a life of luxury. I would like to argue that her character is partly shaped by the model of the post-Stonewall, successful gay man. Her urban, career-minded life, without family commitments, represents the experience of many well-off gay men. This economic prosperity is a result of a shift in the status of gay men in Israel, as well as in other parts of the Western world. Noah, on the other hand, represents the stereotypical all-Israeli heterosexual man, with his plain, modest way of living, his vocation, and his neglected appearance. As such, he finds himself completely out of place in Talila's universe. The film attempts to describe a clash between two traditions in Israeli reality of the early 1990s: on the one hand, the ever-growing consumer culture in Tel Aviv and other wealthy areas in Israel, and on the other, the more modest way of life, reminiscent of the Zionist ideal. Of all the characters in the film, Noah is the only one called up into the army. By doing his reserve duty, even though in a noncombat unit, Noah's character is portrayed as one who participates fully in Israeli life, as opposed to the Tel Aviv crowd, a group of hedonistic, career- and money-driven professionals.

The film captures a certain shift in Israeli society, namely the construction of an escapist, hedonistic culture, which is defined by and based on consumerism. The film begins with a short series of shots showing shop window displays, long aisles in a large, neon-lit supermarket, and crowded cafés. Similarly, Talila's feelings for Noah are expressed by exchanging goods: she buys him new clothes. The majority of scenes in the film take place on elaborate sets. In his interview with *The Jerusalem Post,* Fox said, "I didn't want the film to focus overly on image, but the element of how things appear is very important to these people's lives. They are slaves of fashion and design. They work in the field, they enjoy it, and it even acts as a substitute for other things missing in their lives" ("Twentieth Century Fox" 13). The film is full of brand names, and as one review commented, even the Israeli flag, usually a contested symbol in Israeli cinema, is seen in the frame numerous times like the American flag in Hollywood films, as if it were just another logo (Raveh). Its presence, however, does not invite further debate, as the film does not engage with politics; it is simply there.

The ever-growing process of consumerism in 1990s Israeli society has influenced the way different identities have been shaped and defined. In the gay arena, the power of consumerism is of special importance. For some gay men, it seems, consumerism has replaced revolt and protest as a means of achieving social mobility. This, of course, does not apply to every gay man or lesbian: not all members of the "imagined" gay community are middle class, professional, and urban. In the United States, as Michael Bronski argues, gay men and lesbians come from very different, varied backgrounds, geographically, ethnically, and economically (177–78). The same can be said about the Israeli gay community (some of the documentary and autobiographical films discussed in chapter 4 explore different identities within Israeli gay society, based on different ethnic, socioeconomic, and gender identifications). It might be more accurate to discuss two types of gay "communities." One is expansive and as such aims to include as many gay men and lesbians as possible, not only those who correspond to the image of the gay community as portrayed in the media. The other is a highly visible, although restricted, group of mostly Ashkenazi professional gay men. This is the group Eytan Fox belongs to and to which he mostly refers in his films.

Although gay men and lesbians are not all urban high spenders, their image as consumers bears a special political significance. One of the reasons for this, Bronski suggests, is the strong link between financial independence and personal freedom, the philosophy of "liberation by acquisition," which is the backbone of many contemporary gay narratives (179). Similarly, Alexandra Chasin writes about consumption as an important route for American gay men and lesbians to political and social empowerment (101). As *Song of the Siren* shows, in Israel as in the United States, consumption and financial independence enjoyed by formerly disenfranchised groups such as gay men and gay or heterosexual women have facilitated the social mobility of these groups.

Paradoxically, *Song of the Siren* celebrates an Israeli version of Western urban gay sensibility, without actually including a gay character in the plot. But if gay men are absent from the film, heterosexual men appear to be "queered" by the filmmaker. The urban male characters in the film take on the traditional roles gay men have performed in society, namely bending the rigid boundaries of gender and sexuality. If gay men are often seen as "naturally" inclined to appropriate what are perceived as "feminine" interests, it is the profession as well as the urban setting and social status of the heterosexual characters that allows them to define a new kind of masculinity based on consumerism and self-indulgence as symbols of individualistic society. It is therefore not accidental that the story partly takes place in an advertising agency, whose role is to present a prettified version of reality and drive consumption.[23] This is an industry that, according to Frank Mort, who has written on the influence of advertising on postwar Britain, invites a "liberalised stance on masculinity" (118).

Indeed, part of the expansion of Israeli consumer culture is the creation of more daring and imaginative models of masculinity, often in sharp contrast with traditional values such as militarism and heterosexism (consumer culture is also a reaction to some socialist values such as asceticism, which Israeli society was built on). As a concept, the use of a "gay sensibility" outside the gay world has had far-reaching implications on the advertising, marketing, and fashion industries as well as in the arena of sexual politics.

Song of the Siren presents, through two of the male heterosexual characters, a new, hybrid masculinity that blurs the boundaries of fixed definitions of gender, allowing, for instance, heterosexual men to dress and act as if they were gay men, borrowing their unique "sensibility." One of these is Ofer (Yair Lapid), a successful adman from a rival office, who abandons Talila after two years of living together but ends up proposing marriage to her. Talila rejects his proposal, claiming she cannot marry a person whose life looks like a lifestyle magazine. This remark is not accidental: Mort sees the invention of lifestyle magazines, for men in particular, as the epitome of consumer culture, which gave birth to this new type of man (18). Talila refuses to marry Ofer because he has never told her he loved her but instead told her "how to dress, how to do my hair, what coffee to drink and where to eat," replacing intimacy with a list of consumer goods.

The other is Ronen Marko (Charlie Buzaglo), Talila's boss, who left Israel for Amsterdam just before the war broke out because he was afraid of what was to come. He is portrayed as an obsessive shopper "who is afraid the missiles will ruin his $500 shoes," as Talila claims. These two men, although heterosexual, act in a narcissistic and stereotypically "feminine" or "gay" manner (they love beautiful things, they are cowards, they have difficulty making commitments). They also fulfill the stereotype of gay men by obsessing over their looks. Like gay men, they seem to be left outside collective Israeli society, seduced instead by Western trends. Whereas Noah is portrayed as a modern version of the muscular Jewish pioneer or the patriotic Israeli fighter, both Ofer and Ronen, as well as Talila before she meets Noah, are portrayed as his opposite: rootless Israelis, alienated from Israeli reality and culture, and reluctant to contribute to the national cause. Instead, they are part of a new global civil religion, the religion of consumerism and accumulation of goods.

The subversive element in both the book and the film is that none of the three really cares about their dissociation from Israeli reality. Unlike the core of the gay community that sought integration with and approval of the majority, the Tel Aviv–based characters in *Song of the Siren* do not seek to be included in the Israeli collective but rather create for themselves an alternative sphere in the city. When Talila tells one of her colleagues about her visit to her father's house in Petach Tikva (a provincial town east of Tel Aviv and one of the first Zionist settlements in Palestine, established in the late nineteenth century), he says, "I heard people went mad since the war broke out, but Petach Tikva?" Similarly, Talila asks herself where Mazkeret Batya is when she is first invited to Noah's place and refuses to go to Jerusalem with her family (many residents of Tel Aviv left for the capital during the war, believing it was safer), stating she would prefer to suffer a missile attack to leaving Tel Aviv.

Although the film is in tune with current urban trends in Tel Aviv (which are influenced by global ones), its tone is satirical. Instead of celebrating a secular, urban, and less politically engaged group of people, it depicts them as complacent and out of touch with reality. This is emphasized by the construction of a Tel Aviv-Mazkeret Batya (city-country) binary. Whereas Ofer and Talila represent the universal city and its false, dangerous charms, Noah represents the local Zionist-Israeli settlement life and values. He is more "real" than Ofer, who is portrayed as a shallow, two-dimensional model from a lifestyle magazine. Noah can offer Talila what Ofer will never have: real emotions. In the end Talila does choose him and turns her back, symbolically at least, on her former life. As much as the film comes to validate a less nationalist, politicized life in Israel, its creators do preach, to a certain extent, a return to the old Zionist values.

Despite this confusion, the film has a special importance in depicting a defining cultural, unequivocally urban, moment in Israeli society of the early 1990s and its link to the evolving gay culture at the time. Fox dealt with gay themes in later projects and chose, as he did in *Song of the Siren*, to do so through Hollywood-style, commercialized work frames. He used Tel Aviv for his TV series *Florentine* (1997), in which he depicted the life of a group of young men and women in their twenties, two of whom are gay, who have moved to the city from Jerusalem. As in *Crows*, Tel Aviv is described as a sanctuary, especially for gay men, a city in which they are free to explore their sexuality and to engage in same-sex relationships.

The limited success of *Song of the Siren* did not stop Fox from becoming a prolific director. All of his projects after his debut film were concerned with gay themes. However, as much as his work assisted in expanding a gay discourse, it did so from a narrow, limited perspective. It is striking, therefore, that his first feature film was more radical in his sexual politics than any of his later films. I shall offer an extensive analysis of the shortcomings in Fox's cinematic view of modern Israeli gay identity in chapter 3.

Reel Dystopia: The Enemy Within in *Life According to Agfa* and *Amazing Grace*

The scene that ends Assi Dayan's film *Life According to Agfa* (*HaChayim Al Pi Agfa*, 1992) instantly became a classic, almost iconic scene. Shot in minimalist black-and-white, it shows a wounded IDF officer and his fellow soldiers bursting into the Tel Aviv bar from which they had been thrown out. Motivated by blind rage they open fire, killing a handful of people, among them the bohemian owner of the pub, the waitresses, the Arab cooks, and a group of hotheaded Mizrahi Jews. It is an operatic scene, meticulously designed and crafted, that manages to disturb despite its deliberate stylization and artificialness. It is the lack of reason that shocks the viewer the most. The scene shows random killing, which seems out of place despite the violence expressed throughout the film and the actions that allegedly provoke and lead to it. These are IDF soldiers who slaughter their fellow Israeli citizens. And this is a bar in Tel Aviv, historically a secular metropolis, which at the time the film was made was still seen as an unashamedly and unapologetically hedonistic haven from the fighting that was scarcely disturbed by Israel's endless wars.

It is important to note that the film was produced before the phenomenon of suicide bombers became commonplace in the life of the city and Israel as a whole, so this could not have been a factor in the making of the film. It is more likely that the film addressed dormant fears of apocalyptic ending, which were evoked by the 1991 Gulf War, a war in which Tel Aviv was, for the very first time, a primary target (a threat that was hardly conveyed in *Song of the Siren*, 1994).

However, the seeds of these apocalyptic images were sown long before, in Israeli cinema of the 1980s, in which expressions of nihilism, portrayal of conflicts and terrorism, a fear of religious fundamentalism, an increasing interest in the Holocaust, and the threat of AIDS all proposed a darker flipside to a Zionist utopia. This concern reached its peak in the early 1990s with films like *Life According to Agfa* and in conjunction with Western postmodern concerns. As Judd Ne'eman argues, "The vision of Israel's apocalyptic predicament relies not only on a Jewish instinct but also feeds upon a postmodern feature" (117).

This concluding section explores the nature of apocalypse and dystopia in both *Life According to Agfa* and *Amazing Grace* (*Hessed Mufla*, 1992), the last film directed by Amos Guttman, also released in 1992. Both films mark the city as a site in which new identifications, based on a new, chaotic, social order, replace old Zionist symbols. Diseased gay men, Arabs, and unhinged army soldiers claim their place in Israeli society after long years on its margins. The fact that they form hate groups among themselves attests to the failure of the Zionist regime in creating an inclusive, tolerant society. This failure culminates in scenes, and themes, of total destruction: massacre in *Life According to Agfa* and AIDS in *Amazing Grace.*

Whereas *Amazing Grace* is both a gay-themed and gay-authored film, *Life According to Agfa* is neither. Yet, both films portray a darker phase in the life of the city in the early 1990s—a time that was marked by war that Israel could not possibly control, with missiles targeted at Tel Aviv and the AIDS epidemic that, although not as prevalent in Israel as in the West, affected gay men and their standing in Israeli society.[24] Above all, both films showed little, if any, respect for once sacred Zionist and Israeli symbols—particularly the army—undermining their influence on culture. By doing

Expressions of nihilism: Nimi (Sharon Alexander), an IDF colonel, opens fire on the patrons of a Tel Aviv bar in Assi Dayan's *Life According to Agfa* (1992).

so, they revealed alternative, less "wholesome," modes of existence, one of which was gay.

Both films show a nocturnal, decadent city, a generator of an "end of days" narrative. The city in the films is a city of seedy bars, violent acts, and disease, a dramatically different portrait from the modernist vision of the White City, a name given to Tel Aviv in the 1930s because of its distinctive International Style architecture. It is different also from the placid, European feel of the city in Israeli New Wave cinema of the 1960s and the permissive, carefree Tel Aviv in Uri Zohar's films of the 1970s. By the 1980s the cinematic representations of Tel Aviv had long since degraded into dystopian projections. The openness and dynamism depicted in previous films, such as Zohar's *Peeping Toms* (1972), which mostly takes place on the city's beaches, or Judd Ne'eman's *The Dress* (1969), were replaced by demarcated, claustrophobic interiors, mainly apartments and bars. Even the parks, which are featured in Guttman's films as cruising grounds, are rendered darkened mazes.

Many of the films of the 1990s show a hardening of the urban surface, which serves as an emblem of increasingly restricted social boundaries. In *Life According to Agfa* there is a curfew imposed on Israeli Arabs from which Samir (Akram Tabwi), the wounded cook, can only barely escape. When Daniela (Smadar Kalchinsky), the drug addict waitress, celebrates the visa she has obtained that allows her to leave Israel for the United States, Samir bitterly comments, "I got a visa to enter Tel Aviv." Almost two decades after the release of the film, Dayan's dire prediction has become more relevant than ever. In the wake of the second Palestinian Intifada, the long series of terror attacks in the city and beyond, and Israel's own policy of seclusion and aggression, Tel Aviv, like the rest of Israel, has become something of a "fortress city."

Amos Guttman's and Assi Dayan's Tel Aviv is a diseased city and is conceived as an allegory for the decline of Zionism within which existing connections between modernity and collective ideas of social progress have become unraveled. The films present a certain perspective in Israeli discourse. In both, the unified front of the Zionist utopia is long gone, and the romantic ideals of "futurism" and "progress," which stood at the heart of the first Hebrew city, have deteriorated to a depiction of death and madness. Ricky (Avital Diker), a troubled young woman in *Life According to Agfa*, sums up the accelerated process of decay by saying, a short while before she jumps to her death, "This city has a sour smell, as if something went bad, like one huge quarrel."

Life According to Agfa marks the loss of boundaries and sense; it is a film in which the city is a battleground and the enemy is the Israeli soldiers themselves, who betray their role as defenders of Israeli society. The traditional positions of enemy and innocent victim, the Palestinian and the Israeli soldier, respectively, are constantly reversed in the film. Nimi (Sharon Alexander), the IDF colonel, was wounded during a military operation the night before the film opens; it is possible that Samir, who appears in the bar with a bandage on his face, was wounded in that same operation, but it is Samir with whom the viewers identify. He makes up different stories every time he is asked about his injury. First he says it happened while he was having "a small political argument." Then he says it was the result of a violent fight with Jews after a football match. Finally he gives the following surreal explanation: "The cross in the church fell on me, so the messiah's thorn got stuck in my head." His changing versions of what caused his injury put the viewers in an uncomfortable position of confusion. Samir's injury, as well as the curfew imposed on Arab villages, is portrayed as unjustified by introducing us to the corrupt and dangerous character of the army colonel, who is one of the key decision makers in the Israeli arena. As Daliah (Gila Almagor), the bar owner, tells Samir, "I read that Zionism is the edgiest movement in history, so take care." It is an unusual point of view in Israeli discourse, in which Jews are traditionally portrayed as sensible and modernized, whereas Arabs are considered primitive and barbaric.

This reversal takes on a more profound meaning when one considers the director Assi Dayan's public persona and familial relations. As Yosefa Loshitzky has observed, the filmmaker and actor, whose father was the legendary general and politician Moshe Dayan, "personified in his early cinematic roles [...] the ultimate Sabra. [...] Nevertheless, Dayan's troubled personal life, the many public scandals in which he has been involved, and his later career as a filmmaker highly critical of Israeli society and its myths, transformed his image from an affirmation of the ultimate idolized Sabra to its negation. If in the beginning of his filmic career Dayan played the idealized Ashkenazi, leftist Sabra then in his later career as a film director he portrayed the grotesque inversion of this Sabra" ("A Tale of Three Cities" 139).

The patrons of the bar—called Barbie after Abarbanel, an infamous Israeli institution for the mentally ill[25]—are prophets of a new apocalypse. The massacre does not distinguish between Jews or Arabs, between Ashkenazi or Mizrahi. Ancient apocalypses, both in Jewish and Christian traditions, as Jonathan Boyarin has observed, included an aspect of judgment leading to reward and punishment (43). The postmodern apocalypse, which is at the heart of the film, on the other hand, is endtime-without-judgment.

Life According to Agfa does not aim to be realistic. Rather, it is a film that invites a constant reflection on its medium. It is shot mainly in black-and-white apart from the last sequence in which Tel Aviv is seen in washed-out colors, a sequence that only further emphasizes the artistic use of black-and-white photography in the rest of the film. Key moments are captured, as the title suggests, on an Agfa film by Liora (Irit Frank), the bartender who is also an amateur photographer. The still photographs that she takes, shown as brief freeze-frame shots, call our attention to the art of representation. This is not life that we see on the screen; this is merely life according to Agfa. Dayan's insistence on exposing the viewers to the mechanism of filmmaking disrupts the flow of the cinematic illusion by constantly underlining the apparatus and its ideological concerns. These disruptions in the moving image can be seen as metaphors for the disruptions that have punctured Zionist ideology and made it collapse.

The film shows the physical and psychological disintegration of the characters: one is dying of cancer; Daniela is a drug addict who gives up her future to sustain her habit; and Ricky commits suicide after having soulless sex with Benny (Shuli Rand), a police officer she encounters in the bar. Having been clinically depressed since giving birth, the young blond, an incarnation of a Barbie doll with a spoiled mind, is looking for company in order to save herself from herself. But the sex act only accelerates the process of her self-annihilation.

Like *Life According to Agfa*, *Amazing Grace* centers on an apocalyptic vision, namely the devastating effect of the AIDS epidemic. The motif of sex as a self-destructive act is repeated in the film in which eighteen-year-old Yonatan (Gal Hoyberger) falls in love with HIV-positive Thomas (Sharon Alexander, who played the IDF colonel in *Life According to Agfa*). Through its overt queerness and the portrayal of a group of people who defiantly refuse to fit in the Zionist-Israeli matrix, Guttman, like Dayan, aims at unraveling the modernist narrative of Zionism. Like Dayan, Guttman offers a subversive order in which day is replaced by night, life by death, reason by unreason.

In her book *AIDS and Its Metaphors*, Susan Sontag examined the way in which the virus was imagined in popular culture.[26] She depicts the virus as an invader that "takes up permanent residence, by a form of alien takeover familiar in science-fiction narratives. The body's own cells *become* the invader" (18). Drawing on this idea, Monica B. Pearl has described the HIV retrovirus as a postmodern virus, a virus that does not succumb to a coherent narrative, by making the body "unable to differentiate between itself and what is external, or foreign, to itself" (24). The way a retrovirus acts, argues Pearl, "does not follow the 'traditional' trajectory of infection, whereby a foreign substance infects the body and is 'conquered' by an army of antibodies, rather it insidiously convinces the body that its very being is the foreign substance, and so the body fights itself" (24).

I would like to suggest that this virus is an adequate metaphor of the postmodern condition in which Israeli society found itself in the early 1990s. As the two films in question show, this is a society so polarized and torn from within that it threatens to destroy itself. In neither film is an external enemy present. The apocalyptic ending in *Life According to Agfa* is a result of a clash between hate groups that were all, initially, taking part in the same utopian vision of the Zionist movement. Similarly, *Amazing Grace* argues for the lack of empathy even in places one would most expect to find it. Depicting the gay community in Tel Aviv as a microcosm of Israeli society, Guttman shows a reality in which envy, strife, and violence dictate the ways one character treats another. This is powerfully conveyed in the bar scene in the film in which the harsh sexual economy of the gay community and its violent side effects are explored.

For both filmmakers, the city of Tel Aviv is both a symbol and a consequence of vanishing Zionist values. In her analysis of Amos Gitai's 1995 film *Past Continuous* (*Zichron Dvarim*), another film that reinforces the connection between the disintegration of the Zionist dream and the decadent city, Loshitzky argues that "Tel Aviv's corrupted body [. . .] signifies the end of old-style socialist Zionism. [. . .] Death and sterility dominate the

Eighteen-year-old Yonatan (Gal Hoyberger, right) falls in love with HIV-positive Thomas (Sharon Alexander) in Amos Guttman's *Amazing Grace* (1992).

life of the film's characters, whose compulsive obsessions with sex result in unwanted pregnancies, children suffering from a lack of fatherly attention, and terminal illness. There is no promise of continuity, or at least of a continuing healthy life, which, after all, was the original promise of Zionism, as well as of Tel Aviv's founders" ("A Tale of Three Cities" 138).

Amazing Grace and *Life According to Agfa*, as well as *Past Continuous*, are often included within a larger group of films made in the 1980s and 1990s that explore the Israeli urban experience. These films offer a counter-image to the chronological, linear, progressive, and phallocentric nature of Zionism by bringing this so-called progression to a halt.[27] Amos Guttman's early films *Drifting* (1983) and *Bar 51* (1985) portray the city as the ultimate haven, even if claustrophobic, for "misfits" marginalized by mainstream Israeli society. The marginality of Guttman's characters is expressed not only through their actions but also through the depiction of the spaces that they inhabit. Thus, the city comes across as decayed and dark, a complete contrast to the "beautiful and blooming land of Israel" of the famous Zionist folk song (see also chapter 2).

Tel Aviv and Gay Identity on the Israeli Screen

This song is featured in both of the above-mentioned films and serves as an ironic comment on the unbridgeable chasm between the reality of Guttman's protagonists and that of the members of "first Zionist Israel." This use of folk songs, which generally praise Jewish combat bravery, is also a prominent feature of *Life According to Agfa.* It is the army colonel and the policeman, the dubious figures of authority, who usually start singing to themselves. One of the most mesmerizing scenes in the film is one in which the young woman commits suicide while the policeman takes a shower and sings in the bathroom. This scene, as well as others, demonstrates the hollowness of these songs and the message they carry. All that is left of the larger-than-life ideals of the Zionist past are the rituals, the uniforms, and the patriotic lyrics.

The city of Tel Aviv has epitomized the Zionist dream since 1909. The ideological foundations on which the city is based represent the Zionist wish for a Jewish sovereignty in a modern, utopian city. Tel Aviv has adopted an image of a city without a past, a counterimage to Jerusalem. Tel Aviv has long since fashioned itself as the ultimate space of secularism, liberalism, and progress. But when the first cracks in the Zionist-Israeli master narrative started to appear, Tel Aviv, through its representations in the arts, and particularly in film, was quick to reflect these changes. In a series of films made in the 1980s and 1990s, Tel Aviv served as the most telling cultural barometer of the dying utopian Zionist narrative. The return of the city to its near past through UNESCO's recognition of the "White City" in Tel Aviv as a world heritage site in 2003 expresses the longing for the lost promise of modernism. Tel Aviv is now looking to its past in order to believe in its future once more.

2

Melodrama, Decadence, and Death in Amos Guttman's Cinema

Amos Guttman, who died of AIDS-related illness in February 1993, was the first Israeli director to portray gay reality in his films. Guttman's pioneering cinema, which confronted the issue of homosexuality in the militantly homophobic Israeli society of the late 1970s and early 1980s, has secured him a special standing in Israeli culture through the controversy it has often provoked. With their unapologetic approach and expressionistic visuals, the films promoted gay concerns that had been mostly overlooked by the "official" gay movement, represented by Aguda, up until then.

Guttman directed three short films—*Repeat Premieres* (*Premierot Hozrot*, 1976), *A Safe Place* (*Makom Batuach*, 1977), and *Drifting* (*Nagua*, 1979). *Nagua* was also the title Guttman chose for his first feature film of 1983. Three other feature films followed: *Bar 51* (1985), *Himmo, King of Jerusalem* (*Himmo, Melech Yerushalayim*, 1987), and *Amazing Grace* (*Hessed Mufla*, 1992).[1] Almost all of his films deal explicitly with gay life in Israel and serve also as an autobiographical statement about growing up gay (mainly in the first two short films), about his life as a gay filmmaker, about being excluded from society and bearing a mark of difference, and about his HIV status. Guttman's cinema brings out the ambiguity and uncertainty that are part of the process of constructing a gay identity in a hostile environment. His films, therefore, express a sense of pride even though they are also saturated with self-loathing. This dialectical tension constitutes a central theme in Guttman's work and will be explored closely in this chapter.

Guttman was the first filmmaker to give Israeli gay men a voice of their own, but his dark, some would even say homophobic, films isolated him from the mainstream gay and lesbian group and its main organization, Aguda. It is not only Guttman's distinctive artistic vision that captured Israeli culture and society at the time the films were made; the reception of his films by gay men and lesbians also attested to the difficulties members of the community were faced with when looking for ways to represent themselves on the screen and beyond.

Guttman titled both his last short film and his first feature *Nagua* ("infected," "diseased," or "contaminated" in Hebrew) long before the devastating effect of the AIDS epidemic became widely known. In light of his death from AIDS-related illness, this choice of title may be perceived as an irony of fate but also as an attempt to emphasize his view of gay life as an alternative to the image of "healthy," wholesome life that Zionist and Israeli mainstream cultures tried to promote. American gay filmmaker Todd Haynes described the use of metaphors of disease in his films (such as anorexia in *Superstar: The Karen Carpenter Story*, 1987) "as a kind of resistance to notions of healthy identities and selves" (Taubin, "Nowhere to Hide" 104). For Guttman, like Haynes, the "diseased" or corrupt body and soul of his gay characters were an alternative to hegemonic culture. But it was not mere rhetoric: Guttman, I argue, actually perceived gay existence as a tragic, doomed experience.

Even without referring to the disease (unheard of at the time the short *Nagua* was made) the two films, especially the feature version, are marked by undeniable gloom and despair. This tone became more pronounced in Guttman's later films. All of Guttman's feature films, apart from *Drifting,* end with the death of one of the characters. In the final scene of *Bar 51* Thomas (Juliano Mer) dies. Realizing that he has lost his sister, Marianna (Smadar Kalchinsky), to her American lover (the two siblings had a sexual relationship), Thomas forces himself on her. Marianna then draws a knife and Thomas takes her hand and directs the knife into his body, declaring, "This is what you want." In *Himmo, King of Jerusalem* Hamutal (Alona Kimchi) gives a lethal injection to the title character (Ofer Shikartzi) as an act of euthanasia. And in *Amazing Grace,* Thomas's grandmother Helen (Hina Rozovska) dies after a long disease just as Thomas (Sharon Alexander), who is HIV-positive, is going back to New York. Even the fate of Yonatan (Gal Hoyberger), Helen's young neighbor with whom Thomas had sex before leaving, is darkened since Thomas was already infected. Like Rainer Werner Fassbinder before him, Guttman has made the human, in particular the male, body "the point at which economic, racial, and sexual oppression are registered" (Silverman 154). Guttman's obsession with disease, death, and the deterioration of the body implies at once the pain inflicted on gay men and the resistance of those who live outside the tradition of the ruling powers.

Focusing on this particular aspect of Guttman's cinema, Raz Yosef has devoted most of his analysis of Guttman's films to establishing a link between the director's work and Leo Bersani's concept of gay sex as a wish for self-annihilation. Indeed, many of Guttman's films contain harshly explicit sex scenes, and it is only in his last film, whose protagonist is dying of AIDS, that tenderness becomes part of the sexual act. The scene in which Thomas and Yonatan kiss toward the end of the film replaces sexual aggression with affection. The effect of this gesture, however, only highlights Guttman's customary themes. The first kiss in his movies is also the last, and death and "self-abolition" still rule. In one of the scenes in *Amazing Grace*, which takes place in a seedy gay bar, a bartender referring to the AIDS epidemic tells one of the customers, "I lost eleven friends in the last two years, a whole ward." The customer corrects him: "twelve: Sylvian is also dying."

Bars play a central role as settings in Guttman's films. They encapsulate the essence of gay life as Guttman perceives it: decadent, lonely, and cold. The scene from *Amazing Grace* mentioned above ends with a violent fight, depicting bars, especially gay bars—metaphorically representing the gay world—as places of danger and hatred. This scene refers to Fassbinder's *Querelle* (1982) with its "outsized vision of the bar and danceclub where the performance of gay fantasy is permitted and encouraged [. . .] the world of *Querelle* is a fantasy construct that highlights desire and sexual availability while also incorporating the harsh truths of competition, envy and strife" (White 23).

Guttman directed his first feature film a short time after Fassbinder finished directing his last. Fassbinder and Guttman, who was heavily influenced by Fassbinder, had similar visions of gay reality, namely that even in a post-Stonewall era it has yet to take part in a real social integration. The interior compositions in both directors' films are symbols of what White calls a "ghettoized environment" (23). The similarity to Fassbinder and Douglas Sirk, his favorite filmmaker, does not end there, as I will show below.

As much as Guttman's films are indeed a fierce critique of both the gay and lesbian community and Israeli mainstream culture, they also express a wish to belong. Reading Guttman's films as autobiographical documents, one cannot ignore his powerful desire to be accepted as a gay man by his family, not only his nuclear one but also the bigger Israeli "family," and as a filmmaker by the establishment. In *Amos Guttman, Film Director* (*Amos Guttman: Bamay Kolnoa,* Ran Kotzer, 1997), a documentary made after his death, friends and peers tell of Guttman's despair following the commercial and critical failure of *Himmo, King of Jerusalem.* After it, he took a five-year break from filmmaking. He felt the same disappointment at not receiving the Israeli Film Academy award, the Israeli "Oscar," for *Amazing Grace* a short time before his death.

As *Amos Guttman, Film Director* shows, the protagonists in Guttman's films are reflections of himself, both in their eagerness to break invisible boundaries and in their failure to do so. Moreover, the actors who play them remind us, through their own personal life stories and struggles, of Guttman's life, for example, the otherness of Juliano Mer (also known as Juliano Mer-Khamis), half Arab, half Jewish and the secret past of Ada Valerie Tal, who starred in three of Guttman's feature films and was revealed to be a transsexual only after her death.[2] Guttman was a sexual and cultural misfit, a Hungarian-born among native Israelis and a gay man in a society that revered machismo. Like the characters he wrote himself into, and some of the actors who brought them to life, Guttman felt cursed, doomed, *nagua.*

This chapter examines Guttman's cinema as a response to and a critique of Israeli society and culture between the late 1970s and early 1990s. I trace the cultural and cinematic influences in the films, both local and global, and contextualize them in the wider nexus of minority discourses and identity politics. This will raise further questions regarding the possibility of challenging nationalist narratives through subversive cultural practices in order to shape cultural and sexual mores.

Departure Point: The Israeli "Personal Cinema" Movement

As much as Guttman deserves his pioneering status, his films could not have been made without the precedent set by earlier "personal" Israeli films. In many ways, Guttman's films are reminiscent of the "personal cinema" movement, which started in the 1960s as a reaction to the heroic-nationalist and *Bourekas* films that dominated Israeli cinema at the time. Ella Shohat comments on Uri Zohar and fellow "personal cinema" directors from the 1960s: "These filmmakers generated a kind of thematic and stylistic paradigm for the personal films of the seventies and eighties, gradually forming a major movement within Israeli cinema, one generally supported by a sympathetic film-critical apparatus" (181). The relative dominance of the personal films in the 1980s, which according to Shohat amounted at times to almost half of film production (183), was also the result of the inauguration of new film institutes, among them the film department at Beit Tzvi school, where Guttman was first a student and later a teacher. Guttman's short films were produced as projects for the school, which also supported him in the making of some of his feature films.

The early "personal cinema" was heavily influenced, in both its aesthetics and themes, by French New Wave films. Filmmakers were characterized by their aspiration to create "universal" films, that is Western films, and their eschewal of what they perceived as "local" themes, locales, and characters. Ella Shohat gives a thorough definition of those films and their filmmakers' ways of achieving what she calls the "effect of universality":

> Often the main characters remain unnamed [...] thus avoiding specific associations with Israeli milieus, locales, or ethnic origins. Elsewhere, the names are "excentric" [sic] or defiantly non-Semitic. [...] Linguistic markers also play a part in this flight from the Middle East, from local habitations and local names. [...] The characters often speak of life "abroad," a term which in Israel almost invariably refers to the Western world, not simply as more accessible than the East for geopolitical reasons but also as a locus of desire for those with the means to travel. Location shooting, finally, tends to exclude the more typical Israeli imagery of streets and people, a device which contributes to the anonymity of locales. At times, the location shooting focuses on interiors... which subliminally metaphorizes the closed world in which protagonists dwell. (201)

Another key feature of Israeli "personal" cinema is the filmmakers' insistence on leaving their unique signature on the films, contributing to a growing awareness of auteur culture. In this respect, too, Guttman's films seem to fit within the category of "personal" cinema. Most of his characters have European, non-Israeli names, such as Thomas, Robby, and Marianna. The presence of "abroad" as a fantasized space is prominent: in the feature version of *Drifting*, Robby's mother lives in Germany, from where she sends him money; in *Bar 51* Marianna falls in love with a dancer and choreographer from the United States who promises to take her there; in *Amazing Grace* Thomas lives in New York City and goes back there after a short visit to Israel and Buffy (Iggy Wachsmann), Yonatan's roommate, leaves for London at the end. Shots of interiors predominate, not only rooms and corridors but also dark and smoky bars, which could be part of the decor of any other big city. Guttman's emphasis on visual, cinematic values, such as meticulous design of the frame, over literary values, such as narrative and content, has been remarked on by several critics. I discuss this aspect of his work at length in the section on melodrama below.

Shohat explains these artistic strategies, and those of other personal filmmakers, as exercising a provincial wish to escape the rough Middle Eastern reality in which they were living, transforming Tel Aviv into Paris and Israelis into French while actually creating an "identityless world" (202). Shohat sees in their aspiration a reprehensible wish to dissociate oneself from a political situation that cannot be ignored and "to eliminate any references to the Israeli context, preferring always to develop an aesthetic of transcendence, abstraction, and 'airy nothing'" (201). Moreover, Shohat criticizes the hypocritical identification of the "personal" filmmakers in Israel with marginality, since "virtually all of the protagonists of 'personal cinema,' like those of the heroic-nationalist films, come from 'First Israel'" (209).

Although Shohat includes Guttman in her account of the evolution of "personal cinema" in Israel, not all of the criteria she establishes can be easily applied to him or his films. Indeed, Guttman belonged, to a certain extent, to what Shohat calls "First Israel": he was Ashkenazi from the upper middle class, an educated artist who had links with the cultural and bohemian centers in Tel Aviv. On the other hand, he was a gay man at a time when only a few other identities were considered more marginal or taboo. By choosing to make his gayness, hence his "authentic" marginality, the central theme of his films, Guttman gave up his position in "First Israel." He replaced the common motifs of Israeli cinema, such as socialism, heroic militarism, and the formation of Zionist subjectivity, with representations of a decadent and destructive way of life.

Shohat mistakenly includes Guttman's first two feature films, *Drifting* and *Bar 51*, in a group of films made during the 1980s that, in her words, "focus on intimist *angst* and on basically introspective, isolated protagonists on the margins, treated through the grid of generally human issues, '*beyond time and place*,' such as love, aging, and the crisis of creativity" (212; second emphasis added). She ignores the direct references Guttman makes to Israeli culture and his blunt confrontation with Israel's hegemonic values but later admits, arguing with regard to *Drifting*, that "although Robby finds Israeli political and cultural struggles irrelevant, he is nevertheless caught up in the country's power structures" (215).

Guttman's films are all about the protagonists' desperate attempts to become part of the mainstream and their failure to do so; about discriminatory and racist Israeli society; about the hypocritical nature of Zionist ideology. The foreign names are instrumental in emphasizing his characters' (and his own) unrealized wish to create a new life for themselves, perhaps in a new place. In *Bar 51* Zara's (Irit Sheleg) real name is Sarah Azulay, a Jewish-Eastern name, and she is originally from Bat-Yam, a poor suburb of Tel Aviv. The more she aspires to escape her past (and present) and to reinvent herself with a new, universal name in a far, Western country (she dreams about starting anew in the United States with her treacherous foreign lover), the more she drowns in the low life of Tel Aviv. Other characters in the film follow the same path: Apolonia, who has a foreign and mysterious first name, is also Goldstein, a common Israeli-Jewish surname. As Igal Bursztyn observes, her name is as ironic as her appearance and gestures, which suggest both stylized and glamorous artificiality and banality (*Face as Battlefield* 182). This contradiction can also be found in the character of Aranjuez (Alon Aboutboul), Zara's gay, "sissy" brother, whose real name is Israel. The new name and identity he adopts for himself do not bring him the redemption he is hoping for, and he remains caught on the margins of society, working as a dresser in the sleazy Bar 51. In *Amazing Grace* Thomas lives in New York but cannot find happiness there. Struggling with his illness, he tells Yonatan, who hopes to study music in New York, how he left Israel for a similar dream but had to abandon it and work in a restaurant instead.

The universalism in Guttman's films, which might make some of them seem outdated or irrelevant in current Israeli reality, is not an "airy" escapism, and his cinema is anything but "beyond time and place," as Shohat suggests. Neither is it evidence of a lack of commitment to Israeli politics and struggles. On the contrary, it is a device Guttman used to portray his characters and Israeli reality in a merciless and cruel manner. The attempt of Guttman's characters to escape a destined future is doomed to fail. This is how Guttman saw his own life story: the quest to be like everyone else and to cure his disease failed, both metaphorically and literally, leading to nothing but a life of alienation and a premature death.

Disintegration of the Nuclear Family

One of the main goals of the "personal films" made in Israel from the 1960s onward was to negate the representation of a unified Israeli community often found in the heroic-nationalist films. As Shohat's analysis of this broad and scattered movement shows, filmmakers adopted different approaches to express their critical views. Guttman's films represented the "other" Israel by introducing gay men, who were at the time mostly invisible. Guttman's approach to homosexuality and gay life was different from that of filmmakers who preceded him. As a self-professed gay man, Guttman was able to offer a semiautobiographical self-representation, rather than a partial, comic misrepresentation. Acknowledgment of the fact that Israeli society also includes gay men cruising in parks for casual sex was a step toward a much broader array of voices. As I will show later, Guttman was interested not only in the gay cause but also in different kinds of exclusion, such as ethnic and racial.

Although most "personal cinema" challenged the traditional perception of the Israeli collective, imagined as one big unified family, Guttman went further by showing the disintegration of the nuclear family. In *A Safe Place* the mother (Bella Ganor) is a dysfunctional, depressed single woman who can barely take care of her children. In the long version of *Drifting*, Robby's (Yonatan Segal) family has lost any stability: his mother lives in Germany, and his father only visits him at his grandmother's house from time to time. The grandmother is herself an eccentric woman who nevertheless cannot accept his lifestyle. Robby insists on living with her although his parents do not understand why he does so and offer him financial help to enable him to leave. In *Bar 51*, Thomas and Marianna, the offspring of a Jewish father and a Christian mother, leave their small northern town for Tel Aviv after the death of their mother. Left on their own (their father died a long time ago), they begin an incestuous relationship that leads to destructive jealousy and eventually to Thomas's death after his attempt to use force against his sister. In Guttman's cinema, values of love, either familial or libidinal, are contaminated by either aberrant (in the case of Thomas and Marianna in *Bar 51*) or exploitative relationships, which all lead to an inevitable tragic ending. The absence of the father and the subsequent shattering of the familial structure also produce a crisis of masculinity.

This recurring theme in all of Guttman's films is best illustrated in *Amazing Grace*, in which he weaves a complex network of familial relationships. The film follows two broken families in both of which there is a gay son. As in his previous films (except for the long *Drifting*, in which the father makes a brief appearance only to urge his son to become heterosexual, as if it were his decision to make, and attributes his son's homosexuality to his not finding the right woman), fathers are absent; they are either dead or gone, and the mothers cannot help their children cope with misery and sickness. The characters of *Amazing Grace* long for a family but they cannot have it. Helen is the mother of Yehudit (Rivka Michaeli), who makes her living as a seamstress. Helen believes her grandson Thomas is destined to die alone, "just like his father," not knowing that Thomas is HIV-positive. It is not just that he will not have a family and die alone; he might also die very young. Both older and younger generations are facing death. Thomas is the last descendant of a family that is about to disappear.

Even though Yehudit takes good care of the sick Helen, the relationship between the two could not be worse. In the opening scene of the film, mother and daughter have a fight. Later on, when Thomas asks Helen to be kinder to Yehudit, she tells him, "I have no time to be nice. I have a daughter who does not care if I'm dead or alive." Helen is convinced that Doris (Ada Valerie Tal), Yehudit's customer, is trying to convince her daughter to send her away from home. Doris herself is excited about meeting her ex-lover for the first time in twenty years. At the end of the film the viewers are informed that he did not recognize her. Once again, the attempt to become part of a family, to feel loved, fails. Like the other characters in the film, Doris is left disillusioned, saying, "I must admit, my love affairs are over."

Yonatan is in love with Thomas. His mother is also his employer and fails to fulfill both roles. His sister, Tova'le (Karin Ophir), sleeps with Suliman, the Arab, for drugs. She becomes pregnant and has an abortion, not for the first time. Yonatan's former lover Miki (Aki Avni) leaves him after they decide to move in together, saying he cannot be in a steady, long-term relationship. Miki himself comes from a broken home. As in the case of Thomas and Yonatan, the father is not present. Miki's mother (Tina Tulin), who cannot accept his homosexuality, sends the military police to arrest him after he has gone AWOL. Miki then tries to kill himself but is rescued.

Secrets and lies play a central role in the film. Miki's mother refuses to acknowledge her son's way of life and instead sends the police to deal with the "problem," and by doing so lies to herself and to her son. Yonatan's relationship with his mother is replaced with an employer-employee contractual agreement. Above all, there is Thomas's silence about his illness; he refuses to share his knowledge with his mother and grandmother, and when Yonatan tries to get closer he claims that he has nothing to say about himself. The word AIDS is not uttered once throughout the film, but there are numerous references to illness and death.

Through his emphasis on the disintegrating structure of nuclear families, from which the father is usually absent, Guttman makes a broader statement about Israeli society. The two are evidently interlinked: as Frantz Fanon claimed in *Black Skin, White Masks*, "The family is a miniature of the nation" and "The characteristics of the family are projected onto the social environment" (142). By using the nuclear family as a microcosm of Israeli society, Guttman's films follow one of the key characteristics of 1950s American melodrama. In Guttman's films, as in the 1950s melodrama, the social and historical conditions in which the text is produced are displaced onto the familial and the personal (Hammond 59). The genre seeks "to denaturalize and explode the myth of the happy, unproblematic founding unit of the family" (Klinger, "Cinema/Ideology/Criticism" 81) and, by extension, to expose the inner contradictions within broader social and national myths.

Dealing mainly with experiences and issues of concern to women, female-oriented melodramas have been referred to as "weepies" or "women's films" to distinguish them from "classic" or "masculine" genres such as the western or the gangster film (Byars 13).[3] Although Guttman did not direct "classic" or "traditional" melodramas, he employed certain aspects of the genre to deliver his agenda. This is most notable in *Amazing Grace*, in which the emphasis on relationships between lonely mothers and their children can be seen as Guttman's tribute to classic melodramas such as Douglas Sirk's *All That Heaven Allows* (1955) and *Imitation of Life* (1959). However, it is also apparent in Guttman's previous films, in which the references to melodrama serve to unmask Israeli reality. In his negative sentiments toward militantly masculine Israeli society and in describing the life of gay men, who are traditionally perceived as weak and feminine[4] and discriminated against like women, Guttman's cinema owes much to the melodrama genre and to Hollywood cinema in general.

Guttman, Melodrama, and the Avant-Garde Film

Hollywood was an important source of inspiration for Guttman, representing escapism and reinvention, while also offering generic structures, especially in the form of the melodrama. As the interest of Hollywood 1950s melodrama "lies primarily in the way that fissures and contradictions can be shown, by means of textual analysis, to be undermining the films' ideological coherence" (Mulvey 75), it is no wonder that Guttman, like Fassbinder, found it an appropriate genre to explore his position as a gay man in an oppressive heterocentric society. Although Sirk's films were made in the relatively puritan 1950s,[5] two decades before Guttman's, there are some struggles that the characters of both directors share. Gay men in Israel in Guttman's lifetime, like Sirk's female characters to some extent, found it difficult to articulate and live their desires openly (hence the concentration on family, inner situation, the emphasis on interior location, melodramatic mise-en-scène, and music, as I will discuss below).

Nonetheless, Guttman's male characters articulate a far more developed political self-consciousness of gay identity than Sirk's female protagonists had of their identity as desiring women. Therefore, although Guttman's films should be studied in relation to Sirk's melodrama, one should be aware of the more permissive context in which they were made, namely an era that saw the formation of identity politics through the rise of minority discourses. Among other objectives, the use of melodrama in Guttman's films may be seen as a challenge to other movements in Israeli cinema, primarily the heroic-nationalist genre films of the 1950s. These often served as propaganda films and as such conjured up "a coherent picture of a world by concealing the incoherence caused by exploitation and oppression" (Mulvey 75).

According to Christine Gledhill, Douglas Sirk offered formal criticism in his Hollywood melodramas using parody and stylistic excess (7). Parody, stylistic excess, and a camp quality[6] are also an inseparable part of Guttman's cinematic language, which was developed in response to both the "realism" of heroic-nationalist cinema and the perceived vulgarity of the *Bourekas* films. The concept of cinematic excess assumes that the filmic text is the site of a complex semiotic heterogeneity that can never be totally reduced to the film's dominant narrative structures, and this heterogeneity is brought to the fore whenever the dominant representational conventions break down. The artificial mise-en-scène, the use of lighting as an expressive tool—usually to render the depressing, dark, and haunted existence of the protagonists—and the theatrical dialogues negate classic realist texts. The last, it has been argued, reproduce bourgeois ideology by representing a coherent, hierarchically ordered representation of the world. The artificial, unrealistic cinematic style serves to address issues that realism comes to repress and deny.

In Israel, as in Europe, realism stood for national cinema, and in contrast to the "studio-look and genre cinema" (Elsaesser, *Fassbinder's Germany* 21). Guttman's decision, not unlike Fassbinder's before him, to import Hollywood melodrama was an attempt to challenge what was considered to be the norm in Israeli cinema at the time.[7] Referring to Fassbinder's *Despair* (1977) and *Nora Helmer* (1973), Kaja Silverman points to the role of the "lavishly etched" windows in "working against the illusion of depth which represents such an important part of the cinematic *vraisemblance*—against that 'impression of reality' to which the classic film aspires" (133). It is indeed Fassbinder's intention to remind us of "the fact that the 'frame' is not a window on the world outside" (Elsaesser, *Fassbinder's Germany* 59).

Guttman's world, mainly in *Drifting*, *Bar 51*, and *Himmo, King of Jerusalem* but also, even if to a lesser extent, in *Amazing Grace*, is reduced to interiors of an apartment, a club, a hospital, or a cruising park shot mostly at night. This is defiantly different to the long shots of vast landscapes in mainstream films to which Guttman ironically refers by using the Israeli folk song, praising the "beautiful and blooming land of Israel." This song features twice in two of his films, as discussed below. Long shots of the Israeli landscape also appear in a few "personal" films, which portray Tel Aviv as an exciting Western metropolis, similar to Paris or New York.

Lintels and doors often fill the frames of Guttman's films. They represent a claustrophobic, demarcated space in which the protagonists are allowed to exist, "a visual expression of oppression and confinement" (Loshitzky, "The Bride of the Dead" 224). These spaces are enclosed, self-contained universes, arenas devoid of any type of jouissance that, notwithstanding, hint at the existence of a different reality, that of "First Israel." Avoiding shooting what seems to be "real Israel," Guttman's films create a feeling of "falseness" similar to that which Fred Camper finds in Sirk's films. Through the "false" look and feel of Sirk's cinema, Camper argues, the director "is able to use the films themselves to suggest that some reality higher than the films does in fact exist" (255).

According to Mike Hammond, "One of the properties of melodrama is that both the irresolvable conflict and that which is repressed return in the form of excess in the mise-en-scene and the music" (60–61). Unlike 1950s melodramas, Guttman's films openly question the power of authority. Nevertheless, the shooting of interiors, the use of dark colors, and excessive, artificial mise-en-scène further reinforce the feeling of detachment from the centers of power created by dialogues and individual characterization. In Guttman's case, the external reality to which his films refer, the reality that stands in direct contrast to that of his protagonists, is that of "First Israel."

The idea that Guttman's films take place in a world of their own and create a different reality is explicitly elaborated in his first short, *Repeat Premieres* (1976). The film follows the protagonist, a puppeteer, as he escapes his earthly existence to his fantasy world. The film opens with the puppeteer, left alone in a costume storeroom, starting to play with his puppets, creating an imaginary world in which it is he, for once, who sets the rules. This can be seen as a parallel to Robby's dream in the long version of *Drifting* of directing his own movie about his own life. As in *Repeat Premieres*, the issue of gaining power over one's situation is central.

The film emphasizes the protagonist's solitude and his illusory world, populated by images of mythical movie stars and motivated by his fantasies. In a later scene he sits in front of a large theater mirror putting on makeup and pretending to be someone else, a Hollywood movie star perhaps. The film ends with the protagonist gazing from his balcony at a group of people skating around a square, an allusion to the famous photograph of Theodor Herzl, taken on the balcony in Basel during the first Zionist Congress (1897), where the idea of the Jewish State was originally conceived. The choice of soundtrack for this sequence, a piece by Richard Wagner, whose anti-Jewish sentiments have made him and his art controversial in Israel, emphasizes Guttman's dissociation from Zionist-Israeli cultural codes. The unfamiliar, beautified architecture and the surreal vision of people skating around a square imply this is a dream sequence. Like the whole film, this sequence emphasizes the protagonist's isolation from the "real" world. His escape from this oppressive world may have a link to his homosexuality.

When considering *Repeat Premieres*, an unusual film in Guttman's oeuvre, Kenneth Anger's cinema, especially *Fireworks* (1947), comes to mind. Like *Fireworks*, *Repeat Premieres* takes place in a fantasized world with surreal elements and is a statement on gay men's state of mind. In both films, following Juan A. Suárez's observation on *Fireworks*, the vagueness of dreams and subjective states of mind result from the rigid rules of the classical continuity system being rejected in favor of loose constructions of action and setting (129). Framing both films as dreams makes their respective protagonists' consciousnesses privileged points of view. In *Repeat Premieres* this is further enhanced by the use of two motifs, which Guttman adopts from Fassbinder: mirrors and dummies. Both elements symbolize the protagonist's escape from the "real" world into his own narcissistic, homosexual self. The mirror, however, is limited in what it can reveal about the self: it can only offer a reflection, an imitation of oneself, either "an opposite" of oneself or an absence. Kaja Silverman has argued that, for Fassbinder, the mirror was another tool to emphasize the artificiality of identities, in particular masculine identity. More often than not, it was the mirror image of the character rather than the character itself that he was interested in capturing on film (133). Similarly, Aaron Betsky has pointed out that although the mirror's space is "free and open," it is constrained by its lack of reality: "As soon as you look away from it, it ceases to function. You can't live in the mirror" (*Queer Space* 17).

In Guttman's cinematic vision, the use of the mirror motif reaches beyond the self-contained, artificially constructed world of the protagonist of *Repeat Premieres* to suggest an interreferential system that encompasses all of his films, the worlds they create, and the characters that populate them; they all incessantly reflect and respond to each other. This is further elaborated by giving two of the films the same title and by using recurring names, such as Thomas, for his characters. Like the classic melodramas

Mirror reflection in Amos Guttman's *Repeat Premieres* (1976): an escape from the "real" world to a narcissistic, homosexual existence.

before them, Guttman's films weave a world of their own, and the characters in them, like those of the classic melodramas, are "each others' sole referent" (Elsaesser, "Tales of Sound and Fury" 56).

This world that Guttman's characters inhabit is what is left for them, having been excluded from the "first," "blooming" world of Zionist Israel. Instead of vast lands they have seedy bars; instead of creating families they cruise in parks. At the same time there is also a struggle to be part of the other world, but this is not possible. Being rejected by society as well as rejecting its false values and beliefs themselves, they remain excluded. Happiness in Guttman's films, as in Sirk's or Fassbinder's, remains elusive, unattainable. Guttman's characters are forever haunted. It is impossible to reach happiness—longing is all that is left.

Desire is seldom consummated in Guttman's films. In *Amazing Grace* Yonatan experiences a brief moment of happiness when he is with Thomas, but as he tells Thomas later, he struggles not to get used to what he knows he will not have for long. In *A Safe Place* the protagonist, Danny (Doron Nesher), finds refuge in the cinema, where life is a reflection, merely an "imitation of life," or experiences desire through mediating objects such as his classmates' shirts left in a locker room during gym class. The realm of fantasy serves as the "safe place" mentioned in the title. In one of the scenes a young man takes the seat next to Danny in a movie theater and makes an unequivocal sexual gesture, but Danny sneaks outside. Earlier in the film, Danny fantasizes about a man, imagining him lying still on a sofa, but when he approaches to kiss him, the imaginary man wakes up and vanishes from the screen, leaving him alone even in his own private world.

In *Repeat Premieres* the protagonist builds a world of his own, reducing his contact with the outer world to a minimum in order to avoid hurt and disappointment. In all of Guttman's short films, the protagonists' separation from the "real" world, their life in the shadows, is further emphasized by the fact that the films are shot in black-and-white. But the viewer knows the protagonist will not be able to run away forever; at some point he will have to confront reality, and in this confrontation he will surely pay the price for who he is. This is very similar to what Camper says of Sirk's films: "They set up the idea of happiness, and often appear to be showing it for a fleeting instant as a real possibility, but the passage of that instant reveals that the feeling can be perceived only in the form of the entire film, and that in this context it is clearly foredoomed. It is quite characteristic of Sirk that the narrative forms of his films suggest that any happiness which appears to occur cannot last" (252).

Guttman and the Rejection of Israel's National Narrative

Himmo, King of Jerusalem tells the story of Hamutal, a young nurse from Tel Aviv, who arrives at the Monastery of the Holy Cross in Jerusalem, now converted into a provisional military hospital. The year is 1948 and Jerusalem is under siege. Hamutal, whose boyfriend has been killed in the fighting, is assigned to work with the most seriously injured patients. She gets to know Himmo, who is waiting to die, and she falls in love with him. Himmo was once "the king of Jerusalem," a handsome and brave soldier who lost his arms and his eyesight in the battle for independence. Shortly before the siege is lifted, Hamutal kills Himmo with a fatal injection. She then returns to Tel Aviv.

Even in *Himmo, King of Jerusalem*, perhaps his least autobiographical film (it was based on Yoram Kaniuk's novel, first published in Hebrew in 1966), Guttman's presence cannot be overlooked. Lying immobilized on his bed wishing for his death, which is the ultimate redemption, Himmo, like some of Guttman's other characters, is *nagua*. Like them, and not unlike Guttman

Danny (Doron Nesher) finds refuge in the cinema, where life is merely an "imitation of life," in Amos Guttman's *A Safe Place* (1977).

himself, Himmo is "the 'Other' of the Zionist (European/Ashkenazi) dream of normalcy" (Loshitzky, "The Bride of the Dead" 222). As Loshitzky points out, the Jerusalem-born Himmo stands out against the "mythological Sabraism, associated in Israeli-dominant ideology with being Ashkenazi and Tel Aviv or kibbutz-born" ("The Bride of the Dead" 222).

Once heroic soldiers, *Himmo*'s protagonists find themselves useless and forgotten by the establishment. When the soldiers hear that David Ben-Gurion has declared the establishment of the State of Israel in Tel Aviv, one of them says to another, "The State of Israel is in Tel Aviv, here there is a siege." Like Guttman's gay characters, the wounded soldiers of *Himmo* cannot be part of the society to which they belong. Loshitzky states that "Guttman's [sic] latent comparison between Tel Aviv's post-modern outcasts of the '80s and the soldiers who were wounded in the battle of Jerusalem during the '48 War [. . .] implicitly poses a critical and disturbing equation which challenges the official Zionist ideology of Israel" ("The Bride of the Dead" 224–25).

Although *Himmo* is a period film, it shares the same grand themes that recur in Guttman's other, more ostensibly gay, films. First, there is the "homosexual ambivalence" (Loshitzky, "The Bride of the Dead" 224) in the relationship between the characters of two of the wounded soldiers, Franji and Asa, which Guttman foregrounds and emphasizes in comparison to Kaniuk's literary original. This, and the central role given to women in the film, contribute to "the gendering of the history of collective memory" (Melman 57). Melman argues that Israeli collective memory, delineated by historians, is deficient because "the concern with the relationship between the memory and myths of 'Eretz Yisraeli-ness' and Israeliness, and the formation of national identities is separated from the historical study of male and female gendered identities" (56). Following Melman I would like to argue that the inclusion of women and the possibility of "homosexual ambivalence" in a nationalist-heroic tale such as *Himmo* encourage a less homogenous and monolithic map of Israeli national memory. Rather than homogenizing the collective who remembers, Kaniuk, and to a greater extent, Guttman, attempted to open up the national memory/story to alternative memories/stories.

Himmo's defiance of the hegemonic and patriarchal Zionist master narrative links it to Guttman's previous films. It was only in *Himmo* that Guttman truly reevaluated the notion of patriotic death, which had been glorified in various heroic-nationalist films, offering instead a dystopian version of one of Zionism's greatest narratives, with the addition of a homoerotic tension between its male protagonists. However, *Drifting* and *Bar 51* also question the "idea of self-sacrifice for the homeland" (J. Ne'eman 136) just by showing those who refuse to adjust to such norms or simply cannot. It is therefore safe to say then that all of Guttman's films represent a clear disjunction between the protagonists and national narrative of the State of Israel.

Laura Mulvey states of 1950s melodrama, whose stylistic and thematic conventions apply to most of Guttman's work and especially to *Bar 51* (see above), that "no ideology can even pretend to totality: it must provide an outlet for its own inconsistencies. This is the function of 50s melodrama. It works by touching on sensitive areas of sexual repression and frustration; its excitement comes from conflict not between enemies, but between people tied by blood or love" (75). Such inconsistencies are manifested in several key scenes in Guttman's films, which delineate the inevitable clash between the official narrative of the state and that of its outsiders. One such scene in *Drifting* shows Robby and his married gay friend Ilan (Ami Traub) walking along the paths of Independence Park in Tel Aviv, named after the 1948 war but better known as a central meeting and cruising place for gay men. There, they encounter three teenage runaways, two gay boys and the sister of one of them, singing a famous Israeli folk song. The three youngsters find a refuge at Robby's place, after he performs a sexual act with one of them in the park. In this scene, quintessential Zionist-Israeli symbols—the park that commemorates fallen soldiers and the folk song—are used, or rather misused, by those who have been excluded from the national myths that spawned those symbols in the first place.

Guttman does not point only to schism between those who have the rights to these national myths and those who have been excluded from the prevailing narrative but also to that which has broken out within the community of the disenfranchised. Back at his home, Robby "auditions" the two boys for the film he hopes to make. He watches them as they undress (at one point he also asks them to perform a sexual act with each other), an action that marks them as "feminine." At the same time, Robby, who is now in the more powerful position (a privilege he abuses) and who is gay and therefore under the gaze of mainstream society, is no less feminine than the two teenagers he gazes at. Guttman manages to show the cruelty of hierarchy borrowed from the heterosexual world and enacted in the gay world. The gay community may try to achieve a communal brotherhood, but it will prove to be difficult.

In this scene Guttman attempts to delineate the mechanism of the penetrative gaze, to make it visible. It is no longer, in the words of Orly Lubin, an "abstract description" but "an actual event" ("The Woman as Other" 306), a transition from metaphor to literalness that exposes the powerful operation and cultural significance of the gaze. Guttman uses the mechanism of the penetrative gaze here, as sex has been seen traditionally as the only arena in which gay men are allowed to act or to be acknowledged by the heterosexist establishment. This scene is a critique of both the wish to form a supportive gay community and of the mainstream view of gay men as primarily sexual beings.

The same folk song that is featured in *Drifting*, describing the "Jerusalem boy and girl" who live in "beautiful and blooming Israel," is repeated in a scene in *Bar 51* in which Apolonia Goldstein, an aging cabaret singer in the shady Bar 51, who has taken the two orphans into her home (Thomas is expected to have sex with her in exchange for this gesture),[8] attempts to commit suicide in the bathroom. Her failed attempt is taking place while Thomas and Marianna are watching Sarah'le Sharon, the Israeli folksinger known for her communal singing events, on television. Sharon is urging an audience full of soldiers to sing along and saying, "There are these days when you think all sorts of thoughts and you feel like crying, but instead of crying you sing and when you sing together, you feel great. I want all of us to experience this great feeling this evening. This is an opportunity to sing only with soldiers, who might be tired but are still eager to sing." This scene points to the unbridgeable chasm between the "wholesome" existence of Sarah'le Sharon and the soldiers she addresses, who represent an elevated form of Israeli life, and that of the two misfit orphans in Apolonia's apartment, now flooded by a stream of blood and soapy water.

The dance sequences in Guttman's films have a similar role in contrasting a "wholesome" reality with low-life existence. As mentioned in *Amos Guttman, Film Director*, Guttman was fond of the Hollywood musical, and his greatest dream was to direct such a film. He placed short dance sequences in almost all of his films, and these can be read as an ironic take on Hollywood musicals or Israeli folk dances, which are identified with the first Zionist pioneers. As one might expect, these dance sequences Guttman directed lack the naïveté and joy attributed to dance sequences in musicals and in Israeli heroic-nationalist cinema. Instead, they take place in sleazy nightclubs and are transformed into unequivocal sexual acts in which the men are eroticized, and hence feminized, as they become objects of desire. Raz Yosef argues that the dance rituals in Guttman's films are meant to dramatize the power relations of sex, its games of domination and submission (*Beyond Flesh* 145).

It is not only the disjunction from the supposed decency of the heterosexual and productive Israel that Guttman's films represent but also his rejection of the politics and dynamics of the local gay and lesbian community, which has submitted itself to the master Zionist-Israeli narrative in order to be accepted as an equal part in Israeli life. Guttman's criticism isolated him from the Aguda. His loathing of the false, politically correct image the gay community was trying to create for itself is articulated in Robby's opening monologue in the feature version of *Drifting*:

> If the film dealt with a social problem, or if the hero at least had a political opinion: if he were a soldier, if he were a resident in a developing town, if he served on a naval destroyer, if he became religious, if he were a war widow. But if he must be a homosexual, then at least he should suffer; he shouldn't enjoy it. The state is burning; there's no time for self-searching. There's a war now. There's always a war. He left the army of his own will, without any reason. The viewers won't accept it. There are too many dead relatives. He's not sympathetic, not thoughtful; he scorns all those who want the best for him. He's not even a sensitive soul, a composed intellectual. Why should they [the viewers] identify with me? Why should they identify with him? (translated by Yosef, *Beyond Flesh* 152)

Caught on the margins of society: Apolonia (Ada Valerie Tal) in the sleazy Bar 51 in Amos Guttman's *Bar 51* (1985).

Guttman's message is clear: if one is gay, one should at least suffer, pay for what one is, be "appropriately gay"—*nagua*. Robby is paying not only for being gay but also for leaving the army, an act that in the early 1980s was perceived as a terrible crime.[9] Of the film *The Night Soldier* (*Hayal HaLayla*, Dan Wolman, 1984), in which the protagonist was exempted from military service against his will because of "personality inadequacy" and, as an act of revenge, murders other soldiers, Judd Ne'eman points out, "According to Israeli mores, rejection from military service impairs the individual's integrity and creates a mark of shame which in turn triggers retaliatory acts of rejection" (140). In *Drifting* Robby is not being rejected (although one can assume he would be if his sexual identity were known, according to the army directive in those years),[10] but he is the one who rejects both the army, hence the State of Israel, and the narrative that the gay community tries to force on him.

Like the protagonist of *The Night Soldier*, Robby passes from "a state of solidarity to the diametrically opposed state of anomie" (J. Ne'eman 141). And like *The Night Soldier*, *Drifting* contains an act of revenge/betrayal when he asks one of the three Arabs—or "terrorists," as his grandmother calls them—he has brought to his home to fuck him. Through this act Robby renounces his supposedly superior position as a "white" Jew and gives himself to the pleasure of being dominated. By doing so he undermines not only the national discourse but also the attempts of the gay community to become part of this discourse. This is perhaps the ultimate expression of the disjunction between the desired image of Israel and Guttman's vision of it, which he maintained throughout his entire cinematic career.

By scripting a sex scene in which a "white" Jew submits to a nameless Arab, Guttman suggests a pact between representatives of two of the then most oppressed groups in Israeli society. In an interview with *Davar* he said, "The Arab protagonists were necessary to the film. They are not gay, but they are a part of the fraternity of the useless" (Wallach 16). Robby's life might be better, materially at least, than that of the Arab man who fucks him, but he is just as socially excluded. In their exclusion from the public sphere, gay men in the Israel of the early 1980s were as much a threat as the three Arabs to whom Robby offers refuge in his home. The scene in question links one oppressed group to another, indicating a certain parallelism between the two.[11] It is one of many that made Guttman's films so hard to watch and accept, both in the gay world and beyond. I discuss the negative reception of the films, especially in the gay community, and the reasons behind it in the next section of the chapter.

Guttman and the Politics of the Israeli Gay Community

Amos Guttman's struggle to finance his films was obviously a result of the subject matter he chose to deal with (as described in *Drifting*'s opening monologue), but it was also a part of a much broader problem Israeli filmmakers were facing in the 1980s and 1990s, namely a severe lack of funds. As Ella Shohat pointed out, the lack of financial aid from the government was a result of its discrimination against the cinema and its favoritism toward other arts (184). Shohat wrote her account of the Israeli film industry in 1989. Her claim about the poor financial support given by the Israeli government was made in the same period that Guttman directed most of his films.

As mentioned above, Guttman's case was even more complex. On one level, he was battling to get support from the state. With his first two feature films, his efforts failed. Three years of negotiation with the Committee to Encourage Film Production (which works through the Ministry of Commerce and Industry) ended with its members deciding not to assist Guttman with the production of the long version of *Drifting*. During this period Guttman and Edna Mazia, the screenwriter, changed the script

Act of betrayal: Robby (Yonatan Segal, right) submits to a nameless Arab in Amos Guttman's *Drifting* (long, 1983).

several times. The rejection by the fund became an important element in the final version. In an interview with the *Canadian Jewish News* before the screening of the film at the Montreal World Film Festival in 1983, Guttman said, "We thought all you need is a good script to get some financial support, which is very limited, from government sources, but getting official approval was most difficult in our experience, so we raised money by ourselves and got the film made" (Lazarus, "Israeli Director Receives Little Support" 25).[12] Moreover, the Israeli consular office in Montreal applied diplomatic pressure to withdraw the film from the festival. As reported by the *Canadian Jewish Press*, the official reason given by the consulate was that "*Drifting* did not meet the standards of taste and quality which should be expected of Israeli films as reflective of the modern Jewish state" (Lazarus, "Israeli Director Receives Little Support" 25).[13]

The trouble caused by the establishment did not come as a total surprise, given the topic of the film and the bold sexual scenes, including the interracial sex scene. However, Guttman had to face objections from a less expected quarter—that of the gay and lesbian community, his "home" base.[14] The community members, represented by Aguda, had their own fight to win at the time, a fight to gain legitimate status by producing positive, "clean" representations of gay life in the media.

Guttman did not find much interest in the community's agenda. In numerous interviews conducted with him in the national and international press, he emphasized that his intention was not to be a spokesperson for the Israeli gay community, acknowledging that most audiences would like the protagonist to be more representative. Like Fassbinder and his self-proclaimed "aesthetics of pessimism" (Thomsen, "Five Interviews with Fassbinder" 86), namely his refusal to create "'positive images' of women, blacks, gays, and other disenfranchised groups, images which all too often work to resubstantialize identity, and even at times to essentialize it" (Silverman 154), Guttman opted for portraying a harsh, self-annihilating existence and heroes whose flaws are well-exposed.

His films, therefore, were not well received. Amit Kama, a prominent gay male activist and the first chair of Aguda, accused Guttman and gay author Yotam Reuveni, who like Guttman was one of the very few Israeli artists to come out during the 1970s, of practicing self-oppression, the ultimate goal of any oppressive mechanism. Kama claimed that "in spite of being the first 'heroes' to publicly come out, and produce gay-themed narratives, they were trapped in self-hatred, and thereby unable to free their works from internalized homophobia" ("From *Terra Incognita* to *Terra Firma*" 141–42).

In Kama's eyes, others often perceive famous gay men as friends, advisers, and role models; they are a source of identification for all gay men and even more so for those who are still in the closet. As such, they are expected to serve as "ambassadors" of the gay community in nongay society (*The Newspaper and the Closet* 27). In this sense, Guttman did betray his audience: his public stance regarding his sexuality was indeed unusual at the time, but it was not used, as one might have hoped, as leverage for creating and distributing "clean" images of gay life. His films did contain what Kama calls "suggested homophobia" (*The Newspaper and the Closet* 37). On the one hand, they represented openly gay men on the screen for the very first time; on the other, the portrayal of these characters enhanced their marginal status and did not assist in eradicating common beliefs about them. Indeed, Robby in *Drifting*, for instance, is often arrogant and he finds himself repeatedly in dysfunctional relationships, whereas his friend Ilan is an exploiter who has married for financial reasons. Most importantly, their supposed corruption seems almost inevitable, a homosexual trait, as the character of Ezri (Ben Levin), the naïve young boy Robby picks up in the park at the beginning of the film, demonstrates. In the course of the film he loses his naïveté and becomes, ostensibly, like the other members of the community, a regular cruiser in the park. He also often has sex with older men for money.

However, these matters should not be oversimplified. What Kama fails to acknowledge is the inevitable effect of living under oppression and the origins of feelings of self-hatred and the desire to become someone else. Furthermore, Kama's essay was written in 2000, many years after Guttman directed his first film and after the gay community in Israel had undergone dramatic changes and become a legitimate, even sought-after, player in the Israeli public arena. As much as the reaction of the members of the gay community to these films is understandable, one cannot deny that Guttman's films describe candidly the difficult process of self-acceptance gay men often go through.

From the perspective of a much more open society, Guttman's films seem sometimes to be not only the cause of a great deal of damage to the gay community but also inaccurate and irrelevant. However, the situation in the early to mid-1980s was different: actor and artist Boaz Turjeman, who acted in both the short and the long versions of *Drifting*, talks in *Amos Guttman, Film Director* about the sufferings he had to endure, caused not only by heterosexual society but also by the nascent gay community in Tel Aviv. At the time the documentary on Guttman was made, Turjeman had been based in Brussels for many years, a decision that might be read as a reaction to his experience in Israel.

As Edna Mazia, who cowrote the scripts for *Drifting* and *Himmo*, claims in *Amos Guttman, Film Director*, the bourgeoisie obviously did not take much interest in their films, but apparently even people on the margins of society, whom the films depict, did not like to see the "truth" about their own lives unfold on the screen.[15] In the same documentary, Amir Kaminer, a film journalist, critic, and key figure in Tel Aviv nightlife and its gay scene, commented, "Guttman showed the imperfections of the gay community—betrayal, casual sex, drugs. This is a part of gay life, besides the beauty one can also find in it. People didn't appreciate this candid approach, also out of hypocrisy. Nobody likes to acknowledge the lesser parts of himself."

As an autobiographical statement, *Drifting* attests to Guttman's difficulty in accepting the role society assigns to gay men. The criticism made against the heterosexual majority is not a demonstration of confidence; rather, it attempts to conceal the wish to be part of the majority, to erase the markings of otherness. It is indeed a wish for self-annihilation and reinvention of oneself as "normal." Guttman's films, in short, represent both a courageous pride and a self-hatred. They are both a celebration of difference, which is manifested in the films' themes and form, and an expression of the wish to be like the heterosexual majority. I explore this contradictory approach in the next section.

Guttman's Conflicting Selves

Like the character of Sarah Jane (Susan Kohner), the daughter of the black maid in Douglas Sirk's *Imitation of Life* (1959) who pretends to be white, and like gay actor Rock Hudson, who produces a conventional, clean-cut image of masculinity in all his films, especially in those directed by Sirk, Guttman's protagonists aspire to assimilation. Since their gayness is not visible[16] (like Sarah Jane, who can easily pass for white although born to black parents)[17] some of them try to pass for straight. The straight-looking man (Ze'ev Shimshoni) in the short version of *Drifting*, for example, hides his gayness from his girlfriend while looking for casual sex with men. Similarly, Robby in the long version of *Drifting* tries to "fix" his deviation by having sex with a former girlfriend.

As Fassbinder pointed out in his notes on *Imitation of Life*, "Sarah Jane wants to be white, not because white is a prettier color than black but because you can live better as a white person" (*The Anarchy of the Imagination* 87). Hudson's sexuality was kept secret in order to secure his status in Hollywood as one of its most popular heartthrobs,[18] but at the same time, at least in retrospect, his appearance did manage to undermine the conventional, mainstream perceptions of masculinity and heterosexuality. For instance, by becoming an object of the erotic gaze—a position assumed to be reserved for female protagonists who are scrutinized by a voyeuristic male viewer—Hudson's husky and manly screen persona was "feminized" (Neale 18). Similarly, Richard Dyer sees Hudson's appearances as a broader attempt to "give away" Hudson's true sexuality and by doing so to subvert the alleged coherence of the films and the reality they come to reflect (*The Culture of Queers* 163). Richard Meyer suggests that "Hudson's homosexuality—however disavowed by Hollywood, by the film viewer, or by Hudson himself—registered in his star image, in the sexual immobility of his masculinity, in the way that women really *could* count on him to maintain his erotic distance" (279–82).

This later critical reading of Hudson's performances, however, eluded most contemporary moviegoers, and the erasure of Hudson's homosexuality from his films achieved a near perfect effect (his homosexuality became public only years later along with the news that he had AIDS, a revelation that shocked many at the time).[19] In both cases—that of the character of Sarah Jane in *Imitation of Life* and Rock Hudson's persona—concealing one's true self suggests a better, more secure life. This is also how Guttman's characters view their lives: they could be better if only they were like everyone else. But unlike Sarah Jane and Rock Hudson, Guttman's characters also have a strong desire to rebel against society's rules. Like Annie (Juanita Moore), Sarah Jane's mother, who believes her daughter's wish to pass for white is a "sin," as claimed by Fassbinder (*The Anarchy of the Imagination* 88), Guttman's gay protagonists know they cannot truly be something they are not.

Whereas social conventions, especially those concerned with attitudes toward nonnormative sexualities, were not, for the most part, openly contested in the United States of the 1950s,[20] Guttman's characters, who live in a post-Stonewall era, act up against their oppression:[21] they look different (they put on makeup and wear "bizarre" clothes), perform gay sex, communicate with the Arab "enemy" (and even surrender and let themselves be dominated by Arabs), and look for sexual partners in the park named after the War of Independence. The characters' acceptance and nonacceptance of their status, lives, and locales give them and the films they populate their sense of ambiguity, confusion, and depth.

The contradictory approach toward marginality, and homosexuality in particular, in Guttman's films can be seen as a manifestation of a fluid state of inner conflicts or contradictions within the subject, a dispersal of selves or identities. As such, it is an enhanced reaction derived from one's marginality, but it can also be seen as a more specific example of society's view of queerness. Kathleen McHugh has suggested that "the experience of queers, many of whom 'pass' precisely because of the phenomenon of heterosexual presumption, gives them a more immediate access to the mystifying figuration of the 'unified' subject. This edge or 'in' sight would not be limited to queers, of course. Anyone who experiences 'passing'—identity disjunctions wherein the nefarious connections between social distinctions, identity, and appearance are revealed, by definition, to the 'passing' subject—would have access to such an edge" (240n5).

As stated above, Guttman's films express a strong autobiographical sensibility. Contradiction, ambiguity, and conflicting views played a central role in his own life and in his career as much as they did in his films. He came out long before other gay artists and public figures had even begun considering doing the same, while directing films that made viewers question the benefits of coming out to such a harsh reality. In his films gay sex lacks tenderness and love, but at the same time heterosexual sex is even more "deviant," as in the incestuous relationship between Marianna and

Thomas and the sex the latter has with Apolonia in exchange for the refuge she gives him and his sister in *Bar 51*. As a filmmaker Guttman wished to achieve recognition both as an alternative voice and as a commercial director whose films would please vast audiences; he aimed both to criticize the "establishment" and to be accepted and funded by it.[22] *Himmo* is perhaps Guttman's attempt to be accepted as an equal in Israeli society, to become canonical. Robby's monologue in the long version of *Drifting*—in which he stresses his wish to create the first Zionist gay film but also to win the Oscar for it—is an example of an inconsistency of the self, which, at times, is also manifested in the incoherence of the cinematic text produced by Guttman. *Himmo*, for instance, functions on two levels: it is both a national fable and a "personal," antinational film with a prominent gay subtext.

Robby's attempt at a relationship with a woman is destined to fail, but this attempt is part of his struggle to live and act "normally." Robby's married friend Ilan is a gay man who goes at night to the park with Robby. He cannot leave his wife, he says, because he cannot give up the economic support marriage gives him. "She is good to me," Ilan says to Robby, "I need a structure. Otherwise, everything is dissolute." Robby himself expresses a wish to get married. "Sometimes I imagine how it would feel to have a family, kids. If I could only understand why I can't have it." Ilan tells him to get used to the fact that he is gay, but Robby cannot accept it: "I can't get used to the idea of growing old with a (male) partner, making tea for each other when we are seventy." At one point a former female lover comes into his life, and she and Robby have sex, but his face remains expressionless. As much as Robby tries, the warm, protective life that heterosexuality offers is not within his reach.

The basic contradiction between the wish to be accepted and the impasse Guttman's characters reach time and again is not resolved even in *Amazing Grace*, which was made in the more liberal and progressive early 1990s and whose protagonists seem to have fewer guilt issues about their sexuality. In the film, both Yonatan and Miki, once lovers, remain miserable: Yonatan for being deserted by Miki after he was led to believe Miki would move in with him, Miki for not being able to be in a relationship, to be loved, or to give love to others (in one scene, after he tries to hug Yonatan and is rejected, he says, "I didn't want us to fuck, I only wanted to hug you. Whatever I do, I'm always left alone"). Fassbinder's comment about *All That Heaven Allows* applies to the contradiction that Guttman, like Sirk and Fassbinder before him, aims to explore: "Human beings can't be alone, but they can't be together either. They're full of despair, these films" (*The Anarchy of the Imagination* 79).

Aberrant love: siblings Thomas (Juliano Mer) and Marianna (Smadar Kalchinsky) in Amos Guttman's *Bar 51* (1985).

The inconsistency of the self, described above, can be read in Lacanian terms as a result of the entry of the subject into the Symbolic order, which is constituted by language, "the network of signifiers" (Hall, "Recent Developments" 158). By entering this order, Hall argues, the formed subject "is no longer the integral and homogeneous 'subject' of Descartes, since it is constituted by unconscious processes; it is not the unitary individual but a set of contradictory 'positions,' fixed by those processes in a certain relation to knowledge and language" (Hall, "Recent Developments" 158). Guttman's films draw attention to the role of ideological discourses in the constitution of the subject. At the same time they fail to offer a real alternative, just as Annie in Sirk's *Imitation of Life* fails to make her daughter Sarah Jane believe she will be able to succeed in life even though she is "colored." As Stuart Hall notes, it is "conceptually impossible to construct [. . .] an adequate concept of 'struggle' in ideology, since (for example) struggle against patriarchal ideology would be a struggle against the very repressive conditions in which language as such is itself constituted. No alternative model has been proposed as to how 'the subject' might be positioned in language without also being positioned in patriarchal ideology" ("Recent Developments" 161).

As Hall shows, "screen theory"[23] suggested strategies of resistance "especially for the unmasking and interruption of dominant discourses" ("Recent Developments" 161), and these strategies are similar to those that Guttman embraced in the making of his films (namely, the unmasking of the patriarchal and masculine nature of Israeli society). However, as Hall further explains, a strategy of resistance does not free one from language or, for that matter, from reigning ideology, as "it certainly does not identify the conditions for the production of alternative languages and discourses. What it appears to do is to establish a simple alternation between being 'in language' (and therefore, inescapably, in ideology) or 'against language.' But a non-patriarchal language cannot be conceptualized in terms of a revolution against language *as such*: this is a contradiction in terms" ("Recent Developments" 161–62). Guttman's films might be "against language," but they still exist in relation to language and ideology. This internal contradiction is manifested in Guttman's public persona as gay activist and in his artistic vision. Guttman resisted the core of Israeli ideology, in some cases combining it with racial issues and in others going as far as to create a completely illusory world. At the same time he was not able to free himself from the need for response, and for financial means—from the mainstream, in other words. Likewise, as much as his protagonists attempt to break away from the dominant ideology, they simply cannot escape it (nor do they want to, it seems). But their attempt to "straighten" themselves with ideology fails again and again, and eventually they either give up or die.

Epilogue: The Success of *Amazing Grace*

Even though most viewers found Guttman's first two feature films difficult to accept, the reception of *Himmo* was a new low for the director. By accepting the offer to direct the film (*Himmo* was Guttman's only project that was a commission), Guttman tried to overcome the obstacles set by his otherness and reclaim his voice in mainstream Zionist narrative. In *Himmo*, Guttman, a misfit in an extremely heterosexist and militaristic society, dared to tell his version of the most heroic Zionist war of all, the War of Independence. Examining the event from his own distinct perspective, Guttman attempted to link different expressions of otherness and practices of exclusion. His reading of the War of Independence was a subversive one. By showing the indifference of the establishment toward its wounded soldiers, Guttman pointed to the disruptions inherent in Israeli society from its very early days. The reality of Israeli outcasts in 1980s Tel Aviv was, in Guttman's eyes, a direct outcome of the seeds of social disintegration shown in *Himmo*.

With *Himmo*'s pessimistic outlook, Guttman experienced, not surprisingly, a traumatic defeat, which almost led to his own annihilation as a film director: the film was a huge commercial and critical flop. Almost all the reviews overlooked the strong connection Guttman made between Israel of 1948 and Israel of the 1980s. Instead, they highlighted the alleged artificiality and lack of sincerity in Guttman's attempt to describe a founding moment in Zionist and Israeli history that was clearly not his own. Even the reviews that did point out the similarity of *Himmo*'s setting to the world of marginality portrayed in Guttman's previous films dismissed this thematic link, arguing that the situation was drastically different and emphasizing that *Himmo* was based on someone else's story, not the director's own. The critics' as well as the audience's response to *Himmo* was a proof that the mainstream majority was not ready, in the 1980s at least, to accept a critical reading of its founding narratives, let alone a subversive reading offered by a gay director.

However, when *Amazing Grace* was released a few months before Guttman's death and five years after *Himmo*, the director was celebrated again.[24] By portraying, once more, gay life as a sad, decadent, and solitary experience leading to an inevitable death, Guttman fulfilled society's expectations of him. Describing homosexuality as painful and marginal, Guttman made *Amazing Grace* easy to accept for those who consider themselves liberal and open-minded. Nachman Ingber, an influential film critic, says in *Amos Guttman, Film Director* that he found *Amazing Grace* a great achievement since "Guttman was dealing with his own materials again," whereas *Himmo, King of Jerusalem* was, according to his account, a huge disappointment: "*Himmo* was a bit beautified, a bit artificial. The connection Guttman made between 1948 and modern times was problematic. He did not have a strong relation to Jerusalem or to the 1948 generation." Ingbar, whose opinion is representative of a wider view of these two films, merely reiterated a common view of gay men and lesbians, which at that time, the early 1990s, was still very much intact.

In a way, *Amazing Grace* and the death of Guttman marked the end of one era and the beginning of another. The late 1980s and the early 1990s brought a sea change for the gay community, on the legal front as well as in other aspects of life. One should not overlook the links between the increased tolerance toward sexual diversity and the overall shifts in Israeli

Himmo (Ofer Shikartzi) and Hamutal (Alona Kimchi) in Amos Guttman's *Himmo, King of Jerusalem* (1987): like Guttman's gay characters, the wounded soldiers of *Himmo* cannot be part of the society to which they belong.

discourse in the early 1990s, from unified categories of identity and of politics toward pluralism. The Oslo Peace Accord and its subsequent optimism about a possible "new Middle East" should not be separated from the new ideologies of identity politics that came to the fore at the time. These shifts have been addressed in two groups of films, those of gay director Eytan Fox and a new wave of gay-themed documentaries and autobiographical films, both of which I explore in the following chapters.

Melodrama, Decadence, and Death in Amos Guttman's Cinema

3

Gay Men and the Establishment in the Films of Eytan Fox

In December 1996 the then president Ezer Weizman was asked for his opinion about homosexuality and gay rights while delivering a speech to high school students in Haifa. Weizman responded, "There are laws in the Bible against sodomy and bestiality. [. . .] To turn it into something where everyone comes out of the closet, this I can't accept. [. . .] I like a man who wants to be a man and a woman who wants to be a woman, not a man who wants to be a woman and a woman who wants to be a man" (qtd. in Walzer 14). After a week of demonstrations, Weizman issued an apology. As Amit Kama argues, the president's apology to representatives of the gay community was an achievement in its own right. He had expressed similar offensive opinions toward other minorities and women before but had never bothered to apologize ("From *Terra Incognita* to *Terra Firma*" 158n31).

The strong reaction to Weizman's antigay speech and his subsequent apology manifest a weakening of the traditional stance, or Labor's (*Avoda*) Zionist ideology, which has shaped Israeli culture and society since the establishment of the state in 1948. Weizman did not only preach traditional Zionist values; they were embedded in his persona: as a heterosexual former pilot in the Israeli air force who fought in many of Israel's wars,

Weizman was the perfect emblem of the "New Jew" and a complete opposite of the effeminate Jew of the Diaspora. As such he could not possibly sympathize with the gay cause and what it allegedly represented. But whereas a few years before a similar statement would have been seen as legitimate or simply ignored, in the social climate of the mid-1990s it initiated a heated debate and strong opposition. Weizman's apology signaled an important change among the old elite of which he was a typical representative as well as in the core group of gay men and lesbian activists.

In his essay "From Nation-State to Nation - - - - State: Nation, History and Identity Struggles in Jewish Israel," Uri Ram charts the evolution of two parallel, interlinked phenomena since the 1970s: neo-Zionism and post-Zionism, "the respective right-wing and left-wing transgressions of classical Zionism" (27). Neo-Zionism is practiced mostly by settlers in the occupied territories, who are represented by extreme Right-wing parties (including parts of the Right-center Likud Party) and regard "the Biblical Land of Israel (identified as all areas under Israeli military control) as more fundamental to Israeli identity than the state of Israel (a smaller territory defined by the 1948 'green-line' borders)" (28–29). Post-Zionism, on the other hand, is recent thinking among middle-class people whose concern is given more "to individual rights than to collective glory" (28). In its acceptance of Palestinian claims about 1948 and criticism of Zionist policy and conduct up to that year, post-Zionism, according to historian Ilan Pappé, envisages "a non-Jewish state in Israel as the best solution for the country's internal and external predicaments" (44).

As Ram further emphasizes, both neo-Zionism and post-Zionism have their roots in traditional, or "classical," Zionism. Their novelty, however, lies in "their one-sided accentuation: neo-Zionism accentuates the messianic and particularistic dimensions of Zionism, while post-Zionism accentuates the normalising and universalist dimensions of it" (29). Together they constitute the current "postnationalist"[1] Israeli collective identity, divided along the lines of cultural pluralism, individualism, and consumerist and postmaterial values. Whereas the younger, secular middle-classes welcome those changes, other, formerly peripheral social sectors, such as the nationalist-religious and ultra-Orthodox groups, see them "as alarming signs of decadence and decline" (Ben-Ari, Maman, and Rosenhek 4).

Situated between these two movements, traditional Zionism is struggling to win back the influence it once had. Although still the dominant social and cultural force in Israel,[2] it is in fact under threat. As Baruch Kimmerling (*The End of Ashkenazi Hegemony*) observes, the political strengthening of groups that have been on the periphery for many years, like

Mizrahi Jews, or were destined to be there, like Russians and Ethiopian immigrants, indicates the end of the rule of the old elite and their successors, those who invented the Sabra and who determined the profile of a country for decades. Ilan Pappé argues that "traditional Zionists are now engaged in a rescue operation. [. . .] The operation is to salvage Zionism from its neo-Zionist enemies on the right and its post-Zionist foes on the left" (45–46).

I would like to argue that the legitimacy and acceptance the gay movement has achieved since the late 1980s and its heightened public profile are a direct outcome of the weakening of traditional Zionism and the old Ashkenazi elite that has shaped it. The Ashkenazi-Zionist elite is more threatened than ever before by ethnic, cultural, and religious groups that have undermined its once undisputed reign. In its struggle to reclaim its past glory the hegemonic Ashkenazi group can no longer turn its back on lesbians and gay men, who have, mostly, fought for the right to integrate into mainstream Israeli society and adopted its core values.

Even though the gay "revolution" had at first certain elements of queer resistance, opposing the heterosexist and militarist values Israeli society was based on, some of these elements gradually disappeared from its agenda. Instead, activists in the gay movement have internalized heterosexist norms, hoping for social acceptance rather than social change. The films of Eytan Fox, an openly gay filmmaker who has become in recent years one of Israel's most prolific and commercially successful directors, best illustrate this new reality. His films, and their dual role in both reflecting and perpetuating the alliance between gay men and lesbians and the Ashkenazi elite, are the main subject of this chapter.

The Conservative Gay Revolution

The conventional explanation of the surprising and rapid changes in the status of Israeli gay men and lesbians in the 1980s and 1990s is the liberalization of Israel, a process that occurred in tandem with the continuing shift of Israeli society from socialist to liberal-capitalist values,[3] as well as the beginning of the peace process between the Israelis and the Palestinians. The Oslo Accord, the short-lived peace agreement between Israel and the new entity, the Palestinian Authority, evoked hopes for what Shimon Peres, the deputy of late Prime Minister Yitzhak Rabin, dubbed "the new Middle East." The hope for regional prosperity, which grew even greater after the signing of the peace agreement between Israel and Jordan in 1994, raised questions about the continued dominance of the Israel Defense Forces (IDF) as a conscription army and the mobilized nature of Israeli civil life. These doubts opened up a space for new models of citizenry in which the army was no longer a key element (see also my discussion of *Song of the Siren* [1994] in chapter 1).

However, there are other versions of the success story of gay men and lesbians in Israel. In his essay on the juridical aspect of the gay revolution in Israeli culture, Alon Harel rejects the common claims about liberalization and suggests an alternative argument. According to Harel, the legal revolution is actually based on the conservative character of Israeli society, which rests on a traditional Zionist ethos and its heterosexist norms. Paradoxically, the wide political support for gay rights has stemmed from the wish to keep the gay community on the margins by preventing gay lobbying and visibility. For example, since the struggle to abolish the antisodomy law created a widespread public debate in the 1980s, one of the very few debates in which homosexuality was at the center, conservative parties, among them religious ones, believed that its abolition would actually prevent the spread of an organized gay movement and discourse. By acknowledging gay rights, Harel asserts, the main parties believed they could control the expansion of the gay movement and, more importantly, keep it separate from mainstream political discourse and national agenda.

Harel agrees that some significant social changes in Israel have taken place in the past twenty years. He also acknowledges the fact that gay men, lesbians, and even transsexuals are now more visible in Israeli culture than ever before. At the same time, he questions the reasons for these changes, and in particular he challenges the assumption that they were the consequences of a focal ideological change, namely Israeli society becoming a pluralist society based on ideals of equality. He also questions the future success of the gay movement in Israel. According to Harel, the acceptance of the gay community into society has meant the loss of its initial militant nature and a growing opposition from conservative sectors as they "realize that the dominance of heterosexism in Israel is no longer an uncontested axiom" (471). This will make it harder for gay men and lesbians in Israel to continue fighting for goals yet to be achieved.

Harel's arguments undermine the conventional interpretation of the Israeli gay revolution. They suggest that more than the gradual fading of conservative, militaristic, and heterosexist values, it was the outcome of the old elite's attempt to keep the Zionist narrative and its values intact by controlling alternative lifestyles that might threaten it. By appropriating otherness, the dominant culture reinforces its position vis-à-vis foreign influences.

I would argue that although Harel rightly rejects the conventional narrative of liberalization, he portrays too pessimistic a picture of the Israeli gay "revolution." His interpretation, although interesting, suggests a simplistic process in which the ruling ideology totally absorbs and neutralizes any kind of opposition in an almost deliberately conspiratorial move. It consequently leads to a defeatist view of the possibility for radical ideas to have any influence on dominant cultures.

Antonio Gramsci's ideas on the creation and maintenance of hegemony offer, I believe, a more accurate explanation for the rise of gay politics in Israel since the late 1980s. Rather than seeing the dominant culture simply as drawing in weaker social groups in order to control and delimit their presence, Gramsci emphasizes the *interdependent* relationship between hegemonic and nonhegemonic groups in society. Since hegemony is based on the consent of the nonhegemonic classes and social forces, it is always in need of being reorganized and reformed. New alliances are required in order to adjust to the changing conditions and to the activities of the opposing forces (Simon 38). New alliances are especially needed in times of crisis, when the ruling forces are endangered and therefore have to undergo dramatic changes in order to defend the current system and to prevent opposition (as does "traditional Zionism" in contemporary Israel). Stuart Hall argues that for Gramsci, "'Hegemony' is always the (temporary) mastery of a particular theatre of struggle. [. . .] Particular outcomes always depend on the balance in the relations of force in any theatre of struggle and reform. [. . .] It enables us to think of societies as complex formations, necessarily contradictory, always historically specific" ("Cultural Studies and the Centre" 36).

Whereas Harel's theory assumes a unitary, totalizing power whose ultimate aim is to deny gay visibility and discourse, an application of Gramsci's discussion of hegemony to the alliance between the Israeli gay movement and the old elite suggests a more complex situation. In Gramscian terms, the rise of the gay movement in Israel is the outcome of a bilateral process in which the two parties—the gay representatives (mostly Ashkenazi, urban, and middle class, namely people who in all but their sexual orientation already belong to the hegemonic social group), on the one hand, and the hegemonic social group, on the other—can join together in a mutual effort to reinforce their respective standings in society.

This alliance, however, does not create a one-way street in which the gay movement is simply "drained of any elements which might challenge the system as a whole" (Ferguson qtd. in Gluzman, *The Politics of Canonicity* 172). Although some people within the gay community, like Eytan Fox, do indeed choose to embrace the values of the hegemonic culture they have allied with, others keep on fighting for either gay-related or other causes. Those who tend to do so nowadays are mostly gay men and lesbians who come from less privileged backgrounds, and whose gay agenda intersects with other identity categories such as gender, race, and ethnicity (as some of the films discussed in the next chapter attest).

Fox: A Voice of the Old Elite

The process discussed above has improved the status of every man or woman who ever experienced discrimination because of his or her homosexuality. However, the main beneficiaries were those who could most easily identify with the Ashkenazi elite, namely, urban Ashkenazi middle-class men, like Eytan Fox. This privileged standing as well as Fox's almost total assimilation into popular Israeli culture is manifested in almost all of his films.

Fox's first short film, *Time Off* (*After*, 1990), was produced when he was a student in the Department of Film and Television at Tel Aviv University. Since then he has become one of the most successful directors (at least commercially) in Israel. He has directed two films for television—*Ba'al Ba'al Lev* (*Gotta Have Heart*, 1997) and *Yossi and Jagger* (2002)[4]—three theatrical feature films—*Song of the Siren* (*Shirat HaSirena*, 1994), *Walk on Water* (*Lalechet Al HaMayim*, 2004), and *The Bubble* (*HaBuah*, 2006)—and two TV drama series—*Florentine* (1997) and *Mary Lou* (*Tamid Oto Halom*, 2009). All of his shorter films as well as *Florentine*, *Mary Lou*, and *The Bubble* deal explicitly with gay reality in Israel. Three of them—*Gotta Have Heart*, *Walk on Water*, and *The Bubble*—were written by his partner, journalist Gal Uchovsky (see chapter 1).

However, as I argue, the reality Fox has portrayed in his films and TV series is based on a patriarchal, at times even homophobic, view of gay life. His films consistently marginalize or exclude certain subgroups within the larger gay community. This contradictory approach may be seen as a consequence of the rapid social mobility some gay men have enjoyed since the early 1990s, which blunted the militant spirit of the 1980s (captured in the films of Amos Guttman and in Ayelet Menahemi's *Crows*). Simply put, once some basic battles have been won and the status of urban gay men has improved, the urgency to continue fighting has lessened.

Fox's films portray gay identity as an inseparable part of Israeli life: his characters serve in the army, usually in prestigious combat units; they feel a strong attachment to the land of Israel; they are the Ashkenazi-white future of Israeli society. Their ubiquity and "normalcy," nonetheless, jeopardizes their status as a distinct group with unique characteristics and some as yet unachieved goals. Leo Bersani's observation that "gays have been de-gaying themselves in the very process of making themselves visible" (*Homos* 32) can be easily applied to Fox.

Fox's films are generally inhabited by gay characters who, unlike Guttman's characters, live in harmony with their heterosexual counterparts, serve in the army, and enjoy steady relationships. In his films, Fox does not shy away from the problematic reality of Israel; on the contrary, he uses some of the most traumatic events in Israel's recent history as the background for the individual stories of his characters. In *Time Off* it is the 1982 Lebanon War; in *Song of the Siren* the first Gulf War and the Scud missile attacks on Israel in 1991; in *Florentine* the assassination of Prime Minister Yitzhak Rabin in 1995; in *Yossi and Jagger* the fatal consequence of Israel's invasion of Lebanon as the ambush the soldiers are sent to, intended to prevent terrorists from entering Israel, ends with the death of one of the two protagonists; and in *The Bubble* the growing threat of terror attacks in Israel since the 1990s.

Yossi and Jagger might be seen as a later version of *Time Off*, as it describes the outcome of the two decades of occupation of Lebanon. The two films, though, are inherently different. Whereas *Time Off* engages, to a certain extent, with the political debate around the 1980s war in Lebanon (seen as the first war in Israeli history that was not imposed on Israel by enemy forces),[5] *Yossi and Jagger* does not. In *Time Off*, this engagement is well illustrated in the Peace Now movement demonstration in Jerusalem and in the debates the soldiers have on their way to the battlefield. Although the action of *Yossi and Jagger* takes place nearly two decades after that of *Time Off*, when the consequences of the Lebanon war were already widely known and criticized, rather surprisingly it disregards the war. This difference speaks volumes about Fox's changing position, from voicing a critical point of view toward a more appeasing stance.[6]

Time Off and *Florentine:* Blurring the National/Personal Divide

Fox's importance lies in his tendency to undermine the hierarchy of the "national" and the "personal" in Israeli society. By using national events as the background for his characters' private lives, Fox blurs the rigid distinction between the private and the public spheres of Israeli life, arguing that they are interwoven and interdependent. *Time Off*, for instance, follows a platoon of Israeli soldiers as they move from basic training to the war front in Lebanon in 1982. The plot revolves around a brief moment in a recruit's life. Stopping in Jerusalem where everyone gets time off, Jonathan (Hanoch Re'im), the protagonist, wanders aimlessly in the town. In a nearby park, a haven for gay men, he spots his tough lieutenant Erez (Gil Frank) cruising. Fox uses the military for staging a coming-of-age drama of sexual confusion and self-discovery, whereas the war and its implications, although discussed and criticized, are left somewhat obscured. The national cause, although referred to, is abandoned in favor of personal, allegedly more important, issues.

Similarly, in *Florentine* Tomer (Avshalom Polak) comes out to his parents while the family is watching the live broadcast of Rabin's funeral. Tomer's father (Yankale Yakobson) responds by asking whether such a "confession" should have been delivered at a time like this, thus emphasizing the importance of the state over private, individual concerns. Once again, Fox attempts to attenuate the boundaries between the private and the public and to challenge the precedence of the national agenda. In the same episode, Shira (Ayelet Zurer), a successful host of a children's TV show, experiences her own life crisis. The viewers are led to believe that her decision to quit her job and to leave her long-term partner is triggered by Rabin's death. She then goes to Jerusalem to visit the mother of Erez, her high school boyfriend, who was killed while fighting in Lebanon. Shira apologizes to the mother for not coming earlier, saying she needed to be alone, an apology to which the mother responds, "My grief is between me and him, your grief is between you and him. There is no such thing as public grief; there is only private grief. I don't want to belong to the family of bereavement."

Toward the end of the episode, Tomer visits Erez's grave. Tomer addresses his dead friend. He tells Erez about the big assembly in Kikar Malchei Yisrael[7] that he attended with the rest of their friends and with Iggy (Uri Bannay), his flamboyantly gay roommate, who will later become his lover. Tomer tells Erez about the artists he liked the most among the participants who sang Erez's favorite songs. Of one particular song performed at the assembly, Tomer says, "With all respect to Rabin, this is your song, this is the song your friends from the army sang in your funeral." This song, Tomer tells him, brought him for the first time to tears in the middle of the square. It was Iggy, standing next to him, who comforted him. "I put my head on his shoulder, and for a moment I didn't know if it was him or you, but I didn't mind," Tomer says. Tomer's confession at the grave of his friend, the combat soldier who died while fighting and whom Tomer confuses for a brief moment with his gay roommate, expresses a wish for the end of gay segregation in Israeli society. Iggy and Erez, who traditionally represent two extremes of Israeli masculinity, become one in Tomer's imagination.

The death of Rabin is the turning point for most of the characters; it urges them to reexamine their lives and enables them to reach dramatic resolutions. For Shira, it triggers her to leave her partner, whom she does not love, and relive the memories of her beloved dead boyfriend. For Tomer, it is the moment he decides to come out as gay. Rabin's funeral is the background for Tomer's coming out to his parents; the memorial assembly is where Tomer gets closer to Iggy, the beginning of a relationship that marks Tomer's complete entry into the gay world. Coming out does not undermine Tomer's connection to Israeli reality and, unlike for Amos Guttman's characters, does not lead to his exclusion from it. The public and the private spheres are complementary: it is in the square, among the enormous crowd, that Tomer finds his own private voice. It is in the midst of the Israeli collective, crying over the death of its prime minister and heroic general, that Tomer comes to terms with his gay identity.

Fox's TV and film output is a striking example of the desire for rapprochement between gay men and the establishment. Fox's cinema at once reflects and contributes to this process of legitimizing the gay community, "the minority everyone loves" (Grant 7). However, Fox opts for a fixed gay identity modeled on the heterosexual majority and refuses to acknowledge any differences among gay men and the gay population in general.

Despite the temporal proximity of the different Israeli civil rights branches and organizations, such as the Israeli feminist movement and the Black Panthers, the gay movement did not coalesce into one unified movement; it has remained, for the most part, an exclusively Ashkenazi male organization. As progressive as it was in transforming the status of homosexual subjects and practices in Israel, it did not fully embrace principles of equality, especially with regard to Mizrahi Jews and women.[8]

Fox's embrace of hegemonic values goes beyond his act of "degaying," to use Bersani's term, gayness. Fox also adopts the exclusionary attitude toward racial and ethnic minorities held by the old Israeli elite. In so doing, he perpetuates the exclusion of the traditional "other" of Israeli society, namely Mizrahi Jews, from mainstream society. This attitude toward exclusion is necessary for the creation of a pseudohomogeneous gay identity. In Fox's view, the gay movement in Israel can work only if it agrees with the terms of the powerful Ashkenazi regime. Consequently and ironically, given the fact that these are gay-themed films, after all, Fox's films resemble in more than one way the pre-state Zionist films such as *Adama* (Helmer Lerski, 1947). These films excluded both the "old," supposedly feminine, Jew of the European Diaspora and the Mizrahi Jew, calling instead for one model of desirable masculinity.

Fox's characters might have a different sexual identity, but they are mostly Ashkenazi, they are straight acting, and they aspire to lead straight-seeming lives. The main limitation of Fox's representation, therefore, is that the empowering of gay men can only be achieved at the expense of others: the Arab, the Mizrahi Jew, the "sissy" homosexual. By trying to impose a heteronormative lifestyle on a specific group of gay men (Ashkenazi, middle class), Fox repudiates many gay men who do not belong to this category. Fox's films illustrate the process described by Diana Fuss, in which "identity is always purchased at the price of the exclusion of the Other, the repression or repudiation of non-identity" (qtd. in Ed Cohen 76).

The following sections of this chapter offer close readings of Fox's *Gotta Have Heart* (1997), *Yossi and Jagger* (2002), *Walk on Water* (2004), *The Bubble* (2006), and *Mary Lou* (2009). *Gotta Have Heart* intersects sexual and ethnic identities. *Yossi and Jagger* deals with questions regarding gay men and the military experience and possible patterns of gay relationships. *Walk on Water*, although gay themed, moves gayness away from the Israeli nationalist discourse altogether. *The Bubble* examines the possibility of a cross-ethnic, cross-national love affair between an Israeli Jew and a Palestinian. And *Mary Lou* intentionally frames gay existence within a fantastical narrative that refuses any link to the community's experiences and struggles. All five films suggest gay existence can be justified or excused only if it adopts a patriarchal set of values and practices of exclusion.

Gotta Have Heart: Fox and the Discourse of Orientalism

Gotta Have Heart (originally titled *Ba'al Ba'al Lev*, literally "a husband with a heart") tells the story of a group of young Israelis, whose lives are at a crossroads. Guri (Tsak Berkman) is waiting to hear whether he has been accepted to architecture studies in the prestigious Bezalel Academy of Arts and Design school; Nohav (Uri Omanuti) hesitates over whether he should join the army or move to Tel Aviv instead; Mitzi (Osnat Hakim), Guri's best friend, is in search of a man with "good husband qualities"; and Merito (Sami Huri) is the dark Arab Jew, a mysterious stranger whom almost everyone desires. Nohav is secretly in love with Guri, but the latter is more interested in Merito. Mitzi is also attracted to Merito and gets to sleep with him first. Disillusioned by the experience, she realizes Merito is not good husband material and settles for someone else. Guri goes through a similar realization. After having sex with Merito, he recognizes that it is actually Nohav he likes.

I would like to argue that by focusing mainly on the character of the Arab Jew and bisexual Merito, the film perpetuates the colonial view of the non-European's body and affirms the restricting concept of "gay identity" as it was first developed in the West. Although presented as a film that celebrates liberal values, *Gotta Have Heart* follows a long tradition of misrepresentations of Mizrahi Jews as members of the exotic yet primitive Orient. With *Gotta Have Heart* Fox constructed a film that "attempts to fix the position of Mizrahi male subjectivity into a space that mirrors the object of Ashkenazi needs and desires" (Yosef, *Beyond Flesh* 166).

As a postmodern tale about gay desire, the film blends Israeli militaristic symbols with salient gay tokens. In so doing, it arguably blurs the rigid boundaries between "gay" and "straight" and undermines macho Israeli society. But what seems at first to be an attempt to broaden the notions of "gay" and "Israeli" identities is soon revealed to be an affirmation of the fixed, rigid meanings of these concepts.

The film is framed as a fantasy: there is nothing realistic in the deliberately artificial-looking studio set designs; the dialogues are overdramatic and often rhyming; and the exact time and place of the events are left obscure. There are a few benchmarks that link it to the present or the near past (openly gay identity, Eurovision music from the past three decades, references to Chelsea Clinton), but the set is reminiscent of a rather more distant past, mainly the 1950s. It portrays an Israeli reality in which there are no enemies or wars but a quiet life in an agricultural village. The main attraction of the young protagonists who live in this dreamlike environment is the daily dancing in the community center to the sound of Eurovision Song Contest music and, as a defiant contrast, to the sound of old Israeli songs that bear significant ideological Zionist connotations. The protagonists' stories unfold in a clichéd coming-of-age drama in which teenagers come to terms with adulthood, their professional expectations, and, most importantly, their sexual preferences.

Gotta Have Heart is a comment on the impact American culture has had on Israeli social aspirations. By using and referencing all-American cultural tokens (from the hot dog stand where Guri and Mitzi work to Nohav's declaration that the only thing Americans need in order to make their life complete is the Eurovision Song Contest), the filmmaker shows his longing for a life designed according to the "American dream," emphasizing Israel's inclination toward the West and its rejection of Middle Eastern culture (a tendency that may be related to Fox's American roots. As stated in chapter 1, the director was born in the United States, and although he moved to Israel as a young child, he tried to establish himself at one time as a filmmaker in Hollywood). The plot, characters, and set design of *Gotta Have Heart* all emphasize the film's disassociation from Middle Eastern Israeli actuality. But it is mainly through the exclusion of the character of Merito, whose skin color and "ambiguous" sexual orientation stand flagrantly in opposition to the Western ideal, that the film's colonial stance is revealed.

Colonizing the "Savage"

Merito is portrayed as the ultimate object of desire. Both Mitzi and Guri are attracted to and seduced by him. But despite his attractiveness, Merito is a solitary and confused character. Although he takes part in the daily dancing ritual, where he entices his accidental partners for the night, unlike the other characters, he is not rooted in the place or, for that matter, Israeli culture. His foreignness is symbolized by his non-Israeli name, which is in contrast to the Israeli-Sabra name that Guri bears.[9] His place of origin, occupation, past experiences and future plans, and likes and dislikes all remain unknown. When asked by Guri about his past he refuses to answer and only says he is about to leave again, this time for Tel Aviv. His sexual encounters lack any sincere feeling of affection. His sexuality is the power he uses over those who surround him. It is only through his sexuality, accentuated by his sensuous appearance and body language, that he becomes visible to others. In the majority of the scenes he wears tight, sleeveless outfit with a low neckline. At the beginning of the sex scene with Guri, he appears almost completely naked, lying on a bed with his legs spread apart, waiting for Guri to arrive.

Edward Said has argued, "What is really left to the Arab after all is said and done is undifferentiated sexual drive" (311). As an Arab Jew, Merito is portrayed exclusively through his sex drive. He is outside the civilized order and in the realm of "the savage body." Examining the work of nineteenth-century English writer Richard Burton, Rana Kabbani argues that he, like other European writers, "shared his century's belief that 'Savage Man' (a term that could incorporate all non-European peoples) was a creature of instinct, controlled by sexual passions, incapable of the refinement to which the white races had evolved. He was so distinct from them that he could well be another species altogether. The native was more like an animal; indeed, Burton often spoke of African and Arab man and beast in one breath" (63). As Yosefa Loshitzky points out, "This nineteenth-century colonial view of the body of the non-European other as a 'savage' was carried over more or less intact into twentieth-century literature" (*Identity Politics* 95).[10] As the example of Fox shows, traces of the notion of "the savage man" can also be found in Israeli cinema of the end of that century.

The sex scene between Guri and Merito is an aggressive demonstration of power. First, it is Guri who Merito seductively asks to come by his house. "You know where I live," he tells Guri, implying an acknowledgment of Guri's attraction to him. When Guri arrives at Merito's place, the latter takes a watermelon and breaks it in half, a suggestive act realized in the anal sex which indeed follows. Merito eats the watermelon with his bare hands, an act that emphasizes his wildness, his being outside the borders of civilized decorum. Although Merito's savagery has the power of seduction, it is Guri who is on top, the "active" partner in the intercourse scene that follows, suggesting that the act of colonization of the "other" by a white man is taking place. On the binary "active-passive" Alan Sinfield writes, "It must be remembered that these are ideological constructs, not natural attributes, and that their primary function is sustaining the prevailing pattern of heterosexual relations" (49). In the relations that Merito and Guri have, Guri is the "man" and Merito is feminized. The sex scene is about power and conquest for both sides: Guri uses his "white" superiority and gets to fuck Merito, but it is Merito, thanks to his exotic sexual allure, who summons this scene in the first place. The forceful nature of their sexual act is further emphasized by the strobe lights that flicker throughout it.

Merito is depicted as the "other" in the film not only because of the color of his skin and Mizrahi features but also because he refuses to adopt a clear gay identity. By doing so he rejects what Raz Yosef calls "the Ashkenazi narrative of 'coming out,'" which "privileges gay identity as the most important task of any homosexual." According to Yosef, "It might also be true to argue that for Mizrahi homosexuals coming from a working-class background, gay identity is not always the prime target" (*Beyond Flesh* 170). Merito stands for non-Western otherness in his appearance as well as in his sexuality.

The film attempts to mark out a local gay identity according to the Western project of gayness. Although transgressing the militarist discourse in favor of the once unpopular articulation of gayness, which has been traditionally portrayed as a threat to Zionist values, the film shows an intolerant approach toward transgression of the rigid Western gay identity, as represented by the character of Merito. His obscure, almost nonexistent personality is a result of his otherness, expressed by both his ethnic, non-European origin and his refusal of a fixed, clear-cut sexual identity. Merito is an example of how the sexual and the racial cannot be separated. As Ian Barnard argues, "Race does not exist independently of sexuality (and vice versa). [. . .] Rather, race is always already sexualized as sexuality is always already nationalized, and so on" (129). Merito's portrayal, which emphasizes both his undiscriminating sex drive and his passivity and rootless existence, derives from the Orientalist discourse, as mapped by Said. According to Said, "An Arab Mizrahi is that impossible creature whose libidinal energy drives him to paroxysms of over-stimulation—and yet, he is as a puppet in the eyes of the world, staring vacantly out at a modern landscape he can neither understand nor cope with" (312).[11]

Unlike Merito, Guri accepts a clear sexual orientation, although he does not believe in the possibility of being gay *and* leading a happy life. The character of Guri represents the clash between gayness and Zionist-Israeli masculinity. Guri is torn between his forbidden desires and his wish to integrate into the virile Israeli atmosphere. Although outspoken about his gayness, he plans to marry his female best friend Mitzi if they are both still single by the time they are in their mid-thirties and to have children with her. He also believes that serving in the army and becoming an architecture student, whose task, like that of the Jewish pioneers in Palestine, is to reclaim the desert and build the Jewish land, is of great importance. Guri's character presents the difficulty of reconciling these seemingly contradictory traits.

More than the other characters, that of Nohav corresponds to the Western idea of what it means to be gay. He hopes to leave his small town for Tel Aviv, depicted as a city of opportunities and freedom. He does not think of joining the army, as he cannot accommodate the army life to his homosexuality. His obsession with the Eurovision Song Contest, a kitsch musical event that has become a significant gay and camp token in Europe and in Israel, symbolizes his inclination toward the West and away from the local, militarist mentality he was brought up in. At the same time, he appreciates Israeli culture and is equally obsessed with Israeli folk music and dancing. Furthermore, his decision to consider enlisting in the army after all, encouraged by Guri's insistence that he do so, suggests his attempts to reconcile his gayness with local reality. His character conveys the message that reconciliation is indeed possible: one can be an Israeli and a proud gay man at the same time.

Guri's initial reaction to Nohav calls this possibility into question: Guri is hostile to Nohav because he is too "sissy." When Guri visits Nohav at his home, Nohav tells him of his dream to live happily ever after with the man he loves. Guri says that this will never happen, because he is different: "You will have to accept the fact that you will never get married and that you will not have kids." Although accepting his gayness to a certain extent, Guri views the heterosexual blueprint of marriage and children as the only framework that can bring happiness and can make one's life complete. His alienation from Nohav's universe, which exceeds the boundaries of Israeli existence musically and idealistically, is manifested by his disapproval of Nohav's idea of evading military service, as well as by ignoring him in a gay club in Tel Aviv (as he later ashamedly admits to Nohav).

Even though he is portrayed as an all-Israeli man who has served as a combat soldier in the army and is about to start his architecture studies at a prestigious institution in Israel, Guri needs, at the end of the film, to reevaluate his life. His decision in the last scene to dance with Nohav and not with Merito is a statement that makes his gay identity clear, for him and for others. By choosing Nohav over Merito, Guri also rejects the confused, incoherent sexual identity and ethnic otherness Merito represents. In a short sequence while they are dancing, Guri and Nohav are shown as longtime lovers in the future, a reaffirmation of Nohav's fantasy of living happily with his partner. The music they are dancing to—a Eurovision hit and an old Israeli folk song—is sung by Mitzi, who imitates the two original female performers. This scene is a materialization of yet another fantasy of Nohav's, told earlier to Guri, in which his two favorite divas synchronically sing their most famous songs. In his fantasy, Nohav builds a bridge between East, represented by the Israeli-Yemenite singer who performs an old Israeli folk song, and West, represented by the French singer singing her Eurovision hit. This is a bridge between local and global, straight and gay existence, proving these immanent differences can be reconciled.

However, the character of Merito undermines this reading. More than the others, Merito, with his undefined sexuality and mixed cultural influences, represents the potential of hybridity, which "resists the binary opposition of racial and cultural groups [. . .] as homogeneous polarized political consciousnesses" (Bhabha, *The Location of Culture* 207). But Merito's potential is not fulfilled. Having neither past nor future, Merito is merely used as a vessel to illuminate the colonial desires and fears of others. The film borrows from colonial discourse by representing the character of Merito as the dark, sexually confused seducer who comes from nowhere and whose future is unknown even to himself, as opposed to the other characters who have clear vocations: Nohav, it is implied at the end of the film, will probably join the army, and Guri will begin his architecture studies; Mitzi, on the other hand, will get married and bring up children, future soldiers, as she declaims to Guri.

Although *Gotta Have Heart* advocates gay rights and the integration of gay men and lesbians into Israeli institutions such as the army, Fox opts to portray gay existence from a narrow, primarily Ashkenazi and middle-class, perspective. *Yossi and Jagger* takes this tendency a step further in eliminating any notions of "sissiness" or effeminacy from Israeli male gay identity, suggesting it is only straight-acting gay men who can, and should, be accepted into mainstream Israeli society.

Yossi and Jagger: The Reappearance and Disappearance of the Sissy Jew

Homosexual desire and the negotiation of gay identity within a hostile environment stand at the heart of *Yossi and Jagger*, a short Israeli gay-themed drama written by Avner Bernheimer and directed by Fox. Originally produced for Israeli TV, it became one of the best received Israeli films of 2002. It garnered mainly favorable reviews, and in 2003 was shown at numerous film festivals around the world, following the major commercial success of its limited preview theatrical release in Israel.

The film, set in an outpost near the Lebanese border in the late 1990s, depicts the secret love affair between Yossi (Ohad Knoller), a young company commander, and his deputy Lior (Yehuda Levi), nicknamed Jagger "because he looks like a rock star," as explained in the film. Following the unexpected visit of Yoel, their chauvinistic colonel (Sharon Raginiano), Yossi learns that he and his soldiers will launch another ambush the same night, the third in a row. Yossi's attempts to change the colonel's decision fail, and his fears are fulfilled: the ambush ends fatally at dawn, with the death of Jagger.

Even though the film was released into a relatively receptive social climate (the outcome of a series of legal battles in the previous two decades), it was largely perceived as breaking new ground, as it gave the marginalized the right to rewrite their role in Israeli culture, from which they have been excluded. The portrayal of a gay love story between two men, who happen to be IDF officers, was perceived as controversial partly because the IDF authorities refused to assist Fox with the production.

Fox was taking the implied homoerotic feelings that often characterize male bonding—"feelings of desire and affection between members of the same sex, but not necessarily their physical expression" (Ellenzweig 57)—a step further. Although homoerotic relationships had been portrayed in earlier Israeli films as an immanent part of the military experience, actual gay relationships in this environment were seldom explored, probably because of the army's official antigay policy, which was finally changed only a few years ago. Even though Israeli gays and lesbians have never been officially restricted from serving in the army, they could not serve in certain "sensitive" positions in which their sexual orientation was considered a security risk (see note 10 in chapter 2).

The film, however, reinforces the existing power structure. As I argue, *Yossi and Jagger*'s covert message reaffirms the old regime, which oppresses gay men and constructs them as the "other" of a heterosexist society. Although the viewer may tend to read it at first as a subversive work, the film actually rules out a real possibility of gay existence, both in military and civilian life.

The IDF serves as a quintessential symbol of a male-dominated, homophobic society. The army is more than a functional organization; it is the people's army, an all-Israeli cultural signifier. As Baruch Kimmerling observes, the military has become an inseparable part of civilian life in Israel, as large portions of the hegemonic political culture have a military-minded orientation (Kimmerling, "Militarism in Israeli Society" 123–40). Thus, the prohibition of gayness in *Yossi and Jagger* should be seen as a statement about the position of gay men in contemporary Israeli society in general, rather than as the particular circumstances of the military. This may be why Fox chooses not to take a clear stand on the actions of the Israeli military: he wishes to explore the cultural significance of the military within Israeli society more than the orders it carries out.

It is important to note, however, that the lack of explanation of the fighting can be read as a statement against the occupation and Israeli policy. Naming the outpost *Havatselet* (Hebrew for lily) and using the word *Perach* (flower) to describe a casualty in a code language, as well as the portrayal of the colonel, are ironic comments on the horror of an unnecessary war and the attempt to euphemize it with propaganda. Furthermore, Jagger's death is rendered superfluous, as the piece of land the soldiers are protecting was in fact returned to Lebanese control after the time represented in the film. In many of the heroic-nationalist genre films, which were very popular in the first two decades after the establishment of the State of Israel, as Ella Shohat has suggested, the concluding Israeli triumph was a result of "numerous heroic acts of individuals whose death was necessary for the birth of the nation" (59). In *Yossi and Jagger*, however, Jagger's death does not lead to a triumph, but quite the opposite; it delineates an unnecessary loss that is followed by an admission of a failure, namely Israel's withdrawal from Lebanon. At the same time *Yossi and Jagger* adopts the one-sided, agitprop view of the prolonged Israeli-Arab struggle that was explored in previous heroic-nationalist films. As in *Give Me Ten Desperate Men* (*Havu Li Asara Anashim Meyuashim*, Pierre Zimmer, 1964), for instance, so too in *Yossi and Jagger*: "The Arabs do not appear in the film but perform the narrative role of abstract agent of death, since it is an Arab mine that kills the hero's beloved" (Shohat 60). This confusion indicates not only the uncertain position of the film concerning state politics issues but also its lack of clarity on political sexual issues. Just as Fox does not take a clear stand on Israel's contribution to the escalating situation, he is torn between his wish to challenge existing sexual norms and the impossibility of escaping them.

When it is not silenced, the love affair between the two protagonists in the film adopts the heterosexual model. The gay voice and body are stereotypically constructed in the film, and they are eventually eliminated, both literally and metaphorically. Thus, the controversial display of intimacy between two men does not fulfill the promise for a progressive view of gayness. Two pivotal scenes in the film best exemplify the tension between what is seen on the screen and what is actually implied. In the first scene, which I refer to as the "snow scene," the two lovers, Yossi and Jagger, leave the compound for an isolated area where they consummate their desire.

The Snow Scene

It is only outside the borders of the military compound, hence metaphorically outside the borders of society, that Yossi and Jagger's love can thrive. Their isolation from Israeli society is symbolized by the white snow, which is not a typical sight in Israel, better known for its warm weather and desert landscape. Not only is the place where they are lying an alien landscape, but in fact it is not occupied by Israel any more. The IDF had withdrawn from these territories two years before the film was produced. Even if it is just a coincidence, it nonetheless intensifies the feeling that these two lovers do not belong in the Israeli narrative or the Israeli landscape. Furthermore, the fact that this particular scene, like most of the film, takes place in an area that the IDF had occupied—an act that was widely condemned as immoral and wrong both inside and outside Israeli society—implies that Yossi and Jagger's love, parallel to the act of occupation, may be perceived in the same way. The film does not provide a "safe" locus for gay love/desire. It is dangerous to be or act gay within the boundaries of the consensus (the military compound), but it is also highly dangerous to cross them. The place where Yossi and Jagger consummate their love is not the peaceful haven it seems to be but a part of a battle zone, not too far from where Jagger eventually meets his death after being detected by the enemy.

Although there are verbal references in the film to the alleged sexual potency of gay men, there are no explicit sex scenes. The semen stain on Jagger's uniform confirms the two had sex, offscreen. The boundary between what is seen and what is left offscreen is not unintended. In his analysis of Andy Warhol's 1964 film *Blow Job*, Roy Grundmann writes, "The film's self-censorship separates not only the visible from the invisible but also the acceptable from the taboo. Thus, the frame's function can be considered a conceptual analogy to a guard patrolling the (metaphorical) border between civilization and barbarity, rigorously regulating its permeability, ardently stemming the tide of unregulated eros on behalf of civilization's course: Only what passes for 'advanced' may cross over" (43–44).

The "metaphorical" border Grundmann mentions in regard to *Blow Job* becomes an actual border in *Yossi and Jagger*: their sexual act is external to the border of the frame as well as to the border of the State of Israel. The area where they make love is the place of the uncivilized, with a rabbit that the two lovers spot a symbol of wild nature and the lurking terrorists (who are not seen in the film and whom the viewer becomes aware of through the events that follow) a symbol of barbarity.

The moderate and suggestive love scene is another reason for questioning the presumed controversial nature of the film. It is reasonable to assume that had the film dealt with heterosexual lovers, more graphic scenes would have been included. Nonetheless, this scene delineates the strict gender role division that is to be found in Yossi and Jagger's relationship. This division is an adoption of a linear, generic model of sexual identity formation, which cannot accommodate the dynamic and fluid nature of sexuality that queer politics aims to explore, and as such is also heavily based on a stereotypical, heterocentered outlook on gay men. Jagger is the "femme," Yossi is the "butch," in the tradition of the 1970s gay macho "clone" look, "whereby gay men," as Richard Dyer has argued, "no longer saw themselves as intrinsically different from their objects of desire but made themselves into those objects of desire" (*Now You See It* 112). By sticking to this portrait, the filmmakers reaffirm Dyer's claim that "it is virtually impossible to live, imagine or represent sexuality between men as if it is not informed by awareness of the difference between men and women" (*The Culture of Queers* 5).

The role-oriented division between the two—Yossi, the muscular, rational commander versus Jagger, his effeminate, sensitive, irrational deputy—is meticulously constructed throughout the film. The snow scene implies the protagonists' sexual roles although it is far from being explicit. Unlike the sex scene in *Gotta Have Heart*, it does not include actual intercourse.[12] At the same time, like the scene from *Gotta Have Heart*, the snow scene delineates the power balance between the two protagonists: Yossi is the "top," the active lover, whereas Jagger is the "bottom," the passive one, traditionally perceived as connoting femininity and powerlessness. The clear-cut division is heightened by Jagger, who, while his body is under Yossi's, asks ironically, "Is this rape, sir?" The viewer's gaze is mediated through Yossi's gaze that symbolizes the power Yossi is exercising over Jagger. Yossi knows, however, that he will lose his status in the army if he comes out. His power as a commander is granted to him as long as he keeps pretending to be someone he is not. He trades his true self for his position. Gay power is not allowed in the film: as Jagger attempts to force his wishes on his longtime partner, namely that they both come out, he is punished and dies.

In his analysis of Rainer Werner Fassbinder's *Querelle* (1982), Richard Dyer discusses the marking of the characters in the film "in terms of masculinity/femininity, above all through the equation fucker = male, fuckee = female" (*Now You See It* 92). According to Dyer, "It is in the fucking that the social realities of sex power—of gender, of heterosexual status—enter into gay desire" (*Now You See It* 91–92). As stated above, gay intercourse is not present in *Yossi and Jagger*, but the strict division Dyer describes is reflected in the scene in which Yossi is physically on top of Jagger, unzipping Jagger's coat, discovering he is not wearing his uniform underneath, and telling him that he (Yossi) usually puts his men in jail for less than that. Even though this remark is spoken lightheartedly, just before they start kissing, it comes as an affirmation of Yossi's authoritative and masculine character compared with the feminine Jagger, who is at his mercy. Both positions serve as stereotypes fashioned by heterosocial norms, debasing the efforts to expand the concept of "gayness," and sexuality in general.

By playing the role of the masculine, heterosexual soldier, Yossi reflects the national discourse. His masculine traits are even encapsulated in his typical Israeli name. In comparison, Lior's nickname, Jagger, a non-Israeli name, refers to Mick Jagger's ambiguous sexual persona. On the surface, the character of Yossi is the manifestation of the ideal muscular Jew, envisioned by Zionist Max Nordau (see introduction) and envisioned cinematically as a link in a long chain of characters who convey, in the words of Yosefa Loshitzky, "a powerful eroticized counter-image to the diasporic Jew" (*Identity Politics* 1). His character embodies the eternal connection of the warrior, Muscle, and heterosexual Jew to his ancient land.

By contrast, Jagger is represented as an irrational and impulsive character who, in insisting on coming out and therefore on putting his own needs and ambitions before the interests of the state, violates the normative, heterosexist power balance. Jagger's gestures and good looks (one of the soldiers tells him, "You are beautiful like a girl") suggest that he is more stereotypically gay than Yossi and contribute to the reading of his body as feminine—an outcome of an ideology that, in the words of Lee Edelman, "throughout the twentieth century, has insisted on the necessity of 'reading' the body as a signifier of sexual orientation" (*Homographesis* 4).

"Is this rape, sir?" Yossi (Ohad Knoller) is the "top," Jagger (Yehuda Levi) is the "bottom" in Eytan Fox's *Yossi and Jagger* (2002).

The marking of Jagger's body as "different" is a result of "the homophobic insistence upon the social importance of codifying and registering sexual identities" (Edelman, *Homographesis* 4). Even though not necessarily suspected of being gay (he is not humiliated by his fellow soldiers, but it might be his higher position that prevents the others from questioning his sexuality in public), Jagger is perceived as the "other" from the beginning, and his otherness will eventually lead to his death.

Yossi manages to avoid being marked. He masks his homosexuality and becomes his own self-oppressor. This is illustrated in the scene in which he blackens his face, camouflaging himself, before setting out on the ambush. As he examines his reflection in a broken mirror, a symbol of his fragmented, homosexual self, he adds even more camouflaging paint, although his face is completely blackened already. The uniform and rituals that create the ethos of the military as the ultimate melting pot experience by blurring any racial, socioeconomic, or educational differences between soldiers are also a device to blur his homosexuality and to produce "a flawless surface of conventional masculinity" (Dyer, *The Culture of Queers* 163).

Dressed in his uniform, putting on an act as straight commander, Yossi is "safe" inasmuch as he reveals the undisputable connection between performativity and masculinity. He passes for straight, that is, only because of his clothes and acquired gestures. This performativity is emphasized at one point in the film in which Jagger—angry with Yossi after he refuses to come out with him and blames him for not caring about their militaristic, nationalist cause—mocks Yossi, declaiming dramatically archaic macho phrases such as "Yes sir, let's kill some charlies, sir!"

The fear of being marked leads Yossi to play down his homosexuality to the extent of total nonvisibility and even absurdity: Yossi, whose secret is known only to his lover, is threatened even by the presence of a rabbit that is watching him and Jagger. The rabbit symbolizes both cowardice (the Hebrew word for "rabbit," *shafan*, also means "coward") and unbridled sexuality, implying Yossi's internal conflict between his gay sex drive and his fear of fully accepting it.

Yossi's masculine traits, as opposed to Jagger's "femininity," are manifested mainly when Jagger insists that they come out together. This option is unacceptable to Yossi, who wishes to pursue a career in the military. His determined refusal suggests that gay love is an irresponsible act that may jeopardize his career. By demanding that they come out together and then celebrate in a hotel room with one "queen-size bed," Jagger establishes the domestic-familial space, stereotypically related to femininity, and therefore gayness, which stands in contrast to the militaristic-masculine space Yossi occupies—a space that cannot accommodate his nonnormative sexuality. Thus Yossi tells Jagger they can either keep going on his terms, discreetly, that is, or break up: "I am sorry I don't surprise you with a ring, it is not an American movie," he says. His gayness is a dream or a fantasy, and just like a Hollywood film it differs from reality.

The two lovers are aware of the role division between them, and they refer to it throughout the film. As they lie in the snow, Jagger starts singing along to his favorite song, which happens to be playing on a small portable radio he brought. The song "Your Soul" is sung by Rita, whose dramatic pop music and ultrafeminine appearance made her one of the most successful female singers in Israel and a gay icon. As the viewer expects, Yossi does not share his partner's love for Rita: "Your musical taste is so gay," he tells him. Jagger then accuses him of preferring Meir Ariel to Rita. Ariel, the late Israeli singer, was an archetype of the Sabra, who made derogatory comments about homosexuals in an interview in September 1998 (Walzer 35).

The connection between Yossi and homophobic Ariel stresses his self-hatred. The lyrics of Rita's song bear an even more explicit gay connotation when Jagger sings them, as they address a man (Hebrew, unlike English, for instance, marks gender explicitly). By singing them loudly to Yossi, Jagger reveals how he sees his lover. The lyrics (by Miri Feigenboim) describe a life of lies as a dark and lonely experience, encouraging the addressee in the song to come to terms with his own "true" self:

> Let's dispel the foggy curtain
> Let's stand in the light, not in the shadow
> Until when will you keep on running?
> To games of power.
> You can cry sometimes,
> When you break inside.
> Tell me about your moments of fear;
> It is much easier to be afraid together.
> When cold winds will storm outside,
> I will send hot fire through you.
> One day you may stop running
> Between the shadows
> In your soul.

It is no wonder that two versions of the song—the original and a cover version recorded by Ivri Lider, a popular and openly gay Israeli singer—are played several times, in addition to the two times Jagger sings it. Jagger alters the lyrics from "It is much easier to be afraid together" to "It is much easier to stick it up the rear" and by doing so emphasizes the original lyrics' covert gay meaning.

It is important to note that in all of Fox's films the use of music in the soundtrack is paramount. Female singers' voices, Eurovision pop music, and Israeli folk songs all carry a special meaning in Fox's cinema. For Fox, music is the "excess" that the lush Technicolor and mise-en-scène of the melodrama were for Douglas Sirk, namely a tool to imply that the film is reaching beyond dominant narrative structures. Although the majority of Fox's films present explicit gay themes, they often correspond with hegemonic ideologies. The use of music is an act of subversion that allows him to hint at a different reality.

In his analysis of *Time Off*, Raz Yosef explores the way in which the gay experience, namely the relationship between the soldier and his commander, is denied at a visual level but then surfaces and is reconfirmed at an aural level.[13] According to Yosef, music in *Time Off* "becomes an instrument through which the two men, distanced by ranks and Zionist ideals of proud Sabra heterosexual masculinity, subvert the oppressive military phallic laws and express queer identification" (*Beyond Flesh* 160). In a place where the visual image of the "other" is distorted, the voice serves as a potential alternative. According to Yosef, Fox's understanding of the limitations of the cinematic frame for establishing a gay subject within the patriarchal ideology of popular cinema led him to make use of the aural dimension. I would argue that Fox's use of soundtrack often offers a compromise of a sort between his wish to appeal to a wide nongay audience and his desire to construct a gay subjectivity on the screen.

The Death Scene

The first and last time Yossi softens is when he realizes that Jagger has been injured and is dying. Jagger's death, the emotional climax of the film, enables Yossi to come to terms with his own sexual identity, implying a possible fissure in the wall of silence. In these moments, while waiting for rescue, he tells Jagger things he never dared say before. He declares his unconditional love, not the least bothered by the presence of another officer, who for the first time realizes the two officers are lovers.

This self-realization follows a prevalent universal pattern in gay narratives, in which, in the words of David M. Halperin, "The weaker or less favored friend dies. [. . .] Death is the climax of the friendship [. . .] and it weds them forever (in the memory of the survivor, at least). [. . .] Death is to friendship what marriage is to romance" (78–79). Thomas Waugh reinforces Halperin's claim by arguing that death is a narrative device used to make sure the gay romance will not last: "The protagonists of this alternative gay rendering of the conjugal drive, unlike their hetero counterparts, seldom end up coming together. We don't establish families—we just wander off looking horny, solitary, sad, or dead. [. . .] Gay closures are seldom happy endings" ("The Third Body" 145). This pattern is especially prominent in Israeli films that deal with homosexuality. According to Raz Yosef, the disposal of the homosexual body is essential for keeping Israeli heterosexual hegemony intact ("The Military Body" 26).

Jagger's death is the first time Yossi adopts some of Jagger's "reckless" behavior, as he breaks the barrier between the public and the private, the domestic and the militaristic, while rushing to Jagger's side not as the latter's commander but as his grieving partner. This gesture could be read as an irrational and emotional, and therefore feminine, reaction, at odds with

A fissure in the wall of silence: Yossi (Ohad Knoller, left) and injured Jagger (Yehuda Levi) in Eytan Fox's *Yossi and Jagger* (2002).

what the viewer has learned to expect from Yossi. Unfortunately, this moment of self-realization can only be experienced at Jagger's death.

However, it is important to note that the film defines a gay identity, not so much by portraying homosexuality as natural and neutral but rather by denouncing heterosexual courtship and relationships as hollow and abusive, employing the same arguments usually made against gay men. The two gay lovers in the film are ironically shown to be more committed than their fellow soldiers.[14] Goldie (Hani Furstenberg), one of the female soldiers, replaces intimacy with abusive sex—as shown in her power-oriented sexual relationship with the married colonel (her declared refusal to commit herself to a relationship—"I am here to have fun, not to get married"— is probably more a protection against hurt than a sign of liberation). Yaeli (Aya Steinovitz), the other female soldier, cannot have her love object. Being desperately in love with Jagger, she remains blind to the fact that he is gay. Like the others, she can read the signifiers, describing him as "gentle" and "different from all the other men," but fails to interpret them. As a gay couple, Yossi and Jagger adjust themselves to the heteronormative model, and they succeed in doing so more than their heterosexual counterparts.

Gay Men and the Establishment in the Films of Eytan Fox

The latter are conventionally stereotyped: the colonel abuses his power and the female soldiers are either whores or virgins. Thus, they become a grotesque representation of male chauvinistic norms.

Reversing the norm of Hollywood films, it is the straight characters in *Yossi and Jagger* who illuminate the gay protagonists and are used as a critical reflection of heterosexual, militaristic morals.[15] Being the primary target, the colonel not only cheats on his wife with one of his soldiers but also abuses his power in order to do so. At one point in the film he orders his sex partner to move her "fat ass to the car." The colonel refers to the news about the upcoming ambush as good news, stressing how much he likes "the action and the smell of burnt flesh in the morning" although he is not there with the soldiers to smell the burnt flesh the following morning.[16] When Yossi tries to change the colonel's decision, the colonel accuses him of becoming a "homo" and a "sissy" and of worrying about his soldiers as if he was their mother (thus, stereotypically connecting homosexuality with cowardice and motherhood, hence femininity). In his reaction to what will prove to be justified concerns, the colonel reveals not only his unenlightened opinions regarding women and homosexuals but also his erroneous judgment.

The character of the colonel and the longing of the other soldiers for love that is not within their reach reflect the shortcomings of straight relationships compared with the stability and warmth that are to be found in the relationship of Yossi and Jagger. Furthermore, Yossi's judgment is proven to be better than the colonel's, suggesting that although Yossi is the misfit in a heterosexist system he can surpass those who are supposed to be superior to him in the military hierarchy. The film, therefore, inverts the balance of power between homosexuality and heterosexuality, in which the former is implicitly superior to the latter. This power struggle, however, takes place within a patriarchal domain and adopts heterosexist morals. The greatest achievement of Yossi in the film is his false attempt to play down his sexuality in order to pass for straight. It is Jagger who tries to break with his self-imposed silence, an act for which he is killed, and it is the disposal of his body that secures the existing power structure.

Jagger's death and the discretion that is an immanent part of Yossi and Jagger's partnership violate the idyll. In the end the militaristic and homophobic structure remains intact, and even Jagger's grieving parents, in the final scene of the film, are kept in the dark about their son's sexuality. In the shiva (a period of seven days of mourning) Jagger's mother (Yael Pearl-Beker) says to her son's fellow soldiers that it is only now after his death that she realizes she did not know him at all. This utterance may be interpreted as an expression of a remote feeling she might have that behind the "normative" appearance there was something different about him. The fact that only Yossi knows Jagger's favorite song implies a fracture in the concealed existence of both Yossi and Jagger. To seal this concealment of Jagger's true nature, Yaeli declares her love for Jagger at the shiva, adding she believes he felt the same for her, although they had never talked about it. Jagger's mother is left with the belief that her son had a girlfriend, that he was "normal" by society's standards. Although far from the truth, it is suggested that the parents are better off this way.

Disguised in their uniforms, suffering in silence until the death of Jagger, the two protagonists prove gay men can be a part of Israeli society as long as they accept the existing order and keep their love a secret. The significance of "transplanting" a forbidden desire into the army is undermined by the realization that they surrender without a fight to heterosexist norms. More than anything, *Yossi and Jagger* attests to the difficulty for gay men in Israel to create a new, different vision. If the word "queer," as argued by Ellis Hanson, "invites an impassioned, even an angry resistance to normalization," and "is a rejection of the compulsory heterosexual code of masculine men desiring feminine women" (4), *Yossi and Jagger* is anything but a queer work. The film was made by a gay activist filmmaker known for encouraging famous Israeli artists to make their sexuality public, yet it only shows how prevalent heterosexist norms are to the extent that they have become internalized by members of the gay community itself.

WALK ON WATER: ISRAEL'S GAY ARCHENEMIES

Even more than his previous films, Fox's *Walk on Water* illustrates his engagement with burning issues on the Israeli agenda. This time, Fox attempted to link themes such as the memory of the Holocaust and second-generation Israelis, Israeli current affairs, the threat of terrorism, and homosexuality. The large number of topics raised throughout the film disallows the possibility of in-depth discussion of any. Instead, the film offers only a partial portrayal of the conflicts within Israeli society and between Israelis and Palestinians. The protagonist, Eyal (Lior Ashkenazi), a Mossad hit man, is on a mission to track down an ex-Nazi officer. Working undercover as a tourist guide, he befriends Axel (Knut Berger), the gay grandson of his suspect, who is on a visit to his sister Pia (Caroline Peters) in Israel. During an extended tour of the country, the two men struggle to find some common ground. In order to complete his mission, Eyal goes to Berlin, where he is invited to the grandson's family party.

As in previous films, such as *Song of the Siren*, Fox offers characterization that is based for the most part on cultural stereotypes. In this film, he counters the macho but sensitive and conscientious Israeli Mossad hit man with the liberal, gay young European. More importantly, the film demonstrates a hidden homophobic sentiment, whereby homosexuality is "transferred" to the archenemies, past and present, of Israeli society: the two gay characters in the film are Axel, the German tourist, and Rafik (Yousef "Joe" Sweid), a Palestinian he meets in a Tel Aviv club. Like Merito in *Gotta Have Heart*, Axel and his Palestinian sex partner are marked as "others," and their otherness is manifested, among other things, in their alleged promiscuity. It is not just the single night they spend together that suggests it. In a later scene in the film, Axel counts the many partners he has had and classifies them by their nationality, and in another scene, talking to his sister, he mentions a brief relationship that he had. Infatuated, Axel left Germany for Italy to live with his lover but came back in less than two weeks. His promiscuity is highlighted by the background of his sister's and Eyal's monogamous natures. As much as promiscuity can be seen as a defiant cultural practice against oppressive sexual mores, it has had negative connotations since the appearance of the AIDS epidemic, and even before that. Promiscuity is an ambiguous matter not only within heterosexual discourses (where "'promiscuity' now conventionally connotes 'excessive,' 'indiscriminate,' and often 'insatiable' sexual practice" [Gove 6]) but also in gay circles, and is normally marked as the less desired model for gay men. Ben Gove writes,

> Black and white gay male discourses alike have often had a comparable antipathy toward the term, particularly since the profound backlash against gay sex/uality that much of dominant culture has desperately latched on to in order to "rationalise" the HIV/AIDS crisis. [. . .] Yet this gay male distrust of the term has also been pronounced since at least the 1960s, when, as Steven Seidman notes, dominant discourse (as earlier in the century) "often assumed . . . the inherently promiscuous, carnal nature of homosexual desire, a sign of its pathological or deviant status," or else responded to the actual growth of opportunities for publicly avowed gay male promiscuous sex during the 1970s and early 1980s in the same demonising manner. (13–14)

Leaving aside the debate about whether promiscuity is a model that gay men should follow, I would like to emphasize its negative associations both within and outside the gay world. Taking into account Fox's adherence to heteronormative patterns discussed in previous sections of this chapter, it is safe to assume that he did not intend to use promiscuity as a means of defying the culture that he so wishes to represent. Indeed, not since *Time Off* have Fox's Ashkenazi protagonists sought casual, promiscuous sex. This terrain is reserved for "others." Rather Fox's all-Israeli protagonists have always been, or longed to be, part of a heterosexual-normative, monogamous relationship.

The film revives the old myth of Jews in Israel as both victorious warriors and victims. On the one hand, the dialogues between the Mossad agent and Axel explain to non-Israeli viewers what it is like to live under a constant threat of terror and seek to convince them that the true victims of the situation are the Israelis. On the other hand, the film also seeks to portray Israelis as powerful and "in control." The opening scene, in which the Mossad agent kills a man described in the film as a Hammas activist, is one example. The use of Israeli music in the film also conveys this message; it accompanies most of the scenes, including those in Berlin (Israeli music, for example, is played in the car Eyal is driving in the city). Similarly, the Israeli folk dancing scene in the villa of Axel's parents in West Berlin, not far from where the decision on the Final Solution was made, marks a symbolic victory of the Jewish spirit over those who wanted, and others who still want, to destroy it.

Like *Yossi and Jagger*, *Walk on Water* embraces the heteronormative order and defines some of its most prominent symbols as signs of both mental and physical health. Shortly after he returns to Israel, having successfully carried out a secret mission in Turkey (the "elimination" of the Hammas activist in front of his wife and child), Eyal discovers that his wife has committed suicide. In the note she left for him, she wrote that he kills everything near him. Her death, the viewer is led to believe, evokes a strong emotional reaction in Eyal although he tries to conceal it. His commander insists that he go see a therapist, and his poor results in training imply that he suffers from depression. While in the process of mourning the death of his wife, Eyal is asked by Axel whether he has children. Eyal says that he does not and rules out the possibility he ever will. However, in the epilogue which takes place two years after the main events portrayed in the film, he is seen waking up to look after the newborn child he has had with Pia, Axel's sister. The marriage of a second generation of Holocaust survivors from Berlin and the granddaughter of a Nazi criminal conveys a hope for some kind of reconciliation between the two nations. The common child symbolizes this and more: reproduction represents Eyal's life choice. Overcoming his depression, he has decided to quit his job in Mossad, which is fundamentally about killing people, in favor of agricultural work in the kibbutz, and he has brought a child into the world. This is, the film suggests, the ultimate symbol of happiness and normalcy.

But although the viewer is introduced to Eyal's new, traditional nuclear family, there is no sign of Axel. Through an email that Eyal sends Axel, the viewer learns that Axel is living abroad with his partner. Homosexuality, which has been displaced from the Jewish-Israeli body to those of Judaism's and Israel's archenemies, namely the Palestinian and the German, is also, toward the end of the film, pushed outside the borders of the Israeli state, as much as it is pushed outside the borders of the cinematic frame.

The conflicting approaches to gayness in Fox's films, *Walk on Water* in particular, are further demonstrated by the filmmaker's politics of casting. Whereas in Guttman's films at least some of the actors, most notably Boaz Turjeman and the late Ada Valerie Tal, were gay or transsexual, Fox, although he has touched on gay themes in almost all of his films, has hardly ever chosen self-professed gay actors for gay roles. In *Mary Lou* a group of drag performers play themselves, and another actor, Alon Levi, came out in an interview soon before the show was aired in 2009 (Halutz), but they are an exception that comes at a late stage in Fox's career and only highlights his customary choice of casting. Before that, one of the very few openly gay actors to have taken part in a Fox film is Knut Berger, who plays Axel in *Walk on Water*. As stated above, by shifting homosexuality and gayness away from Israeli roles, and actors too, Fox exposes in his work an unresolved tension between wholesome Israeli life and gayness. Ella Shohat has pointed out that the majority of Mizrahi characters in *Bourekas* films were played by Ashkenazi actors, such as Haim Topol, Yehuda Barkan, and Gila Almagor (135–36). Thus, self-representation was denied. By the same token, I would like to argue that Fox's almost systematic choice of heterosexual actors for gay roles denies gay self-representation.

As in some of Fox's previous films, the hegemonic message of *Walk on Water* is challenged by a subversive use of music. Eyal's favorite singer is Bruce Springsteen. Axel, on the other hand, prefers to listen to female singers. The musical clash between the two is of a gendered kind: the masculine, rough sound of Springsteen versus the delicate voice of Italian singer Gigliola Cinguetti. However, throughout the film, Eyal learns to like female voices, and when he arrives in Berlin he offers Axel an Israeli album by a woman singer as a present. Although music is a tool to explore Eyal's "feminine" side, this exploration only leads to the reinforcement of a heterosexual institution: it is Eyal's total transformation and rediscovery of his "softer" (hence, feminine) side that enables him to marry Pia and have

Promiscuous lovers: Rafik (Yousef "Joe" Sweid, left) and Axel (Knut Berger) in Eytan Fox's *Walk on Water* (2004).

a child with her. Axel is coupled as well, but his progress from a state of promiscuity shown at the beginning of the film to stability is only briefly mentioned.

The Bubble: Till Death Do Them Part

The Bubble, released in Israel two years after *Walk on Water*, seems to be a natural progression in Fox's cinematic path. In this film, Fox's most recent to date, he covers similar themes to those explored in his previous projects, namely the Israeli-Arab conflict, the tension between army and civilian life in Israel, youth culture, and, most importantly, the place that the urban, Ashkenazi gay male occupies in the complex political and cultural life of Israel.

The film's title refers to the way Tel Aviv is often discussed in the Israeli media. Criticized as a hedonistic haven for indifferent people, Tel Aviv is seen as separated from the rest of Israel. The traditional positioning of secular and urban Tel Aviv as an alternative to both the religious nature of Jerusalem and the agrarian, socialist culture of the kibbutzim and the moshavim is now extended to the whole of Israel. Whereas the rest of the country is seen as mobilized and at the frontline, Tel Aviv is in the rearguard, enjoying a carefree, feckless existence. Fox uses this sentiment as the background of the complex plot that unfolds on the screen, a plot that nonetheless comes to refute it. As the film successfully shows, Tel Aviv, being a prime target for terrorists, is anything but immune to the threat of violence and its allegedly complacent existence is disrupted time and again.

Still, Tel Aviv stands for a bastion of normality or, indeed, a bubble, and the decision to set the film at its heart has a special significance. That this bastion collapses and surrenders to the violent and volatile reality of the Middle East leaves little hope for change. As a film that uses Tel Aviv as a barometer of certain cultural tendencies within Israeli society, *The Bubble* could easily fit in with the group of films analyzed in chapter 1. However, unlike those films, which at their core attempted to push boundaries and challenge cultural and social mores, *The Bubble* is a reactionary tale in which the explosive materials, namely a gay love affair between a Palestinian from Nablus and an Israeli Jew from a fashionable quarter in Tel Aviv, are presented in sensationalist and sentimental ways that dilute its dual message against the occupation and for coexistence. Furthermore, Fox's approach to gay relationships and gay existence in general in this film is ambivalent as before: although they do occupy the center of the film for the most part, they are ultimately pushed to its margins. In this sense, *The Bubble* links to Fox's previous gay-themed films that came after *Song of the Siren*, most notably *Yossi and Jagger*.

The two lovers are Noam (Ohad Knoller, who played Yossi in *Yossi and Jagger*) and Ashraf (Yousef "Joe" Sweid). Unlike Rafik, the character Sweid played in *Walk on Water*, Ashraf, as a central character, has been given a history and a background. Originally from Jerusalem and an Israeli citizen, Ashraf grew up in Nablus after the Israeli army destroyed his family home and now is in need of a special permit to enter Israel. He first meets Noam at one of the Israeli army checkpoints on the West Bank. Ashraf is standing in line to be checked by the aggressive representatives of the Israeli forces. Noam is standing on the other side, as a soldier in reserve duty. They both witness the tragic birth of a stillborn baby to a Palestinian woman who has been held up in the queue. Noam is then seen going back to the apartment he shares with his friends Yali (Alon Friedman), a gay man, and Lulu (Daniela Wircer), a heterosexual woman. Their secure urban existence is in sharp contrast to the reality of violence and humiliation the Israelis are responsible for at the checkpoints.

Noam's difficulty in accommodating his pacifist, Left-wing views with the role he assumes as a soldier (even if only temporarily as a reserve soldier) is expressed in his indifference to the strict army rules regarding filming in the checkpoint area (he allows a cameraman to keep filming despite his commander's disapproval) as well as in his elaborate attempt to dissociate

Cross-ethnic, cross-national love affair: Ashraf (Yousef "Joe" Sweid, left) and Noam (Ohad Knoller) in Eytan Fox's *The Bubble* (2006).

himself from what is happening around him: while at the checkpoint and on his way back to Tel Aviv Noam is listening to his iPod. The music has a symbolic power, as in Fox's previous films, in portraying an alternative reality to that seen on the screen.

Shortly after Noam's arrival in Tel Aviv, Ashraf shows up at his door carrying Noam's army ID, which he lost while at the checkpoint (this follows a similar plot move in *Time Off* in which the soldier hands his commander his ID after the latter left it in the park where he had anonymous sex. By handing the ID to his closeted commander, the soldier makes clear that he knows about the commander's homosexuality). This unexpected meeting between the two triggers a passionate affair, which ends tragically with Ashraf blowing himself up in front of the busy Tel Aviv café where Noam and his friends work and hang out. Ashraf and Noam die in the explosion, their bodies lying next to each other, a testimony to the futility of war or, as may be read by others, the hope for peace, a point to which I will return later on. Their death also attests to the futility of gay existence, especially one that dares to defy the existing status quo in Israel, which dictates a total separation between Israelis and Palestinians.

The film follows the tradition of what Yosefa Loshitzky has called the "forbidden love" story in Israeli cinema, that between an Israeli Jew and an Arab. The importance of telling stories of "forbidden love," Loshitzky argues, lies in their power to expose the effects of the conflict and the occupation at the "microlevel": "The displacement, taking place in Israeli cinema, of the Israeli-Palestinian conflict to the territory of forbidden love, makes it easier for the Israeli audience [. . .] to encounter the conflict whose roots are complex and painful" (*Identity Politics* 113). I would like to suggest that for Fox it is not only the characters' racial and ethnic origins that make their love story a transgression of the norm but also, perhaps even primarily, their sexual orientation.

As in Fox's previous films, *The Bubble* blends the political and the personal to maximum effect: not only do the Jewish characters oppose the occupation on moral, political, and ethical grounds, but they also experience the destructive consequences it has in their own lives. The explosion for which Ashraf is responsible was planned by Jihad, his brother-in-law, as an act of revenge for the death of his new wife, Ashraf's sister, who was killed accidentally by Israeli soldiers. They shot her while looking for those responsible (among them Jihad) for yet another suicide bombing in Tel Aviv, in which Yali was severely wounded. Jihad's participation in the planning of those deadly attacks stemmed from feelings of fury and frustration, a direct result of being discriminated against and humiliated by the Israeli army (like Ashraf, he is present in the film's opening scene in which the heavily pregnant woman is giving birth to a stillborn). The two protagonists oppose violent acts and are engaged in political protest, but this, as it turns out, amounts to very little: their main course of action is organizing a rave on a Tel Aviv beach.

This moderate, not to say ineffective, form of "Left-wing" protest demonstrates yet again Fox's full identification with the mainstream and his wish not to upset any side in the debate: the Israeli-Palestinian love affair comes to satisfy those who preach coexistence, whereas the violent acts that follow are used as a proof of the futility of that hope. If anything, Fox seems to be more inclined toward a pessimistic picture that agrees more with the futility of the Left camp in Israel, depicting its followers as naïve. The violent actions on both sides that the protagonists are either forced or encouraged to take part in—Noam as a soldier serving at the checkpoints and Ashraf as a suicide bomber—and their end result is much more pronounced and fatal than their peacemaking endeavors.

As in *Yossi and Jagger*, *The Bubble* seems at first to hail gay relationships as deeper and more committed than their heterosexual counterparts: it is Noam and Ashraf who form a strong bond right from the outset, and even Yali, who it seems has feelings for Noam (while in the hospital, Yali asks Noam why they have never become a couple), starts what may become a serious relationship with Golan (Zohar Liba). Lulu, on the other hand, falls for a man who leaves her after they have sex once. However, the gay relationship that Noam and Ashraf are engaged in is doomed from the start, and its *Romeo and Juliet*-esque ending is anything but unpredictable. It is Yali who comments on Noam's inability to commit himself by falling in love with tourists, straight men, or, in this case, a man who comes from the other side of the tracks. At the end of the film, Yali is still in the hospital and the future of his on-off relationship with Golan is unclear. Lulu, on the other hand, has just started a new relationship with Shaul (Zion Baruch), who has told her he would like them to get married and have children, thus devising a future that Fox denies his gay protagonists. Like Yossi and Jagger, Noam and Ashraf are indeed romantic heroes, but in both films the romance stems from the tragedy that follows.

The allusion to *Romeo and Juliet* suggests that *The Bubble* can be read, at least on one level, as a moral tale. At the same time, the film deals with the here and now of Israeli life and as such is inclined toward a realist portrayal of the conflict. However, the plot of the film relies on a chain of events that for political and cultural reasons is near impossible. To those familiar with the current state of affairs in Israel and Palestine, a story in which two men fall instantly in love while standing on two sides of an army-guarded blockade and then manage to consummate it can only be read as a fairy tale. Although suspension of disbelief allows us to enjoy both cinema and literature fully, it does not work in a film that aspires to be politically sharp and relevant. But the implausibility of the events on screen is only part of a bigger problem, namely the supposedly "leftist" views expressed in the film regarding both the Israeli-Palestinian conflict and the gay rights movement: according to Fox, all that the Left has left to do is organize rave parties, whereas gay men, in the tradition of *Walk on Water* and *Yossi and Jagger*, are excluded, or worse die. In either case, they are denied the future that is promised to their heterosexual counterparts.

Mary Lou: Political Disengagement

Mary Lou, Fox's latest project to date (written by Shiri Artzi), signals an interesting departure from the director's previous attempts to deal with hard politics to a story that purposely lacks any direct references to the place and time in which it was made. Following the international success of the musical *Mamma Mia!* (both film [Phyllida Lloyd, 2008] and theatrical productions), this miniseries is based on the hit songs of singer and composer Tsvika Pick, whose flamboyant appearances since the 1970s have made him a popular culture icon in Israel.[17] The story follows the protagonist Meir's

(Ido Rosenberg) quest to find the mother who left him and his father when he was a young boy. His memory of his mother's admiration for Pick's songs and her wish to become a star leads him to Tel Aviv, where he hopes to find Pick and, through him, his mother. In Tel Aviv he meets a group of drag performers, who look after him and make him a star in his own right.

As in *Gotta Have Heart* before it, Fox meticulously creates a world of fantasy in *Mary Lou*, which is beyond time (the art direction makes conflicting references to different decades) and place (the pastoral environment of the old town that Meir hails from and the depiction of Tel Aviv as the adoptive big city serve as prototypes more than actual places). Not only does the plotline follow some familiar tropes—the search after the long lost mother, urban migration, and self-discovery—but the characters too are shaped according to archetypes, especially the main gay characters. Meir is the effeminate, dramatic young gay man who can only fully express himself in costume and onstage. He is in love with Gabi (Alon Levi), the macho-looking combat soldier, who humiliated Meir in high school for his feminine appearance and gestures, but slowly comes to terms with his own homosexuality. Ori (Yedidya Vital), who performs in drag under the name Miss Sunshine, is a sensitive soul who is in love with Meir. In order to get over this unrequited love, he goes out with closeted Shlomi (Angel Bonanni), but their short romance ends with Ori's death (he drowns in the sea shortly after being rejected by Shlomi, who is still struggling with his homosexuality).

Mary Lou can be read as an attempt to create a thoroughly symbolic representation of life, one that strips down characters, places, and situations to their very essence. Indeed, the four main male characters are iconic, almost caricatured, gay figures who also represent stages of coming out. By doing this, Fox ignores the nuanced complexity of the inner human drama. The generic affiliation of this miniseries to the categories of both fairy tale and melodrama invite a detached reading of the spectacle on screen: the characters who constantly burst into song as much as the portrayal of Meir's hometown as a token of peripheral, backward existence and the club in Tel Aviv as a token of progress, do not actually portray recognizable, lived realities.

Many of Fox's films have moments of fantasy in them. The love story between Noam and Ashraf in *The Bubble*, for instance, is made possible solely by a skewed outlook on the potential of communication between Israelis and Palestinians. In the same manner, some of the scenes in *Walk on Water* are based on fantasized notions of both Israeli and German collective symbols and narratives (the scene in which Israeli folk dancing is

Gay archetypes: effeminate Meir (Ido Rosenberg, left) and macho-looking Gabi (Alon Levi) in Eytan Fox's *Mary Lou* (2009).

performed by Aryan-looking Germans in Berlin is an obvious example). However, with the exception of *Gotta Have Heart,* Fox has always sought to remain grounded in his immediate political and social surroundings. The fantasy that Fox and Artzi create in *Mary Lou* suggests a more significant disengagement from the reality of the occupation, Lebanon, and the memory of the Holocaust that preoccupied Fox and his films in the past.

Of course fantasy can relate to the here and now, and melodrama has traditionally lent itself to the exposure of broken ideologies. In *Mary Lou*, however, the melodramatic elements do not facilitate a shift in the perception of gay men in society, but rather they corroborate the existing classification of them according to already fixed categories of identification, which Fox himself helped to shape in his earlier films. The hypermasculine soldier who struggles to accommodate his homosexuality with the role he fulfills (Gabi) echoes the inner dilemma Yossi is facing in *Yossi and Jagger*; the sensitive gay man who is eliminated from the world of the film for who he is (Ori/Miss Sunshine) follows the path of both Jagger in the above-mentioned film and Noam and Ashraf in *The Bubble*. The drag performers in *Mary Lou* may be flaunting their homosexuality, but they do so in a highly restricted area of Israeli public life. Thus, gay existence in *Mary Lou* seems to stand further apart from Israel's turbulent—whether gay or other—political concerns. Instead, Fox wittingly creates a whimsical gay world as mere entertainment and ready for consumption. That in itself may attest to Fox's current point of view: gay

Gay Men and the Establishment in the Films of Eytan Fox   125

culture is now etched in Israeli collective consciousness to the extent that it can be framed as a generic televised musical.

Some Concluding Remarks

In the short history of gay filmmaking in Israel, Amos Guttman and Eytan Fox are often regarded as its two pivotal figures. Although equally influential, the two directors' respective styles and agendas could not be more different. Whereas Guttman made a point of emphasizing the distance between the gay minority and the Israeli collective, Fox has made a name for himself as the gay filmmaker whose films set out to prove that the two can live together. Whereas in Guttman's films the protagonists are excluded from the Israeli collective, in Fox's films they are engaged in what is taking place around them, they are an inseparable part of their surroundings. They fight and get killed for the national cause (in *Yossi and Jagger* and also partly in *Mary Lou*); they dance to Israeli folk music (in *Gotta Have Heart* and *Walk on Water*); they are part of the crowd mourning the tragic death of Rabin, the "architect of peace" (in *Florentine*); they experience the Israeli-Palestinian conflict and protest against it (in *The Bubble*).

The "normalization" of the gay community and the shift from the "ghettoized environment" in Guttman's cinema to a total integration into Israeli society, shaped by its conflicts, patriotism, and grief, is Fox's trademark. He insists on showing gay men (lesbians and transgendered people do not appear in any of his films) as an equal, in some cases even a superior, group in Israeli society. However, his films undermine this very goal. This is manifested in narrative choices—in which the gay story often "succumbs" to mainstream conventions, reflecting gay men's dependence on hegemonic culture rather than their equal standing—and in Fox's politics of casting. It is their "surrender" to heterosexist norms that has contributed to their popularity among nongay audiences in Israel and abroad. Indeed, the impact Fox's films have had on nongay viewers cannot be underestimated: both *Florentine* and *Gotta Have Heart* were produced for channel 2, which until 2002 was the only commercial TV channel in Israel, and is by far the most popular one. *Yossi and Jagger* was produced as a short film for Israeli cable TV, but its preview screenings in movie theaters in Israel were, unexpectedly, an enormous success.

Fox's films reflect the change of status of certain gay groups in Israel. *Time Off* was made in the midst of the gay legal "revolution" and a few years before the restrictions on recruitment of gay men to certain units in the army were fully lifted. Therefore, the film expresses a certain degree of militancy, especially in its political stance toward the war in Lebanon. His more recent films, however, reflect the alliance between the old elites and the gay community. The contradictory approach Fox takes in those films regarding gayness, namely the simultaneous celebration and denial of it, suggests he creates from a confused position. As both Fox and the gay establishment become more accepted, it becomes harder for both to challenge what still needs to be changed. This task, it seems, is now in the hands of the less privileged and less well-established young filmmakers.

Like Guttman, Fox and his films have become a reference point for many new filmmakers who portray gay life in Israel. It is this influence, among other tendencies, I would like to explore in the last two chapters, which are dedicated to new gay—both documentary and fiction—filmmaking in Israel.

4

Real Lives

New Israeli Nonfiction Gay Cinema

In the past two decades Israeli cinema has been characterized by an increased interest in the private domain. The focus has shifted away from grand, national narratives to personal stories about individuals or minority groups who have been, after long battles, granted their own agency. If early Israeli cinema was a major tool in forging a national identity in the first decades after the establishment of the state, contemporary Israeli cinema has gradually become an important site where a fragmented society and identities are explored. There were, of course, precursors. The "personal cinema" of the 1960s, the Tel Aviv films of Uri Zohar, and the gay-themed films of Amos Guttman were all significant cultural events that questioned and challenged the mobilized character of Israeli society long before it became a common practice to do so. However, the steady decline in the past two decades of uncontested conformity has meant that "personal cinema" in Israel is now more prominent than ever before.

The new Mizrahi cinema illustrates this trend. After many years of stereotyped representation of Jews who emigrated from countries of the Middle East, North Africa, and the Caucasus in *Bourekas* films, which were mostly written and directed by Ashkenazi filmmakers, the 1990s and 2000s signaled a shift in the mode of representation. Films like *Shchur* (Shmuel Hasfari, 1994) and *Late Marriage* (Dover Koshashvili, 2001), both of which are fiction features that portray non-Ashkenazi communities from within, have been publicized as autobiographical, in contrast to the earlier portrayal of these communities.[1]

Amy Kronish and Costel Safirman have shown how personal existential dilemmas have become a prevalent topic in many recent Israeli films, a development that stems from "the new emphasis on human portrayals of the 'now' generation" (15). One of the main beneficiaries of this new trend, they argue, is the gay community, and the growing number of gay-themed films made in Israel every year bears this out. It is no coincidence that the majority of those films are nonfiction. The shift toward the personal, which has led to further meditation on the construction and expression of selfhood (vis-à-vis national and/or collective identities), has also manifested itself in a search for new cinematic forms of self-expression, namely documentary, autobiographical, and "hybrid" films, in which "autobiography mediates a mixture of documentary, fiction, and experimental genres" to explore "people in transition and cultures in the process of creating identities" (Laura Marks qtd. in Loshitzky, *Identity Politics* 87).[2]

Recent years have seen young filmmakers examine previously unexplored aspects of gay life in Israel, using the "authentic" appeal of the nonfiction film to great effect. This has been facilitated by their predecessors' achievements: Amos Guttman's trailblazing cinema and Eytan Fox's commercial success have generated interest in gay-themed films. Moving on from both Guttman's isolation from and Fox's embrace of Israeli core values, these new filmmakers have broadened the boundaries of the discourse, taking for granted the social and cultural acceptance that the gay community has achieved.[3] Once some of the initial struggles fought by the gay movement had been won (such as the passing in December 1991 of a bill outlawing workplace discrimination based on sexual orientation), other issues and problems could be brought to the fore, such as gay parenthood, male prostitution, and AIDS. Equally important is the production of lesbian narratives. For years, Israeli gay cinema focused solely on the male experience. But the current wave of gay nonfiction filmmaking in Israel has paved the way for lesbians to narrate their life experiences.

The economy of film production has played a significant role in the rise of gay nonfiction films. Documentaries usually do not require large financial investment, as there is no need to employ professional actors or build sets.[4] Makers of autobiographical nonfiction films often use relatively low-cost digital videotape. Further advances in technology have enabled even cheaper and easier ways of putting a film together. The majority of these low-budget films then find their way into television broadcasting.

The Israeli state channel's loss of its monopoly to a wide range of channels (public, cable, and satellite) has generated many more hours of broadcasting and the creation of many more niche audiences. Furthermore, the arrival of commercial TV in Israel in 1993 created a new TV culture that comfortably housed this type of film. Influenced by the American and British culture of talk and reality shows, local TV production has adopted a "confessional" mode in which the personal (the more bizarre and unique the better) has been celebrated. In a prescient essay "Israeli Television and the National Agenda," published in 1995, Yuval Elizur predicted the impact that the proliferation of channels would have on Israeli society: "Television will lose its 'agenda setting' role. No longer will it be able to exercise a unifying influence or concentrate the public's interest around national goals" (116). It is ironic that two decades after the state channel banned Ron Asulin's moderate gay-themed drama *A Different Shadow* (1983) due to its allegedly provocative content, Yair Lev's *Yakantalisa* (1996), discussed later in the chapter, was rejected by the same channel for being "boring," as claimed by the then head of documentary, Natan Kaspi (*Ha'ir* 23 Aug. 1996). According to the film producer Yael Shavit, the film—which tells the life story of artist Hezi Leskly, who died of AIDS in 1994—was simply not "juicy" enough (*Ha'ir* 23 Aug. 1996).

Nonfiction Film and the (De)construction of Gay Identity

In the history of documentary filmmaking, the Direct Cinema period signaled a strong inclination toward "objective" observation. In order to achieve this, the presence of the filmmaker was silenced. This, Michael Renov suggests, was "the symptomatic silence of the empowered [...] white, male professionals" (*The Subject of Documentary* 181). In sharp contrast to the strict principles of the Direct Cinema filmmakers, the self-enactments of the current generation of documentarians are a transgressive act. Their self-referenced films speak the lives of those who have lived outside "the boundaries of cultural knowledge" (Renov, *The Subject of Documentary* 181).

A particularly vital and dynamic element within this trend, Renov suggests, is a growing group of gay filmmakers who, rather than conforming to any particular template, test and try new ways to explore their sexual and cultural identity (*The Subject of Documentary* 180). Trying to define nonheteronormative identities, or to defy notions of fixed identities altogether, gay documentaries and autobiographical films (made by both gay and heterosexual filmmakers) become "queer"; they blur boundaries, mix genres, and create new modes of filmmaking. The blurring of distinctions between documentary and fiction as two separate genres reflects the blurring of lesbian and gay sexualities as discrete identities and is accompanied by the celebration of queerness as a strategy of confounding identity. In this sense, contemporary gay nonfiction films are often more interested in deconstructing or questioning gay identity than in constructing/corroborating it. These films, and the filmmakers, indicate "the myriad possibilities of representational tactics available to apprehend [. . .] very elusive subjectivities" (McHugh 225).

The many techniques that some gay nonfiction films employ attest to the elusive, undefined quality of the "truth" they come to convey. In their cinematic approach and narration, the filmmakers make a point of rendering the films' artificial, constructed, discursive nature as transparent as possible. The films expose the fabrications, prejudices, and artifices that dominate our culture and shape the ways we perceive ourselves, as well as others. The films allow us to explore further the ways in which one rewrites one's self, interprets one's life, and gives meaning to one's existence, especially when one is a gay man, a lesbian, or a transsexual.

A prime example of the new directions in which documentary filmmaking is heading is Jonathan Caouette's autobiographical film, *Tarnation* (2004). Caouette famously made the film using the iMovie software on his computer. Mixing old home movies, popular culture footage (clips of TV shows and films), and newly filmed materials, Caouette told his story of growing up gay in Texas in the shadow of his mother's mental illness. Although omitting any references to his Jewishness as well as to his son from a past heterosexual relationship, as noted by Alisa L. Lebow (118–19), Caouette still managed to produce an unusually candid document about his life. His chaotic upbringing is well illustrated not only on the narrative level of the film but on the formal level too. Focusing on the missing element that is Caouette's Jewish identity, Lebow nonetheless describes *Tarnation* as a film "that matches the instability *in* the text with the instability *of* the text, a film where almost nothing is too outrageous or excessive to mention or depict, a film that leaves no personal boundaries uncrossed" (118). Some of the key elements in *Tarnation*, especially the use of found footage of old home movies, the suggestive use of music, and the emphasis on how the autobiographical can be read through the larger paradigm of society and culture, can be found in a few of the works discussed below.

One of the aims of this chapter, therefore, is to explore the use of new means of documentary filmmaking, such as dramatization and the incorporation of found footage, in recent Israeli nonfiction films. I will attempt both to tackle the uniqueness of these films as they blur the once clear distinctions between the objective and the subjective and to examine the nature of their contribution to the notion of gayness in contemporary Israel. It is important to note that not all the films included in this chapter follow these experimental lines. The majority of them, formally at least, are conventional documentaries. However, a few of the filmmakers, most notably Anat Dotan and Elle Flanders, forge a link between formal experimentation and the challenging of fixed identities.

It is precisely the variations of themes and forms found in the films discussed below—from the more traditional "talking heads"–style documentary (*Yakantalisa*) to Dotan's mixture of fiction and nonfiction techniques in *Last Post* (*Michtav Meuchar*, 1997)—that are indicative of the plurality of modern Israeli gay experiences, shaped, among other factors, by ethnicity and class. Taken together, these films show the different, often contradictory, directions various groupings within the Israeli gay community are heading.

Last Post: Fables of the Reconstruction

The short film *Last Post* was written and directed by Anat Dotan as her final project at the Sam Spiegel Film School in Jerusalem and was first screened in 1997. The film is an elegy for Amos Guttman, with whom Dotan had a professional and personal relationship. Like Guttman, who incorporated autobiographical elements into all of his films, Dotan deals with real-life events in her film but employs fictional storytelling devices. The emphasis is on dramatization in the form of restaging, reconstruction, and reenactment of events. As the actress Sigal Tzuk, who plays her in the film, declares in a voice-over at the beginning, "His films were always about himself. He didn't know how to make films about anything else. I think that was another thing that connected us. He told me to make films so I could tell my stories."

Like Guttman's *Drifting*, *Last Post* draws the viewer's attention to the gap between reality and its imaginative, distanced reconstruction. Dotan does not try to create the illusion of autobiographical transparency. On the contrary, she critiques the notion of an accessible and verifiable personal history. As Judith Butler has stated in the new preface to her 1990 book *Gender Trouble*, although she does not believe that poststructuralism entails the death of autobiographical writing, "it does draw attention to the difficulty of the 'I' to express itself through the language that is available to it" (xxiv). Drawing on this, Dotan opts for a richly constructed account of selfhood, which is as playful as it is opaque. This allows Dotan to conflate personal revelation with a broader sociocultural critique.

Dotan mixes genres and crosses the boundaries between fiction and nonfiction, meditating on the artificial, reconstructed quality of our memories and histories. As she moves away from the traditional documentary style into a performative[5] section (and then back, toward the end, where a short clip of the "real" Guttman shortly before his death is shown), she points to autobiography as, in the words of Keith Beattie, "an act in which the author 'performs the self'" (109).

Using dramatization and reenactments, Dotan offers her unique interpretation of real events as she remembers them, expressing her longing for her dead friend. The film stresses the importance of the way we think about the past rather than the accuracy of our memories. As Marita Sturken has observed, writing about the production of cultural memory, "We need to ask not whether a memory is true but rather what its telling reveals about how the past affects the present" (2). It seems that more than offering "objective" documentation of past events, the film, or rather the making of the film, had a therapeutic function for Dotan and may be similarly therapeutic for the viewer. This, as Bill Horrigan has argued, is often what documentaries about AIDS, made by people who are directly touched by HIV, aim to offer (171).

Dotan's story is told in a nonlinear way: the viewer is not shown the history of Dotan and Guttman's relationship, and questions such as where and when they met for the first time remain unanswered. The film comes across as an attempt to visualize Dotan's memories and inner thoughts about Guttman and her relationship with him. The past, the film suggests, needs to be created and reimagined. Questions of authenticity and proximity to the "real," which were integral issues in discussions of biography, testimony, and documentary making for many years, lose, in Dotan's view, their value. Instead, questions regarding the elusive quality of our memories and of an objective "reality" are raised. As Andreas Huyssen claims, "Rather than leading us to some authentic origin or giving us verifiable access to the real, memory, even and especially in its belatedness, is itself based on representation. The past is not simply there in memory, but it must be articulated to become memory" (qtd. in Sturken 9).

The staging of subjectivity in the film exemplifies the notion of *Nachträglichkeit*, or "deferred action," which Michael Renov borrows from

Freud: "The manner by which experiences, impressions, or memory traces are altered after the fact as a function of new experiences and are thus rendered capable of reinvestment, producing new, even unexpected, effects of meaning" (*The Subject of Documentary* 114). Following Lacan's reading of this Freudian idea, Slavoj Žižek argues that "psychoanalysis is [. . .] not concerned with the past 'as such,' in its factual purity, but in the way past events are included in the present, synchronous field of meaning" (202). Dotan's filmmaking, then, follows the psychoanalytic process in that it gives meaning, retroactively, to past events, a meaning that derives from their reorganization into a symbolic network.

Last Post starts with Dotan's character entering Guttman's (Sean Karlin) apartment for the first time and getting to know his close circle of friends, whose detachment from the society around them is emphasized by their childlike activities. One of them, for instance, is riding a toy horse in front of a TV screen. In her voice-over narration, the character of Dotan says that she was also considered a new "toy" in Guttman's surroundings that had to be explored and tried. Guttman's apartment comes across as the Israeli version of Andy Warhol's Factory, an alternative space in which art and non-normative cultural practices and sexualities are encouraged. This scene, like the look and feel of the film as a whole, suggests that although it indeed comes to tell a story, it also serves a greater purpose, namely intensifying and reinforcing Guttman's myth. It also may attest to Dotan's difficulty in culling her own personal memories of Guttman from the way the media have remembered him. It stresses the power of the image and of the performative act in the constitution of subjectivity. The scene raises questions regarding Guttman's "authentic" character. Was Guttman different from the characters he created on screen? Can one separate the one from the other? Guttman's "true" self and the "true" events that he and Dotan experienced go through a process of disintegration and fragmentation in the film.

Dotan opts to present her personal story—falling in love with the openly gay director—by distancing herself from it. It is told as a fictional story, using actors and scripted sequences, which are inspired by Guttman's films as well as serving as a homage to them. Dotan's memory of Guttman is fed by the cultural, public, memory of him and his work (as an "outlaw" filmmaker) as much as it feeds it. The opening sequence in the film shows Guttman's character walking down a busy street in Tel Aviv at night. At one point he goes past a couple of peepshow bars. The elements that are played out in this short sequence—a nocturnal stroll in downtown Tel Aviv amid sleazy sex bars—seem as if they were taken from Guttman's *Bar 51* (1985) or *Amazing Grace* (1992). Another sequence takes place in a decadent bar, a leitmotif in almost all of Guttman's films. Dotan's character watches "Guttman" kissing another man and, feeling hurt, refuses to talk to him afterward. Another sequence takes place in a battered car and looks like a meticulous reconstruction of American road movie aesthetics. Not only in the narrative but also in the images Dotan creates the boundaries between memory and sight, fantasy and actual vision, become blurred.

At one point in the film, Dotan's character tells in a voice-over about a dream she had, which is visualized in detail as she speaks. It shows her character entering a bright, white room in which two men are having passionate sexual intercourse. Then she is having sex with one of the men while another woman is taping them. While watching the tape, Dotan's character says in a voice-over that she notices Guttman sitting on a tall chair, watching the action and laughing. The images that accompany the narrating voice create a dreamlike sequence. Another sequence, earlier in the film, shows the characters of Dotan and Guttman as husband and wife on their wedding day. The sequence is shot in washed-out colors, which code it as fantasy. In the voice-over she explains that Guttman, while under the influence of recreational drugs, suggested that they get married. But when the effect of the drugs faded, it remained, mainly, her private fantasy.

These two sequences allude to Guttman's early short films of the late 1970s in which the protagonists find refuge from their oppressive life in imaginary worlds. The use of dream/fantasy sequences in the films of both Guttman and Dotan can be seen as a tribute to a long tradition of gay filmmaking, embracing in particular the American experimental filmmakers of the 1960s such as Jack Smith, Kenneth Anger, and Andy Warhol, who participated in and created from a culture of pleasure, perversity, and the unconscious. Although mostly used in fiction films, elements of fantasy can also be found in films that have been considered, to a certain degree, documentaries. In his discussion of Jack Smith's 1963 avant-garde film *Flaming Creatures*, for instance, Marc Siegel comments on its contribution to the expansion of the term "documentary," especially in gay filmmaking. Siegel has argued that "while *Flaming Creatures* may have been 'impure,' too invested in cinematic fantasy to be accepted as a cinema vérité documentary, it also expressed a 'new kind of cinema truth,' one that saw in artifice, in performance the possibility for creating a more fabulous, more livable reality" (92).

Indeed, gay documentary filmmakers in the United States and Europe in the post-Stonewall years did not aspire to produce a "realist" text. On the contrary, realism (mainly interactive realism, "the formulaic mix of interviews and archival footage joined by the mortar of observational vérité and musical interludes" [Waugh, "Walking on Tippy Toes" 112]) was avoided at all costs. Instead, Thomas Waugh argues, lesbian and gay documentarians preferred "artificial and hyperbolic 'performance' discourses that pushed through and beyond the realist codes" (Waugh, "Walking on Tippy Toes" 112).[6]

Similarly, Bill Nichols has argued that what is often also called performative documentary "suspends realist representation" and "puts the referential aspect of the message in brackets, under suspension" (Nichols 96–97). Instead of an attempt to achieve a "window-like quality of addressing the historical world around us" (Nichols 94), performative documentaries present "a variable mix of the expressive, poetic, and rhetorical aspects as new dominants" (Nichols 94). In opposition to essentialist models of a stable gay sexuality and fixed gender categories, the nonrealist approach has focused on gender and identity instability and on lack of transparency.

More than gay life in general, I believe, it is the specific challenge of representing AIDS and its effects on people who suffer from the illness and those who surround them that drives Dotan to revisit the experimental gay filmmaking of the 1960s and 1970s in order to find new ways of storytelling. *Last Post* has much in common with works, mainly memoirs, that deal with AIDS as a major crisis in the contemporary era. The film attests to the problem of making a coherent narrative of and giving a meaning to a social event that seems to evade a cohesive meaning. AIDS and being HIV-positive have long been represented as postmodern conditions that do not respond to common tropes or cannot be contained by conventional practices of cultural memory, due partly to the fact that there is still no cure for the disease. As the epidemic has no narrative closure, it cannot be related as a past event ready for inspection.[7]

Distancing herself through reenactments from the story she tells, Dotan chooses, however, to finish her film with real footage of Guttman, shot shortly before he died of AIDS-related illness in 1993, in which she (this time, Dotan the filmmaker, not the character) asks Guttman if he would like to say anything (Dotan is not fully seen on the screen but her voice is heard). Laconically, Guttman says, "no." The shift from fiction to nonfiction at the end of the film has different registers: there is a shift from a reenacted representation to real, documentary footage (which seems even more authentic due to the grainy and gritty quality of the camcorder picture: a grainy image has long been perceived as a signifier of authenticity),[8] from an actor to the real person, and from a healthy state (although the film is framed by Guttman's illness and it is mentioned several times, there are no telltale signs on the actor's body) to a state of illness and then dying (thus, the film also serves as a memento mori). The beautiful Guttman, lively, full of desire, and fictitious, becomes in an instant a washed-out, grainy, laconic, but real figure. These shifts signal the shattering of the protective, distanced fantasy Dotan has created and bring her and the viewer to point zero: in the end, the "reality" (or at least our desire to grasp this "reality") of life, and death, prevails.

FAMILY TIES: THE CONSTRUCTION OF GAY IDENTITIES IN RECENT ISRAELI "DOMESTIC ETHNOGRAPHY" FILMS—*SAY AMEN!*, *ALMOST THERE*, *HAMAVRI*, AND *THE WAY HOME*

Several Israeli gay-themed films of recent years can be described as autobiographical in that their makers are interested primarily in self-examination. A closer look at some of these films reveals the filmmakers' keen interest in their nuclear families and their families' response to the knowledge of their son's or daughter's homosexuality. Those films exceed the limiting autobiographical boundaries to expose the ways in which homosexuality is perceived in different strata of Israeli society as well as to follow the reconstruction of identity and perception of self in other participants of the family drama in light of that knowledge.

This section focuses on three recent gay-themed *and* gay-authored films—*Say Amen!* (*Tagid Amen!*, David Deri, 2005), *Almost There* (*Kim'at Sham*, Sigal Yehuda and Joelle Alexis, 2004), and *HaMavri* (Ayal Goldberg, 2001) and one TV series—*The Way Home* (*BaDerech HaBaita*, Tomer Heymann, 2009). All four fall under the category of "domestic ethnography" defined by Michael Renov as an expansion of both autobiography and traditional ethnography.[9] With domestic ethnography, argues Renov, the work "engages in the documentation of family members or, less literally, of people with whom the maker has maintained long-standing everyday relations and has thus achieved a level of casual intimacy" (*The Subject of Documentary* 218). Admittedly, says Renov, one could say that domestic ethnography is a kind of supplementary autobiographical practice; it functions as a vehicle of self-interrogation, a means through which to construct self-knowledge through recourse to the familial other. At the same time, its outward gaze reaches beyond the mere autobiographical as "nominally, at least, this mode of documentation takes as its subject the father, mother, grandparent, child, or sibling who is genetically linked to the authorial subject" (*The Subject of Documentary* 218).

Unlike the ethnographer, his domestic counterpart is not granted a fully outside position from which to observe as "blood ties effect linkages of shared memory, physical resemblance, temperament, and, of course, family-forged behavioral or attitudinal dysfunction toward which the artist [...] can fashion accommodation but no escape" (Renov, *The Subject of Documentary* 219). The impossibility of escaping one's family is poignantly put into words by Caouette, relating to his mother in *Tarnation*: "She lives inside me. She's in my hair, she's behind my eyes, she's under my skin, she's [...] downstairs" (qtd. in Lebow 39). Indeed, the need to carve a space not afflicted by family incursion, and the only partial success in accomplishing this, is manifested in all of the films discussed below.

Domestic ethnography is, for Renov, an extension of autobiography but also has the potential to tell us about cultures and societies at large. This potential, I would like to argue, is fully realized in all the documentaries I look at: the four produce a broader statement about how homosexuality is perceived and treated by different groups within the Israeli collective. What they reveal is often at odds with the dominant narrative of a seemingly unified gay community as it has been constructed in many fiction and nonfiction films and the media in general. That narrative indicates a near perfect assimilation by focusing mostly on a limited gay experience, namely that of a middle-class, Ashkenazi gay man, and ignoring weaker subgroups within it such as transsexuals, lesbians, and Mizrahi gay men, the last two are at the center of two of the films I will discuss shortly.

It is not surprising that gay filmmakers often choose to focus on their own family dynamics. This is motivated by both the wish to be accepted in light of the potential risk of familial disowning that the act of coming out entails and the need to investigate the roots of their difference. Both nurture and nature, the two factors in the ongoing debate about the causes of homosexuality, take us back to the nuclear, biological family as a starting point as well as a likely source.

Say Amen! and *Almost There*

It is the threat of disowning that is at the heart of David Deri's 2005 *Say Amen!* In this film, Deri, the youngest son of religious, conservative, Moroccan-born parents, documents, over the course of five years, the response of his family to his homosexuality. The film bears a special importance in its exploration of Deri's gay identity vis-à-vis his ethnic and religious background and as different from that of his Ashkenazi secular counterparts, which has been perceived as the backbone of the Israeli gay narrative. The film has a home movie quality that reveals itself in the cinematography as well as in Deri's detailed and intimate study of his family's patterns of relating to each other.

For many years Deri has been avoiding his family's expectations that he will get married and have children. He is under increasing pressure to settle down. Two of his sisters, who know about his sexuality (Deri's coming out to them took place before the time of the film), voice contradictory opinions regarding his planned confession. Whereas one warns him of the effect it will have on their parents and brothers, the other says she cannot keep it secret anymore from the others, who, sensing something is "wrong," are putting great pressure on her to tell. Deri himself, it seems, is torn between telling and not telling. While refusing to accept one sister's demand to keep silent, he also keeps avoiding his brothers' direct question about why he does not get married or at least have a girlfriend. But the family pressure for "good tidings," namely a wedding plan, prompts him, in the end, to come out to them.

In *Say Amen!* Deri situates himself in the familial order, witnessing "the difficulties of accommodation within rigid family structures to queer sensibilities and life choices" (Renov, *The Subject of Documentary* 180). For Deri, it not only his homosexuality that needs to be accounted for but also his profession, his secularism, and the fact that he lives in Tel Aviv ("a stupid and stupefying city," as one of his brothers tells him). By making the film, Deri attempts to close the split between his two identities—the one influenced by his family and upbringing and the other shaped by his urban, gay life—and to create, in the process, the "imagined singularity" (Smith qtd. in Beattie 105) perceived as the self. Deri hopes to do this by getting his family's acceptance of his "condition." The film traces the way identities are shaped and changed by interaction, not only Deri's identity but also, and perhaps more importantly, the identities of the people who are directly affected by the realization that he is gay. One of Deri's brothers expresses a concern that if people knew his brother was gay they would see him, too, in a different light. Another brother asks Deri to consider the pain of others caused by his homosexuality rather than focus on his own. And one of his sisters tells him that she was never worried about him but about the family, the parents in particular. These anxieties, explicitly expressed in the film, may have played a part in the family's decision to stop the planned screenings of it in 2005.[10]

The dramatic nature of *Say Amen!* is a result of the immense gap separating the two worlds—the secular, gay-friendly world in Tel Aviv and the traditional world of Deri's family. Deri seems to be aware of the dramatic potential of his "news" and deliberately postpones the moment he tells his brothers. He carefully scripts the story of his coming out, intentionally prolonging the act in an attempt to create suspense.

The film omits any references to Deri's romantic life, social circles, or professional networks in his adoptive city, Tel Aviv, and in so doing undermines the importance of those, which are often seen as an alternative to the nexus of the nuclear biological family in gay discourse. At the heart of the film is the biological family and the change of its dynamics in response to his act of coming out. For this reason, Deri does not seem to be the center of the film, although he is the generator of this change. Deri may be mostly an invisible participant—being the main cameraman means that he is left outside the frame on many occasions—but he is in full control over the execution of his coming out operation. One of his sisters defends his right to film the meeting in which Deri comes out to his siblings. The camera, she explains, serves as his shield. His hiding behind the camera, however, is not a sign of passivity but rather a full exercise of his authority as a filmmaker, the subject of the gaze rather than the object. This authority is challenged time and again when his family members question him about his constant filming, try to get the camera out of his hand, or threaten to break it. The mother both threatens to damage the equipment as an act of protest and promises to allow him to film her as much as he would like if he gets married. Only once does Deri willingly relinquish his authority by encouraging his father to take the camera into his hands and film him—David—against the Torah scroll in the synagogue.

Deri realizes that the real drama does not lie in his sexual preference in itself but in the reaction of his family to it. Therefore his life in Tel Aviv is rendered irrelevant, and his appearance in the film is kept to a minimum. When he is seen, he is often filmed from behind, or his figure is blurred, framed, or seen through mirrors. This comes to suggest the various ways in which Deri as a gay man is framed by and reflected to others, tendencies that he actively defies by becoming the man behind the camera who holds the power to frame and orchestrate the others. His deliberate indecisiveness regarding his coming out means it is his siblings and parents who, by putting constant pressure on him, initiate and prompt it. Deri, thus, wittingly triggers the others to conduct the operation for him and move the plot forward. By doing so, he places the emphasis on their struggle to come to terms with the notion of homosexuality, which is so alien to them, rather than on his own struggle.

When in the frame, Deri is mainly seen with his family at his parents' house in Yeruham, a poor development town in southern Israel, or at family gatherings. This enhances the sense of Deri's full engagement with them. The constant presence of the Deris—siblings, brothers- and sisters-in-law, parents, and grandparents—intensifies the drama. Indeed, Deri's identity is bound up with those of the others, despite their disapproval. The film portrays the conflicting emotions that come into play in both sides' attempt to reconcile. Deri's sister's declaration early on in the film that he (David) will never have their parents' support and sympathy in this is challenged several times throughout the film. Although this view is verified by the initial reaction of Deri's other relatives as well as that of his parents, we also witness a growing understanding on their part.

At one point in the film, Deri's mother, disappointed at her son's refusal to promise he will start praying in order to change, tells him that she will disown him. In the next scene Deri is seen in his flat in Tel Aviv talking on the telephone with his mother, who caringly asks him if he has eaten. Another scene captures the feeling of warmth between David and his brother Itzik, despite the harsh things the latter says about homosexuality. Similarly, in a conversation between Deri and one of his sisters, she warns him of the strong reaction that their brothers may have to the news, but in a meeting they have later on, one of the brothers insists that he is more open-minded than they think. One of the last scenes in the film documents a surprise party that the family has organized for the parents. David is cohosting the event. He later poses with his parents in front of the camera. The film ends with Deri asking his parents for their permission to take their picture, encouraging them to look at each other. They are shyly smiling at his request. This scene, as well as the inscription at the end of the film ("to my parents with love"), signals some kind of reconciliation, although it is clear that the parents and some of the siblings are still incapable of accommodating the idea that their son and brother is homosexual.

Deri has followed the prominent gay "urban migration narrative," namely the exploration of one's gayness in an urban environment, by moving to Tel Aviv and building a life that signals a significant break with his former religious and peripheral existence. At the same time, he cannot fully leave his family behind, as the film he made attests to. In his account of queer filmmaking in Israel, Raz Yosef has argued that "the assumption [. . .] is that everyone comes out the same way and that all families are the same. However, unlike the stereotypical Ashkenazi nuclear family, the extended Mizrahi family provides a source of support against ethnic discrimination, which cannot be so easily replaced by other social systems" (*Beyond Flesh* 168). Similarly, Esther Saxey has maintained that "across various minority ethnicities, many people living in white-majority cultures describe their family as a mainstay of their racial or cultural sense of self. They feel conflicted about adopting a sexual identity that might negate or devalue this" (121). Indeed, Deri succeeds in shedding light on the ways in which gay

A possible reconciliation: David Deri with his parents in Deri's *Say Amen!* (2005).

men and women of multiple identity categories come to terms with their homosexuality.

Similar concerns to those expressed in *Say Amen!* are also explored in Sigal Yehuda and Joelle Alexis's 2004 *Almost There.* Structured as a road movie, *Almost There* follows Yehuda and Alexis in their search for a new home in Greece. They travel from village to village until they settle on Mykonos, an island known for its cosmopolitan and gay-friendly atmosphere. Their house hunting is a catalyst for other inner journeys. Questions regarding the couple's Israeli, Jewish, and lesbian identities recur, and their relationships with their families are constantly discussed. They turn the camera on themselves, using it as a tool for exploration of the self and for situating subjectivity within broader familial and social contexts.

Almost There is one of few films made by or about lesbians since the first Israeli gay-themed films were introduced in the mid-1970s. It is also unique in that it explores homosexuality in Israel through a narrative of emigration from Israel. Whereas most Israeli male gay films emphasize the integral role of gay men in the public sphere, the lesbian makers of *Almost There* express an uncommon wish to start anew elsewhere. They prove that home can be built and experienced away from the homeland, in a different land. *Almost There* explains the reasons for the couple's decision to leave Israel but does not seek to justify it. It is clear that it is not the search for a better material life that is the couple's driving force. Rather, it is their families' response to their homosexuality, especially Yehuda's, as well as the violent atmosphere in Israel that encourage them to leave. Yehuda's growing feeling of estrangement from her brothers and sisters after coming out to them and her fear of coming out to her parents prompted her to seek a place where she could live her life freely. It is important to note that like *Say Amen!*, *Almost There* was not shown in Israel because Yehuda did not want to expose her family to it. In a question and answer session after one of the London Lesbian and Gay Film Festival screenings in April 2004, Yehuda explained that although three of her siblings (there are ten brothers and sisters in the family) know about the film, they are not interested in watching it. Their refusal to acknowledge Yehuda's lesbianism, a reaction that, although it did not lead to ostracism, is still painful, is brought up several times in the film.

Yehuda's parents immigrated to Israel from Iran. They were lower middle class, living at the economic and cultural margins of Israeli society. Reflecting on her childhood, Yehuda remembers a dark home and poverty but also a great sense of warmth. However, these strong feelings of love could not be challenged by Yehuda's nonnormative sexuality. In order not to risk her status in the family, Yehuda preferred not to come out. In one scene, on Yehuda's return to Greece after her father's funeral, she is talking on the telephone with her mother. As the conversation, full of expressions of love, is continuing, Alexis's voice is heard in the background, saying, "Now and then I listen quietly to her talking to her mother. What can she talk about if she's hiding so much? And yet I can see she's emotional by the expression on her face. It seems they've found a place where words aren't important."

Unlike the prominence of the Deris on screen in *Say Amen!* and the presence of Alexis's Belgian parents in *Almost There*, Yehuda's family remains a rather abstract notion, almost a specter. Her family members are seen only in old still pictures with the exception of her mother who is filmed from behind cleaning the kitchen in the modest family house. The still pictures express a strong union between the siblings as children that stands in contrast with the current state of affairs. The mother's traditional role in the household is pronounced by the choice to film her in the kitchen and the frequent references to her fine cooking (at some point, Yehuda is seen trying to emulate her mother's famous *kube*, an Mizrahi meat pastry). Yehuda refers to it later in the film when she tells Alexis about how her parents met in Iran. According to Yehuda, whereas her father fell instantly in love with her mother, her mother married him only because it was expected of her. She didn't want to raise ten children, Yehuda says, but to sing and perform. This revelation, and the fact that the mother is the only family member who is featured in the film, suggest a unique understanding between the two. It is possible that the mother senses that her daughter deviates from the norm but passively allows her to follow her desires as a way of making up for her own unfulfilled dreams. If this is indeed the case, she presents a radically different approach to that of Deri's mother who puts endless pressure on her son to get married.

Although *Almost There* portrays emigration in an unapologetic way, Yehuda and Alexis stress their conflicting feelings about their decision and the difficulty in cutting themselves off from both their families and their country. Those ambivalent feelings are expressed in the couple's choice of destination. They agree on Greece because of its geographical proximity to Israel—its landscapes, scents, and nature constantly remind them of what they left behind. For Yehuda, a lemon tree in the courtyard of an old house reminds her of her parents' home where she grew up, and an old local man of her father.

At the same time Greece is a country whose language they do not speak and whose contemporary culture is hardly known to most Israelis. If immigration to a new land implies a wish to become part, if not assimilate completely into, the adoptive culture, Yehuda and Alexis show little motivation to do so. The film portrays a different type of migration, one that is not aimed at integrating but rather recreating a private sphere unaffected by the couple's setting. For this reason, it is not clear whether Yehuda and Alexis could be considered migrants at all: they do not talk about migration as such even though it appears that they have no intention of going back to Israel.

The fact that the couple chooses in the end to settle on an island is symbolic. Severed from Greek culture by the cosmopolitan nature of their surroundings in Mykonos and from Israeli reality by geographical distance, they cut themselves off from both societies. They create an island within an island, a space filled entirely with their own presence. In this sense, the film paints an exceedingly romantic picture of lesbian life in which all Yehuda and Alexis need is the love they have for each other. However, although the couple seems to be content in their new home, it is clear that they are not ready to be reconciled with their previous life in Israel. The migration narrative is only partly successful in both Deri's and Yehuda's attempt to construct their gay identity, and their distance from their families and home cultures is a crippling, as much as enabling, experience.

HaMavri and *The Way Home*

Having referred to two autobiographical/domestic ethnography films made by a gay man and a lesbian of non-Ashkenazi origin, I believe it would be interesting to compare them with two other Israeli gay filmmakers' attempts to make sense of their position within and vis-à-vis their families—the short *HaMavri*, directed by Ayal Goldberg in 2001 as his final project at the Bezalel Academy of Art and Design in Jerusalem, and *The Way Home*, an eight-part TV series directed by Tomer Heymann in 2009 (Heymann is one of the most prolific documentarians working in Israel today. Two of his earlier films will be discussed in the next section of this chapter).

HaMavri[11] deals with similar issues to *Say Amen!* and *Almost There*, namely a family coming to terms with homosexuality. Goldberg documents the daily routines of his family—parents, two sisters, and grandparents. As the film progresses the viewers learn that Goldberg is gay. However, the films are also different: whereas *Say Amen!* documents the moment, or rather moments, of telling and those that precede and follow them, in *HaMavri*, Goldberg's homosexuality is already known to both parents and sisters. More importantly, the compassion and support that Goldberg's parents demonstrate is in sharp contrast to the refusal of Deri's parents to accept their son's homosexuality and Yehuda's fear of telling.

Goldberg's parents, who, unlike both Deri's and Yehuda's, are secular, upper middle class and scions of Ashkenazi families who settled in pre-state Israel many years ago, still find the news regarding their son's gayness hard to deal with. But their response shows empathy and resignation that cannot be found in that of the Deris and, most likely, the Yehudas. Whereas the Deris try to find a "cure" for their son by asking him to pray, Goldberg's mother says, jokingly, that Ayal's sexual orientation is a result of "mixed up genes," implying it is nobody's fault and unchangeable. The parents', especially the mother's, resignation is extended to the act of filming itself, which in the aforementioned films is so emotionally charged: the family not only lets Ayal film them, but in the course of the film they are also seen watching family footage that was already edited into the final version (seen by the viewer at an earlier stage). The viewer then gets a glimpse of the family's eventual approval of their own documentation on screen and of Goldberg's project in general.

Love and acceptance: Ayal Goldberg and his mother in Goldberg's *HaMavri* (2001).

    Although the mother's pain at her son being different from the norm is expressed in a couple of monologues in which she tells of her desire for a "normal" family, at the same time she says, "It's a fact, there's nothing we can do about it." This family acceptance is further demonstrated in the editing: Goldberg chooses to break the continuity of the family portrait with short clips of himself with a few of his lovers. In the final one, in which he is seen with a partner in his apartment, filming the two of them, the voice of his mother can be heard leaving him a loving message on his telephone. The juxtaposition of the picture, showing an expression of gay love, with the voice of the mother, symbolizes the coalescence of these supposedly opposite worlds, a coalescence that although aspired for is not fully accomplished in *Say Amen!* and *Almost There*.

    Thematically, *The Way Home* shares a similar outlook to that of *HaMavri*, but the two projects differ greatly in scope. In contrast to the limited framework in which *HaMavri* operates (showing only snippets of Goldberg's family dynamics in a rather loose structure over less than an hour), *The Way Home* runs over 240 minutes and has epic dimensions: Heymann documented his family for thirteen years, a documentation through

New Israeli Nonfiction Gay Cinema   *147*

which the complex relations between its members—parents, siblings, and nephews—are delineated. The personal vicissitudes of his family as well as of his love life echo those of Israeli reality during that time period.

Heymann is one of five sons who were born to an Ashkenazi, "salt of the earth," parents in a pastoral moshav in Israel. In an attempt to assert his masculinity, Heymann chose to join the paratroopers as part of his compulsory army service. It was only after his time in the army that he started to explore his gay desires and came out to his family. He started filming his family when his homosexuality was already known to and accepted by them and without having a firm idea where the filming would lead. The act of filming becomes, in his eyes as well as others, almost an obsession. Heymann's friends, lovers, and family—all frequently featured in the frame—often comment on it. Heymann himself seems to ask the same questions: what is the source of his need to film and what ends does the filming serve? The camera, it is suggested, serves as a screen that separates Heymann from himself. By looking outward, Heymann obviates the need to look inward. But the end result reveals more than Heymann possibly wished to expose: through his attempt to learn about those close to him, both they and the viewer learn about Heymann himself.

Over the course of filming, Heymann's parents divorce and three of his brothers and their families leave Israel for the United States. At the same time, he becomes a successful documentary director, and his films, in many of which he is also featured (see next section), are shown in festivals around the world. He also forms three long-term relationships, the most recent one with a German dancer whom he met in Berlin after a screening of one of his films. The series focuses on Heymann's relationships, the family rupture followed by the parents' divorce and the siblings' departure, and the special bond between Heymann and his mother, a strong-minded woman whose love and warmth are often compromised by her dependence on her children. Naturally, her presence fills the frame on many occasions.[12]

Like the other three films discussed in this section, *The Way Home* attests to the way in which the filmmakers' nuclear families, the parents in particular, are entangled in their coming out and their construction of an independent gay identity project. However, whereas in *Say Amen!* and *Almost There* the presence of the parents is seen as an obstacle to overcome, in *The Way Home* (as well as in *HaMavri*) the parents, and especially the mother to whom Heymann is closer, have a radically different view of their son's gayness. When inquiring about whether she sees his gayness as a personal failure, she replies that it is not a failure at all: "You are gay, so what? You're happy with your life, you're creative, what else do I need?" At the same time, she does add that she would have been happy if he decided to have children, but even this sounds, for her, like a real possibility, one that Heymann can easily achieve if he only puts his mind to it. The fact that Heymann, unlike three of his brothers (and the protagonists of *Almost There*), decides to remain in Israel suggests a strong bond to the place and his family and, in particular, his mother, who sees in Israel "the only place in the world for the Jews." It attests to his comfortable position in his community and family as a gay man—a sentiment that is absent from both *Almost There* and *Say Amen!* Interestingly, the few disapproving comments on Heymann's sexuality come from his younger nephews, who find it hard to believe that one can fulfill oneself outside the realm of the traditional nuclear family that they know. But this too changes as time passes. When Heymann asks his niece, a few years into his project, whether she knows he is gay, she replies that she does and she does not mind it at all.

Some striking similarities can be drawn not only between *HaMavri* and *The Way Home* but also between the latter and the now canonical *Diary* (*Yoman*, 1973–1983), the late David Perlov's documentation of his personal life and family (wife and twin daughters) against the backdrop of national events. Perlov's film diaries have gained a pioneering status in Israeli cinema for bringing together, perhaps for the first time in its history, private and public life and personal and collective impressions. The footage of family and friends is contrasted with Perlov's voice-over, added later in the editing stage, which frames the images in what can be read as a detached, constructed structure. His voice-over gives meaning, finds allusions, and links the extremely private images on the screen to theories about art and film.

Structurally, Heymann borrows the diaristic structure of *Diary*, organizing the footage into fragments, pieces of personal and collective history, separated by intertitles. In the case of *Diary*, the intertitles refer to dates and the people who appear in each segment. In *The Way Home*, the intertitles give the number of cassette on which the segment was taped and the people appearing in it or the general topic of the footage. Heymann also borrows the distinctive use of the voice-over, added while editing (this also exists in Alexis and Yehuda's *Almost There*) and the conscious decision to mix the private and the public to maximum effect. In *Diary* we witness the atmosphere in the streets of Tel Aviv during the first days of the Yom Kippur War as well as the reports on TV, the dramatic 1977 general elections that brought an end to the almost thirty-year-long Labor rule, and the demonstrations against the invasion of Lebanon in 1982. In *The Way Home*, Heymann films the highly political gay pride parade in Jerusalem and the

TV reportage of the wave of suicide bomb attacks in Israel at the beginning of the 2000s.

The presence of the camera in both *Diary* and *The Way Home*—as well as in the other films discussed above—is constantly felt and directly referred to by those being filmed, thus raising questions about the possibility of documenting "real" or "natural" human relationships under such terms. Both Perlov and Heymann use the camera to provoke reactions from those who participate in their projects, although it seems that Heymann takes it further, especially when filming (and often interviewing) his lovers and family members. His mother in particular understands her integral role in the series and allows her son to film her at some of her most vulnerable physical and emotional points: right after the separation from her husband; during her time in the hospital after surgery and then while recovering at home; and when she says goodbye to three of her sons, who, one by one, are leaving with their families for the United States.

More than Perlov in *Diary*, Heymann provokes highly charged emotional reactions from his subjects and the viewer. This is further amplified by the use of nondiegetic music, hardly used in *Diary*, and old home movies. If Heymann celebrates the melancholic streak in his nostalgic longing for the past by recurrent use of home movies from his childhood that suggest happier times, Perlov firmly avoids it: "The resurgence of the past [. . .] is rare in this journal devoted to the present and obsessed with the documentation of everyday life" (Bluher 30). Despite those apparent differences, Heymann, like Perlov, tries to exercise his power as the filmmaker in organizing his life according to a well-constructed script. Perlov's words about his project can thus relate also to Heymann and his series: "When you shoot a diary, the film replaces life. [. . .] As long as you are at an editing table it's also a great pleasure because you're in control of your life—its crises, its pains. You can recreate life, fragment it. Above all, you can strive for harmony. When you return to life itself, it is much less harmonious, much longer than six hours" (Klein 22).

As shown above, the link between *Diary* and Heymann's project is evident. However, Perlov's seminal work has influenced the other filmmakers discussed in this section too, in the links it draws between the filmmaker, his family, and the world around him. Indeed, all four films, after *Diary*, exceed their limited autobiographical scope and formulate a broader statement about both the families of their makers and the society in which they live. The similarities, however, should not overshadow the differences in experiences of gay life that the four films highlight. In sharp contrast to *HaMavri* and *The Way Home*, *Say Amen!* and *Almost There* shed light on the status of homosexuality in less liberal, affluent, and established parts of Israel, and in doing so, challenge the "white," male, middle-class hegemony of the Israeli gay community. Although the filmmakers' hope for integration into both their families and the wider gay community is not fully realized—in *Almost There* the protagonists leave Israel, and the future relationship between Deri and his family in *Say Amen!* as well as his level of integration into gay circles in Tel Aviv remain uncertain—these films are nevertheless another step toward a greater acceptance of diverse voices in the gay community.

Staging Sexual and National Identities: Performance and Performativity in *Edinburgh Doesn't Wait for Me*, *It Kinda Scares Me*, and *Paper Dolls*

In many ways Tomer Heymann's *It Kinda Scares Me* (*Tomer VeHasrutim*, 2001) and *Paper Dolls* (*Bubot Niyar*, 2006) and Erez Laufer's *Edinburgh Doesn't Wait for Me* (*Edinburgh Lo Mechaka Li*, 1996) conform to the general rules of a realist documentary: foremost, they follow the principles of observational vérité. By focusing on performativity and its role in the constitution of gay and national identities, however, the films invite the viewer to question the alleged authoritative role of documentaries as representing "objective," "true" realities and ask whether these true realities exist in the first place. The films stress the performative aspect in the lives of most gay men and lesbians and raise questions about socially fabricated identities in general. The different gay identities explored and presented in the films suggest there is more than one way in which one can respond to society's expectations. Yet, all three films show how gay identity, like any other, is also conditioned and governed by society.

Theories of documentary often emphasize the fictional elements to be found in the nonfiction story, such as the construction of a character, the use of poetic language and narration, the use of music, and the creation of suspense through editing. I would like to argue that although these points apply to all documentaries, many gay documentaries tend to foreground artistic intervention, those moments in which fiction and nonfiction meet. The exposure of the "seams" of documentary filmmaking implies the artificial, constructed nature of reality itself. In a queer manner, it comes to oppose an essentialist approach to sexual and identity categories and, at the same time, the claim for objective cinematic observation.

Through their focus on performance, the three documentaries under this subheading foreground performativity as a central aspect in the construction of sexual identities: in *It Kinda Scares Me*, Tomer, the youth leader, and the group of teenagers he instructs are putting on a play. In the process of writing and directing the play, Tomer will come out to the teenagers, and his homosexuality will be raised in the final version of the play. In *Paper Dolls* we meet Heymann a few years later, now involved in the life of a group of Filipino transvestites who live and work in Israel and perform in drag in their free time. Often referring to themselves as women, their performances allow them to express a feeling and affiliation that are otherwise—for some at their workplace and in society at large—discouraged. The film shows Heymann's hesitant attempts to shed his masculine appearance when dressed in drag, attuning to the performative act that is part of "becoming" a woman and through that to the performative elements in his supposedly "natural" masculine identity. In *Edinburgh Doesn't Wait for Me*, a group of young, mostly gay, Israeli actors and their director are bringing their theatrical show, based on gay monologues about love, coming out, and matters of identity, to the Edinburgh Festival. Although the actors talk freely about their fears and concerns regarding their profession and the international exposure they may receive at the festival, the viewer learns more about their life from their monologues (during rehearsals and in the festival).

It Kinda Scares Me and *Paper Dolls*

It Kinds Scares Me, Heymann's second film and the first to receive warm feedback from audiences and critics alike, follows his work with a group of teenagers from Azur, a poor suburb of Tel Aviv, as part of a project called Youth Promotion. They are mainly high school dropouts, some of them with criminal records. Heymann is sent to help them reform, an achievement that may be symbolized, as the film suggests, in their enlisting in the army. The film starts with a short text appearing on the screen, explaining the principal goals of Youth Promotion: "(The project) is a national organization, the declared goal of which is to assist and support youths who are at risk, and to integrate them in normative and accepted frameworks in Israel, including enlistment to the IDF. These young boys and girls, who live on the fringes of society and whose future does not seem promising, drift easily and naturally to drugs, violence and crime. The Youth Promotion project supplies them with an alternative in the form of consistent and varied activities supervised by experienced professionals."

The film crew joins Heymann and the boys in their second or third year together. The viewers learn about the history of Heymann and the group

Tomer Heymann relinquishes his "straight" appearance in Heymann's *Paper Dolls* (2006).

through a series of short texts, appearing on the screen before the film begins. The viewers are informed that the first year ended in a crisis, with the boys stealing Heymann's motorbike and destroying it. This incident led to a long break, but eventually Heymann agreed to try again, and the meetings between him and the group resumed.

The film follows Heymann and the group's attempts to put on a play based on their real-life stories. Heymann hopes to overcome the boys' resistance through this creative activity. Writing and performing a play is a means to encourage them to open up to him and, by extension, to the audience in the Tel Aviv theater where the show is eventually staged and to the viewers of the film. In the play the group and Heymann are encouraged to reveal their "true" selves, to let their fears go. The film documents the long and often frustrating process of building trust between the two parties. During that time, Heymann gradually becomes a more active participant in the lives of the teenagers. The film tries to convince us that by the end of it, Heymann is no longer a youth leader from a privileged background, but one of the boys.

The film builds toward a climax, timed roughly half way through the film, in which Heymann comes out to the group. Heymann's homosexuality is hinted at beforehand: at one point he asks the boys what would be the most difficult thing for them to find out about him. This is presented as a teaser for both the viewers and the boys, who speculate what Heymann's secret may be. When he learns that one of the teenagers spotted him in a gay club in Tel Aviv, Heymann finally decides to come out to them. His homosexuality and the complex feelings this new knowledge evokes in the members of the group will be expressed in the play. At the point of revelation there is a significant shift in the film: it no longer focuses primarily on the boys and their lives but also explores Heymann's homosexuality and the way it can be perceived and understood outside his home in Tel Aviv. The sharp contrast between the two worlds is best portrayed when eighteen-year-old Yacov, one of the dominant figures in the group, whom Heymann forms close ties with, arrives in the fashionable Tel Aviv café where Heymann works as a manager to discuss the details of the play. Yacov, who up to this point in the film is portrayed as a fearless, if sensitive, teenager (he calls himself "a reformed criminal" who was an experienced user of LSD and cannabis before he turned seventeen, and at one point in the film he appears at a hearing in a juvenile court) is too embarrassed to come in.

The revelation of Heymann's homosexuality puts the group, at first, in a state of confusion and distress. It requires them to separate the preconceptions they have about gay men from the impression of the person they have known for several years. It also makes them question their own sexual preferences. Although some of them are certain about their heterosexuality, others confess to having thought about physical contact with other men, even if they have never intended to actively seek it. Although homophobic remarks are made, some in a humorous, teasing way, and fears are raised that Heymann may be attracted to one of the boys, they gradually accept this new information and come to respect it. Heymann tries to uproot some of the preconceived ideas about homosexuality and gay sex. He mainly opposes the boys' initial view of gay men as only interested in sex. He urges them to look at gay relationships in the same way they look at heterosexual relationships: like their heterosexual counterparts, gay men also seek love, courtship, and respect, he insists. The success of the play (they perform to a full house in Tzavta, a famous institution in Tel Aviv) signifies not only the acceptance of the teenagers by mostly Ashkenazi, educated Tel Aviv society but also the acceptance of Heymann, the gay café manager from Tel Aviv, by the rougher edges of Israeli society.

Interestingly, the film, similarly to Eytan Fox's, reverses the old order of things regarding the standing of homosexuality in society. It is suggested in the film that gay men are no longer excluded from positions of power but can hold them equally. Heymann is portrayed as the representative of authority: he is hired by the state to work with youth on the fringes of society (formerly the place of gay men) in order to bring them back to its center. In the Israeli context, the center of society means enlistment in the army (another institution that discriminated against homosexuals for many years). The identification of Heymann with the state is further emphasized not only by the act of violence the boys carry out against him (stealing and destroying his motorbike) but also by Heymann's support of the right of the mayor of Azur to deliver a speech at the end of the play in Tzavta. In their harsh reaction to this idea, the boys express their fierce antagonism to any form of authority and the establishment. In this case they accuse the mayor of stealing the limelight and taking the credit away from them, since he had no real part in the work on the play. Heymann then urges them to reconsider. After all, it was the mayor who, by allocating money, made it possible for the group to perform in the prestigious Tel Aviv venue.

The fact that Heymann functions as a figure of authority in his work with the group, despite his homosexuality, can be seen as showing progress in the way the members of the gay community are perceived in Israeli society. It is, however, important to note that Heymann's authority is exercised while working with a group of people who have been equally disenfranchised: the teenagers come from poor backgrounds and are mostly of Mizrahi origin. It is not very clear whether Heymann would have been granted the same power in a different context (among privileged, Ashkenazi, and straight people, for example). Also, it is not very clear whether Heymann would have been trusted in the same way had he performed a less-than-perfect masculinity and made his homosexuality known right from the start. The boys are in a state of shock when they first find out about their leader's homosexuality, because it is indeed shocking: this is the last thing one would expect from the virile, straight-acting former paratrooper Heymann. As one of the boys says to the others in the film: "We always said Tomer looks like he gets to fuck loads of babes, and then you find out he's gay. It's weird."

This leads me to the use of performance, performativity, and visibility in the film. As I claimed above, Heymann's straight acting was a cause for misunderstanding. It was also, I believe, what made it possible for him to lead the group in the first place. However, the issues of performance and performativity are not only linked to Heymann's homosexuality. Rather, they are used as an integral tool for Heymann and his group in their attempt to understand each other and build trust.

Destroying Heymann's motorbike is an act of power on the part of the teenagers, a performative act against authority. Heymann's coming out to them is yet another act of performance, like any act of coming out, but even more so here, as Heymann uses it to expose his own weakness. By coming out to the group, Heymann comes across as vulnerable and different, which is how the teenagers see themselves. His newly acquired "vulnerability" places Heymann and the boys together at the margins of society. It also proves to them that although they came from an underprivileged position they can overcome the obstacles and succeed, as Heymann did. Thus, Heymann's coming out does not necessarily seem an "authentic," brave step in the nascent relationship between him and the boys, but a planned performative act that comes to serve both his work with the group and the dramatic pace of the film. After the expected expressions of confusion, the teenagers gradually overcome their aversion to this kind of difference and join Heymann in the pride parade in Tel Aviv, yet another grandiose act of artificial and excessive performance (the drag queens, shirtless muscle men, etc.), which is meant to serve entertainment and political ends, as visibility has long been connected with concepts of power.

The continuous presence of an audience—Heymann is the teenagers' audience and they are his, while the audience in Tzavta is watching the play in which the group and Heymann reveal some of their most intimate secrets—and the constant presence of the camera, of which the group and Heymann are always aware, mean that all their behavior is essentially performative. Yacov tells Heymann that putting on the play would prove they are not just "a group of hooligans," as they might seem to others. In one scene, dancer Sharon Eyal urges the group to express their emotions using their bodies. When some remain frozen, embarrassed about how they may look to others, she says, "Why do you care what others may think of you? You should do what makes you feel good." The emphasis placed on performance and the importance both Heymann and the group give to matters of representation can be seen as techniques to deal with the invisibility that has been imposed for years on both the teenagers (as representatives of other, non-Ashkenazi, underprivileged Israel) and Heymann (as a gay man). Although both parties, Heymann and the boys, share the same historic, internalized feeling of exclusion, Heymann stands now as living proof that such a shift of status—from invisibility to visibility, from exclusion to acceptance—is indeed possible. Through performances and rituals (the military service, for example) the boys, like Heymann before them, will be let into the heart of Israeli society.

Heymann's coming out serves both him and his film as it dispels, to a certain degree, the ethnographic feel the film may otherwise have produced: a young filmmaker from the center who travels to the periphery to document the lives of people on the fringes of society, aspiring to make them transparent to others. Despite being quite a conservative text, close in spirit to Eytan Fox's films, which have celebrated the success story of gay integration in Israel without taking into account the sacrifices made for it (the adjustment to heteronormative institutions and ways of thinking and the exclusion of other forms of otherness in the gay community), Heymann's film blurs the hierarchic divisions between him and the teenagers he tutors. His decision as a filmmaker to include in the final version of the film several sequences in which the members of the group urge him to open up to them and share his secrets comes to show his equal standing in the film. He also takes part in the confessional project, which the play and the film are about. He is not there just to document. At one point in the film, one of the boys tells Heymann, "You are not our therapist. There is no reason why we should tell you our secrets, but you won't tell us yours." Heymann aims to make the viewer believe that not only is he not the boys' therapist, he is also not an ethnographic documentary filmmaker. By placing his own life on the same level as the boys', by writing his own experience into their play and into the script of the film, Heymann, manipulatively or not, practices new, allegedly nonethnographic, performative documentary making.

It seems that the attempt to deny an ethnographic approach instructed Heymann in yet another documentary film he directed and appeared in. *Paper Dolls* (*Bubot Niyar*, 2006), based on a TV series of the same title first broadcast in 2005, attempts to tackle the acute issue of foreign workers in Israel, especially their precarious immigration status. The film follows the life of five Filipino transvestites who work in Israel as health care providers over a period of several years. At night, they perform in clubs as the drag act "Paper Dolls." Heymann examines the special relationships they form with the elderly people they look after, their desire to succeed onstage, their longing for home, and their constant fear of being deported. The film explores the juxtaposition of two forms of marginality—sexual and ethnic/racial. Indeed, some form strong relationships with the people they work for and their families. This is especially true of Salvador Camatoy, known as Sally, who looks after the elderly Haim until his death.[13] Both Haim and Sally describe their relationship as similar to that between father and daughter. But more often than not, the Paper Dolls' attempts at fuller integration into society are doomed to fail. Their dream of performing at TLV, the largest gay club in Tel Aviv, is realized with the help of Heymann but soon turns sour. Greeting the crowd dressed in Japanese kimonos to look like geisha, their national and cultural identity is completely erased. Following this performance they decide to continue performing only within their community.

Similar to the way *It Kinda Scares Me* emphasizes the bond Heymann forms with the teenagers he tutors, *Paper Dolls* comes to demonstrate his sincere desire to become part of the group of people whose lives he documents, or at least to come across as such. He is not only the film director

The Paper Dolls perform as geisha in a Tel Aviv club in Tomer Heymann's *Paper Dolls* (2006).

but also the subjects' client (the film starts with a scene that shows him having his hair cut by one of the members of the group who also works as a hairdresser), their manager (as stated above, he facilitates their performance at TLV), and above all, their friend, who shows up in the detention facility where one of the members is being held for staying in Israel illegally after his visa has been instantaneously and unexpectedly revoked. Here, perhaps even more than in *It Kinda Scares Me*, Heymann seems to position himself in the role of the conscientious filmmaker who is fully involved in the intricate reality of the lives of the Filipinos he follows.

However, the gaps that separate Heymann from the members of the Paper Dolls are even more pronounced than those that separated him from the teenagers of *It Kinda Scares Me*. These are no longer only social and cultural gaps but now also religious and national ones. The Filipinos' unpredictable legal status in the country further signals them out as outsiders (in the end they all have to leave Israel, despite the number of years they have worked in the country, their fluent command of Hebrew, and other forms of attachment to the land and its people). Although Heymann is an openly gay man like them, and *unlike* the teenagers of *It Kinda Scares Me*, the sexuality of the Paper Dolls is only one factor contributing to their marginal position (if anything, Israel is described by them as a place of relative sexual liberation, especially when compared with their native land). Furthermore, the manner in which Heymann perceives his homosexuality is significantly different to the way the Paper Dolls perceive theirs. Those differences are conveyed in the way both parties—Heymann and the Paper Dolls—perform their gay identity. Heymann is pushed to examine the type of identity he performs, holding on at first to his "straight" appearance and mannerisms but slowly adopting, if only for the dramatic effect, overt expressions of femininity through the act of drag, with the constant encouragement of the Paper Dolls.

Although fascinated by the liminal space that the Filipino workers occupy as transvestites, Heymann makes a deliberate effort at the beginning of the film to assert his masculinity in relation to them, saying to one of the performers, "It's strange to me. I'm not used to seeing such things. Sometimes I even find it a bit repulsive. Like, aren't you ashamed, shaving your entire body and all. . . . Aren't you ashamed of that?" Admitting that he has never dressed up as a woman, Heymann agrees to let the group dress him up. While having his face made up he says, "I'm embarrassed. That's how I grew up. If you dress like a girl, it's like . . . embarrassing. As a man, you have to act like a man, not like a woman." Once the makeover is complete, he comments, "When you did the first time with the long wig and I looked . . . I was shocked, I said . . . it looks like a woman. I felt embarrassed about it. . . . What does it mean? Maybe it's not good?" Through the performative act of drag, Heymann is shifting from one acquired category of identity, that of the virile Israeli male, to another, one that sees in drag and femininity possible components of gay existence, exposing in the process the artificiality of both.

The interlacing of national and sexual identities lies at the core of the film. Both the Paper Dolls' Filipino looks and feminized appearance stand for an exoticism that both excites and frightens Heymann (as well as the manager of the aforementioned club, who, by dressing them in traditional geisha attire, expresses his desire to see in them an archetype of the Orient). But it exists also in the persona that Heymann adopts for himself as an Israeli gay man. His initial discomfort about other forms of gayness can be read, to a certain extent, as yet another expression of the wish of Israeli gay men (at least, one branch of them) to assimilate into the mainstream culture around them. However, his eventual opening up to different modes of self-expression through his act of drag serves as an acknowledgment of and enquiry into the practice of performing identities and the ability to freely move between them.

Edinburgh Doesn't Wait for Me

Edinburgh Doesn't Wait for Me, Erez Laufer's 1996 film, is, like *It Kinda Scares Me* and *Paper Dolls*, mainly a film about the connection between homosexuality and the performative aspects of identity construction, gay identity in particular. The film is divided into two parts. The first half documents the six weeks of rehearsals in Tel Aviv of *Words of His Own*, a play based on short sketches portraying gay male experiences in 1990s Israel. In the second half, the film follows the arrival of the cast and crew at the Edinburgh Festival and their performances during it. The director focuses mainly on the struggles the group encounters in Edinburgh. The play did not prove to be the immediate commercial success everyone expected. The film does end, however, with a happy resolution, in the form of a series of sellout performances. In the background, the dynamics between the actors (two of them are gay, one is straight), the gay director and text editor, and the rest of the production crew unfold on the screen. Gradually, the reality of the play and that of "real" life merge, and it becomes increasingly difficult to tell whether the actors and crew express authentic feelings of stress and joy or merely play their part to the camera. Curiously, in an interview about the making of the film, Laufer said that he could not use the material he shot in the very first days because of the actors' "nonnatural" performances (Zimmerman, "Chadira El Toch Merchav Prati").

This confusion is not only because the documentary's stars are actors. The performative mode, which dominates the film, on- and offstage, comes to illuminate, and sometimes resist, the cultural meanings given to constructed sexual categories. Both the gay actors and director and the sole heterosexual actor respond to what is expected from them. The gay group comes across as flirtatious (one of the two gay actors, Hagai Ayad, is sharing a bed with the straight actor, Tzahi Grad, and the alleged sexual tension between them, at least on the part of Ayad, is extensively discussed; humorously, Ayad "makes a move" but is gently refused) and promiscuous (the director, Noam Meiri, is having a brief sexual encounter with a local man in Edinburgh whom he calls sarcastically "my new boyfriend"). It is little wonder that Itzik Cohen, the other gay actor, compares gay relationships to fast food. Talking about the immediacy and speed of communication between gay men, his use of this term also raises associations of cheapness and unhealthiness.

Tzahi Grad, on the other hand, plays the role of the heterosexual Israeli "macho." The fact that he is open enough to take on a gay role in the play is understood as part of his "bohemian," artistic persona and of his dedication to his vocation. The fact that he is the only straight man in this tight-knit group is emphasized right from the start when Meiri is coaching him on one of his monologues: "Unlike us, you are required to do pure acting. If I were on stage, I would have opened a small window into my life and it would be there on stage, just like that. But it is different for you." At the same time, the filmmaker keeps hinting at Grad's potential, dormant homosexuality. Although his heterosexuality is repeatedly mentioned, it is never practiced.

Unlike Ayad and Meiri, who are seen kissing and socializing with local men, Grad does not respond to his heterosexual call when a young woman shows an elaborate, unequivocal interest in him (he does, however, talk at length about how gay men take a sexual interest in him time and again). His heterosexuality remains theoretical, suspended, waiting to be proven, just like his potential homosexuality (Grad says toward the end of the film, when asked once again about the possibility that he would ever consider experiencing gay sex, that "theoretically" he would have considered this, but, in practice, he simply cannot). The lack of conclusive evidence regarding Grad's heterosexuality, apart from the discursive, rhetorical, and performative means that he and the others employ, intensifies the enigma surrounding him and his motivation to take part in such a show (a play, as we learn later on, in which he has also invested his own money) and adds to the tension that is built up in the film. Moreover, it reflects the belief, common in gay and queer thought, that there is the potential for same-sex attraction in any human being.

The film links different forms of marginality: sexual, national and religious. The experience of sexual otherness the performers and crew feel is amplified by their national and religious marginality in Edinburgh. The narrative of the film makes extensive use of some tropes common in earlier fiction Israeli films (and in Israeli culture in general). The script portrays the production team's sincere attempts to win people's hearts in Edinburgh as a battle of few against many, which is eventually won, almost against all odds. When they find out they have been evicted from the second venue because the owner of the place "did not want any more gay men in there," Meiri says, "We've been surviving for 4,000 years, so why should we give up now to some gentile?" Cohen shares Meiri's determination in saying, "If there's an audience and a torch, I will perform." Earlier on, after facing yet another defeat, one team member compares their situation to that of the biblical figure Job. And throughout the film, the cast and crew express their wish to "conquer" Edinburgh. The etymological root of the verb to conquer in Hebrew (*lichbosh*) recurs in Zionist terminology in phrases such as *Kibush HaAvoda* (the conquest of labor) and *Kibush HaShmama* (the conquest of wilderness).

Ticket sales in the first week or so are very poor, and there are some technical problems at the first venue. At one point it seems as if the production is in danger. However, the initial disappointment gradually vanishes as the play becomes a great success. In the process, the film shows the crew coming up with inventive ideas on how to market the play (among other things, the actors engage in drag shows on the streets of Edinburgh and exhort people to come and see "the holy gays"). The film ends with a triumphant series of shows, which conforms to the formulaic narrative ending of the heroic-nationalist genre films: in the end, the good and the just always win.

In its portrayal of a group of jovial actors, the film offers a comic, uplifting depiction of gay existence, in which gay men are presented as either sexually obsessed or ultrafeminine. Cohen, who was at the time a member of the popular drag act *B'not Pesya* (The Pesya Girls), is shown in drag several times during the film. Ayad is shown in drag once. At one point in the film, Cohen is seen putting on makeup, while one of the female members of the production team is saying to the camera, "How can I possibly compete with such a perfect femininity?"

The director's use of ready-made formulas, both in his representation of gay men and in the way he decided to construct the narrative (telling a victory story of how Edinburgh was finally conquered by only a few "holy gay men") has a special significance apart from the filmmaker's wish to create an accessible, commercial film. On one level, the film conforms to patterns of thinking prevalent both in the gay community and in Israeli society. Thus, gay men are designated as different from the norm by the emphasis on their uncontrolled femininity. As Israelis, who represent their country at a prestigious international festival, their story follows the well-trodden plot, as victimization is replaced by a sweeping, almost miraculous victory. The viewer is led, with the actors, from despair to triumph. However, perhaps unintentionally, the film also stresses the *un*natural process of becoming, whether it is becoming a gay man (often literally, as the act of drag shows) or, indeed, Israeli. In both cases, the work of myths and symbols cannot be easily dismissed.

Positive Story and Yakantalisa: Living with and Dying of AIDS in 1990s Israel

Yakantalisa (Yair Lev) and *Positive Story* (*Sipur Chiuvi*, Ran Kotzer) were produced in 1996. They were first screened at the Jerusalem International Film Festival of that year and were both nominated for best documentary film. The films deal with the AIDS epidemic and do so through the life stories of two individuals. *Yakantalisa* was made for the state television channel, but its planned transmission was cancelled. Kotzer tried to interest various broadcasting bodies in Israel in producing *Positive Story* but was rejected. Eventually, the film was produced as a graduation project for Tel Aviv University, where Kotzer studied, and was also broadcast on TV's channel 2.

The similarities between the films, however, end there. *Yakantalisa* tells the story of a victim of the AIDS epidemic, the poet, choreographer, visual artist, and journalist Hezi Leskly, who died in May 1994 at the age of forty-two. The protagonist of *Positive Story*, Avinof Frumer, on the other hand, is a person with HIV who hopes the disease will not catch up with him: "No one's proven that it's inevitable that eventually I'll develop AIDS. I believe I will get sick, but I'm constantly trying to convince myself that perhaps I won't. Seven years is a long time and it can extend to ten and even fifteen or twenty years." Frumer is in almost every frame of the film, a presence that comes to emphasize his vitality, his choice in life.

Yakantalisa, by contrast, although it centers on the character of Leskly, hardly features him. Only once, toward the end of the film, is he seen, as a young artist reading one of his poems at a poetry evening in Tel Aviv in 1974. The quality of the clip, found in the archives of the state television channel, is poor, with a blurred image and soundtrack. It is hard to see Leskly or to hear him reading. These indecipherable images and sounds, however, reflect the enigmatic character of Leskly well. The story of his life is told by the people who knew him, through the places where he lived, studied, and created, and through his poems. Lev has argued that this was an intentional decision he made while making the film: "I wanted to make a film in which I wouldn't create on the screen a character of a person who no longer exists. On the contrary, I wanted to deal with the absence of this person, with the fact that he no longer exists. [. . .] I turned his absence into a presence through the things that he left behind—words, lyrics and friends" (Lev Ari, 44–45). This absence is illustrated well in one of the very last shots in the film in which the camera roams the empty rooms and corridor in Leskly's apartment in Tel Aviv, creating an eerie feeling of void.

Yakantalisa is epic both in terms of its subject, a prominent figure in the media and cultural scenes in 1980s Tel Aviv, and in its production values. The film's running time is seventy-nine minutes, and it was shot in different locations in Israel and the Netherlands. *Positive Story*, on the other hand, is told by Frumer and is constructed as an interview. Its running time is half of *Yakatalisa*'s (forty-two minutes), and it looks like televised reportage.[14] Despite these differences, the films work together as a testament to a growing tolerance toward and interest in the disease and the people who suffer from it, whether they are well-known cultural figures such as Leskly (or

Amos Guttman, whose autobiographical feature film *Amazing Grace* came out in 1992) or ordinary people like Frumer.

The protagonist of *Positive Story* takes the filmmaker, and the viewer, through the different chapters of his life story—the realization of his difference at school, coming out, first sexual encounters, the day he found out he was HIV-positive, coping with this new knowledge, and the attempt to keep living. The film follows Frumer's routine checkups at the hospital, his shows as a drag queen, a demonstration against the indifference of the government to people with HIV/AIDS, and his workplace. It also includes still pictures of Frumer's former boyfriend Richard whom he met at an international conference for people living with HIV/AIDS in London in September 1991, and who eventually died of the disease. The film can be read as an educational tool in the fight against the disease and stigmatization. If *Yakantalisa* glorifies its subject—Leskly—and emphasizes his extraordinary qualities as a person and as an artist ("as part of the efforts of the community in Tel Aviv to create for itself a pantheon of mythological heroes," as was pointed out by the critic Amnon Lord in *Tel Aviv Magazine*), *Positive Story* needs to portray Frumer as a person that every young Israeli, or at least every young gay Israeli, can identify with.

When he is filmed in the stationery shop where he works, Frumer insists his life is not as dull as it may seem. However, it is precisely this "dullness" that the filmmaker celebrates in order to get his message across. At one point in the film, Kotzer asks Frumer if he and his friends ever talked about the disease when he came out as gay. Frumer says the subject was discussed in the sex education program in high school and that he wishes he had internalized it: "Like everyone else, I thought it won't happen to me. And it did." The film tells the story of someone who is "like everyone else" whose medical condition has disrupted his plans, which were like everyone else's: completing the military service, going to university, falling in love.

Yakantalisa was made two years after Leskly's death. The film goes to the places where he lived and that inspired him: Givatayim, a small town near Tel Aviv where he grew up; The Hague and Amsterdam, where he lived in his early twenties; and Tel Aviv, where he made a name for himself in the 1980s. The singularity of his life and art is the focal point of *Yakantalisa*. At one point in the film the Israeli artist Maya Gordon, one of Leskly's closest friends, tells Lev about her first encounter with Leskly in Amsterdam: "He looked unreal, a creature." Whereas *Positive Story* points to the effort of its protagonist to lead a "normal" life under very harsh conditions, *Yakantalisa* creates a myth, a larger-than-life existence. It weaves the story of Leskly's illness into his life, which was, even before he was diagnosed with the disease, characterized by breaking conventions (unlike Frumer in *Positive Story*, Leskly was not recruited to the army after declaring he was a homosexual) and a strong impulse for self-destruction.

This, it is suggested in the film, is a result of Leskly's tragic circumstances: he was born to Holocaust survivors after eight failed pregnancies (his mother gave birth to four stillborn babies). His father, who lost his first wife and a child in the Holocaust, yearned for a boy. Being a homosexual, Leskly could not possibly live up to his father's expectations. His mother, too, preferred to pretend that she did not know he was gay and that he had AIDS. She refused to help Lev with the making of the film after she found out that her son's homosexuality and the cause of his death would be discussed. According to Rivka Bin-Noun, Leskly's cousin and an interviewee in the film, Leskly's mother wished to believe in Leskly's respectable facade, to believe he was someone he was clearly not. According to Ronit Weiss-Berkowitz, a close friend and another interviewee in the film, "Leskly's mother was one of the last to realize what a great man her son was."

Leskly, presented in the film as the Israeli version of Jean Genet, used to go to S&M clubs and saunas while living in Amsterdam—both for casual sex and out of an intellectual interest in this underground world. The scholar and literary critic Ariel Hirschfeld comments in the film that for Leskly "homosexuality was a journey into a certain kind of knowledge, a particular underworld he was designated for." For Leskly, as he claimed in his writing, which is quoted in the film, S&M was an extension of the language of sex, and he was interested in the extension of languages.

Each film takes a different approach, conceptually and visually, to frame the disease and its victims. Whereas *Positive Story* tells the story of an ordinary person, whose "dullness" is celebrated as an expression of resistance, *Yakantalisa* aspires to create a mythical, enigmatic story about a mythical, enigmatic character. The absence of any footage of Leskly, except for the blurred clip at the end, leaves the task of portraying him to his friends and the places he inhabited. Frequenting S&M clubs (described by Gordon as "hell in intermission") and expressing his thoughts in a complex poetic language or through dance, Leskly is portrayed as an extraordinary character. His premature death from a fatal disease is seen as almost predetermined fate.

It is no coincidence, however, that the two films came out in the same year, not long after Amos Guttman's death from AIDS. It seems as if it was only then that the Israeli media could finally start dealing with the disease and its aftermath.[15] The films signal a turning point in the way the illness was thought of in Israeli discourse—from a token of the dark S&M clubs of Amsterdam to the vital presence of Frumer, whose strongest wish is to integrate into Israeli mainstream culture. Although the two individuals, Frumer and Leskly, are gay, and therefore AIDS is still portrayed as a "gay disease,"[16] they represent different modes of existence with and in relation to the disease.

Alternative Parenthood and the Demise of Gay Partnership in *Family Matters*

Rather than dealing with the construction of a gay identity, the documentary film *Family Matters* (*Mishpuche*, David Noy and Yoram Ivry, 2004) focuses on the process of its dissolution as it enters a heterosexual arena. The film follows a gay couple—Kai, a German flight attendant and Itamar, an Israeli lawyer—who wish to have a child together. They meet Daphna, a single, heterosexual Israeli woman, a professional flautist, through a forum of "alternative parenting" in Israel. The couple agree that Itamar will be the biological father, so he forms a close tie with Daphna. At first it seems that the three of them will indeed be able not only to achieve their personal goal to become parents but also to create an "alternative" form of nuclear family, with two gay fathers and a mother. But soon after they meet, the relationship between Kai and Daphna sours: they both feel abandoned by Itamar. Daphna feels left out when Itamar goes back to Kai (who later becomes his husband, as they marry in Germany), and Kai feels excluded because he is not part of the genetic creation that connects Itamar and Daphna.

The film begins with a shot of Kai strolling in the narrow streets of the Old City in Jerusalem. His partner is at the Tel Aviv hospital where Daphna is giving birth. He hears the news of the birth over the telephone, and he and Itamar both cry. The film then cuts to eighteen months previously, to the point where Daphna, Itamar, and Kai are just starting to get to know each other and are still devising an ideal future together. Initially Daphna describes Kai as an equal partner, and the fact that Itamar is the biological father seems to have no special significance.[17]

Yet, as Daphna's pregnancy progresses, she and Itamar form a unique relationship of their own, which feels, as Itamar calls it, like a betrayal. It becomes clear that Kai has no place in the process. At an early ultrasound checkup, Kai is still present in the room with Daphna and Itamar, but he is no longer a fully equal partner: while he holds Itamar's arm, the camera moves slowly toward Itamar, who holds Daphna's leg with his other hand. This subtle detail indicates the power structure between the three. At this point, Kai still believes he will be with Daphna and Itamar at the hospital when Daphna gives birth, but her facial expression betrays her disapproval. Daphna's feelings are elaborated in a later scene, in which she shares her concerns with her girlfriends.

In order to secure their relationship in face of the new threat, Kai and Itamar decide to marry in Germany. Ironically, the marriage functions as a reaction of a heteronormative kind to a threat that is also part of the heteronormative order (having a child, forming a nuclear family). Although the decision to get married may well be a mutual wish, it is shown in the film as mostly Kai's initiative. It is he, for instance, who insists on a big celebration, whereas Itamar says he would prefer a small, intimate ceremony. When asked about their upcoming wedding, Daphna shows an ostentatious lack of interest and refuses to be there. The wedding, she claims, is Kai's way of displaying his legitimate claim on Itamar.

Kai's exclusion is expressed not only through Daphna's disapproval of him but also through his foreignness, symbolized by his heavily accented Hebrew. At one point in the film he says, "In Germany I am the Israeli, and here I am the German." His somewhat rootless existence is further emphasized by his vocation—he works for a German airline, which puts him in a constant transitory state. The fact that gay partnerships are not as widely accepted in Israel as in his native land adds to his feeling of rejection. When Kai arrives at the hospital, he and Itamar approach the desk and ask for special permission to let them both see the baby, Tal. "I am the biological father, and this is my husband, the nonbiological father," Itamar explains to the woman behind the desk. When they finally get to the room, Kai films the baby with his camcorder, but is then interrupted by another employee who enters the room and asks if they have obtained the required permission to visit. At this point Kai loses his temper. This sequence displays a tension between a liberal, progressive model of relationships and sexuality (even if this model follows heterosexual norms) and a rigid, slightly homophobic reaction to it. It is a pivotal moment, which indicates the heavy price required from those who wish to experience alternative parenthood.

After the birth, the situation between the three deteriorates further, to the point where Daphna refuses to send Tal to Itamar and Kai's place, claiming that Kai's jealousy makes him hostile toward her. This decision is interpreted by Itamar, in turn, as a hostile act, and he then threatens recourse to the courts if things do not change. After negotiations, conducted by a third party, they manage to reach a settlement, and the film closes with Tal's first birthday party. It is a happy ending of a sort, even though it has a bitter undertone. As Daphna says, "We started out hoping to create a different form of family, but that didn't happen. What we have instead is two families: me and Tal, and Itamar and Kai with Tal. I'm OK with it. It is also a kind of peace."

Interestingly, the subsequent breakup of Kai and Itamar's eleven-year relationship is not mentioned, as if not to interrupt the happy family narrative. The story of their eventual breakup was discussed extensively in an article about the film, published before the film was first broadcast on TV. In the article, Kai, who had returned to Germany, said, "Unfortunately, human genetics won" (A. Peled 56). However, the decision to open the film with a sequence highlighting the breakdown of the gay relationship does not leave much room for hope. Alternating the pictures of birth at the hospital with Kai walking by himself in Jerusalem, the opening sets gay relationships and parenthood at opposite poles. Starting the film with a sort of ending, the story of the protagonists unfolds without surprise. Parenthood, the film seems to suggest, remains mainly a privilege of heterosexual couples.

The film touches on a principal tension within the gay world, between the desire to adjust to hegemonic, traditional models and the queer call to defy those structures and develop instead an alternative mode of existence. This tension has been at the core of gay and queer discourses from the start. With every progress gay communities in the Western world make toward an equal standing in their societies (through achieving rights to serve in the army, to form civil partnerships, to adopt children, etc.), more voices emerge criticizing the gay community's subordination to oppressive practices.

One such voice is Lee Edelman's. Connecting the figure of the child in Western culture with the sacred and, in his eyes, fictional idea of a future (which "always anticipates, in the image of an Imaginary past, a realization of meaning that will suture identity" [*No Future* 25]), Edelman expresses hopes for a queer alternative. This alternative will undo the social formation that patriarchy imposes on us and will point out the gap that the dominant culture, caught in the Symbolic order, has already foreclosed for us in the very act of giving meaning and names and of looking forward to "tomorrow."

Edelman acknowledges that queers (by which he means "all so stigmatized for failing to comply with heteronormative mandates" [*No Future* 17]) are also "psychically invested in preserving the familiar familial narrativity of reproductive futurism" (*No Future* 17).[18] However, queerness, he claims, has the power to move us beyond the bounds of identity, meaning, and law to a site that cannot be named or grasped, while in the process continuously undoing social reality, which relies on imaginary identifications, on the structures of Symbolic law, and on the paternal metaphor of the name. In this site, jouissance, loosely translated as "enjoyment," rather than "futurism," is the key principle. By driving us toward the notion of jouissance, Edelman claims that queer culture has the potential to oppose this fundamental expectation for "tomorrow" embodied in the figure of the child. Edelman attacks the desire of gay men and women to perpetuate the illusionary fantasy of tomorrow, embedded, in part, in the desire to rear children. He expresses disappointment, if not anger, at the gay community's failure to form an alternative to the existing social order through emphasis on jouissance. *Family Matters*, on the other hand, represents the attempt to accommodate gay desire within the heteronormative domain. However, it is the ultimate failure of this attempt that the film ends with.

Family Matters is meant to be a bittersweet tale of the joy and sorrow of bringing a child into the world. The failure to establish an alternative family is mixed with the joy of having the baby after all (as Daphna says at Tal's first birthday party, also speaking on behalf of Itamar: "It is a great privilege to be parents, but even more so, it is a great privilege to be Tal's parents"). According to Edelman's view of queerness and its power to challenge heteronormativity, however, the failure of the gay partners in the film is precisely in their wish to have a child in the first place and what that wish really stands for, namely the perpetuation of the existing oppressive social order in the name of its futile hope for "tomorrow."

Zero Degrees of Separation and *Gan*: Gay Identities and Practices and the Israeli-Palestinian Conflict

A recent development in gay discourse in Israel is its engagement with the Palestinian-Israeli conflict. Although the subject was already touched on in Amos Guttman's *Drifting* (*Nagua*, 1983) and Eytan Fox's *The Bubble* (*HaBuah*, 2006) and explored in some depth in films such as *Hamsin* (Daniel Wachsmann, 1982) and *Hide and Seek* (*Machbo'im*, Dan Wolman, 1980), Israeli gay films were mostly exclusive in their portrayal of a closed, homogenized Jewish (mostly Ashkenazi) gay society. The two documentaries discussed in this section explore homosexual identities and practices (the protagonists of *Gan* [Ruth Shatz and Adi Barash, 2003] do not consider themselves gay although they have sex with other men) as they are formed and experienced by Palestinians and Arab citizens of Israel. Although important, sexuality is merely another factor in the life of the protagonists, who face constant threats of deportation and racial discrimination. The films' ideological concerns are directly linked to the activities of Black Laundry (*Kvisa Shchora*), an Israeli group of lesbians, gays, bisexuals, and transgenders against the occupation. Black Laundry, like the two films in question, tries to stress the connection between different forms of oppression—sexual, ethnic, and racial.

Zero Degrees of Separation

Zero Degrees of Separation (Elle Flanders, Canada, 2005) is a unique attempt to link gay activism in Israel with the leftist struggle to end the occupation. The film, directed by Israeli-Canadian filmmaker Elle Flanders brackets together the plight of Palestinians and the struggles that gay men and lesbians face in Israel. Through the stories of two interracial gay couples, the film touches on issues of gay sexualities and relationships, the Israeli-Palestinian struggle, and inner tensions within Israeli society itself.

Surprisingly, it is not the couples' homosexuality that is the central focus of the film. Instead, it emphasizes the daily difficulties they have to endure because of their more acute difference, their ethnic/racial one. One of the most striking points the film makes is the matter-of-fact attitude toward gay identity in Israel compared with the attitude of suspicion and hostility that still awaits Jewish-Arab couples whether they are gay or straight. The film serves more as a critique of the consequences of a long, aggressive occupation and the chasm between Zionist ideology and the crumbling reality more than fifty years after the establishment of the State of Israel and the Palestinian *Nakba* (catastrophe). This chasm is effectively portrayed through Flanders's frequent use of her grandparents' home movies, which triggered the making of the film. In a series of short texts, which appear on the screen at the beginning of the film, Flanders informs the viewers that this film archive documents her grandparents' involvement in the establishment of the State of Israel. Her grandfather was active in Britain's Joint Palestine Appeal, lobbying for the creation of a Jewish homeland, and her grandmother helped Jewish displaced persons settle in Palestine.

Flanders uses this found footage to present two opposing political positions: the Zionist dream, and what it has turned out to be, at least in her eyes and those of her interviewees, who represent the more radical section of the Israeli Left. Whereas the old footage is presented as almost idyllic, showing a group of elegantly dressed, European-looking elderly people touring the still quite empty land, recent footage is of bulldozers,[19] the security fence (or the wall) Israel has started building, and illegal settlements, whose neat houses and streets are then compared with the striking poverty and wreckage of their neighboring Palestinian towns. Recent footage also forms the background to short informative texts on the occupation.

However, the found footage has its own sinister undertone, too: the overdressed people in their suits and expensive jewelry seem foreign, unrelated to the land they claim they have a right to. One short sequence, in which the group of elderly Jewish people is seen traveling in a bus watching Arabs with camels crossing the dunes through the bus windows and their dark sunglasses, is especially effective. The windows and their sunglasses' lenses can be seen as screens, which distance them from the unruly wilderness outside. To the viewer they come across as colonial Europeans, alienated from their environment. This is, in fact, the premise of the film. The fact that Flanders is herself a former Israeli (she emigrated from Canada to Israel with her parents as a young girl but then left) back in the country after many years for the making of this movie suggests an interrupted, fragmentary Jewish existence in Palestine/Israel.[20]

Both old and new footage share a central motif: the land. In the film archive of Flanders's grandparents they are seen in the open space, surrounded by dunes, sprinklers watering the earth, making the land bloom and reclaiming the desert, just like Zionist folk imagery. However, by placing them in montage with the newer footage, the old home movie images take on a completely different meaning. The juxtaposition of recent footage of bulldozers and soldiers throwing hand grenades, for instance, with the pioneering work Flanders's grandparents were supporting, render the latter early signs of brutality and destruction on the Jewish side, which will grow into full-blown violent occupation in future years. According to Ezra, one of the protagonists of the film, the state's current efforts to green the land that was originally appropriated from the Arabs (as stated by him) are actually part of a scheme to keep it out of Arabs' reach.

The chasm between the past and the harsh reality of the present is the main theme of the film and is emphasized not only by visual devices but also through the stories of its protagonists. The film moves between the two couples: the Israeli Edit and her Palestinian girlfriend Samira and the Israeli Ezra and his Palestinian boyfriend Selim (their surnames are not given).[21]

The two couples seem to live similar lives, highlighted by their strong commitment to the fight against the occupation, but their existence is inherently different: Edit is an Ashkenazi Jew whose parents fled to Israel to escape persecution in Argentina, whereas Ezra is a Mizrahi Jew, and as such is doubly marginalized. As a Mizrahi Jew, Ezra's dedication to his political activity, like the relationship he establishes with a Palestinian man, may be seen as an attempt to reconnect with his long lost "Mizrahi" roots, those that have been repressed over the years in order to integrate into

Colonial Zionism: found footage in Elle Flanders's *Zero Degrees of Separation* (2005).

Israeli mainstream society, which is, in the main, constructed according to Ashkenazi values. Ezra makes this connection early on in the film, when he tells Flanders how ashamed he felt as a child to speak to his mother in Arabic, the language spoken at home, on the bus. By transgressing both sexual and racial borders, through a union with a gay Arab man, Ezra shows a stronger affiliation to his original Arab identity than to the forced, artificial Israeli-Ashkenazi identity he has been expected to adopt. Ezra, with his polished Arabic and deep sense of identification with the Palestinians' plight, may be seen as a liminal figure crossing the boundaries between his Israeli/Jewish identity and his Arab identity.

Likewise, significant differences in legal status, lifestyle, and education distinguish Samira from Selim. Samira presumably holds an Israeli citizenship (although her legal status is not made clear in the film) as she is employed as an oncology nurse in one of the largest hospitals in the center of Israel, whereas Selim is under house arrest in Jerusalem at the time of filming and has spent, up to that point, eighty months in jail since the beginning of the first Intifada. Unlike Samira, he does not have a profession. He is an amateur photographer who has not been able to pursue a career in the field because of harsh circumstances. He is eventually deported from Israel, an act that brings an end to his relationship with Ezra.

The difference in status, and in personality, also generates different forms of resistance. Whereas Selim comes across as passive and is shot mainly sitting down in their apartment or engaged in domestic, "feminine" activities such as cooking, Samira comes across as active and outspoken. As she explains in the film, "As a person who suffers oppression, at all levels of identity, as a woman, as a lesbian, and as an Arab Palestinian [. . .] all these threads and complexities of a Palestinian living in Tel Aviv do not allow me to be passive and say 'these problems don't concern me.'" She is seen several times throughout the film in motion, bicycling in Tel Aviv or carrying signs in public demonstrations. She has a proud, defiant sense of self, which Selim seems to lack. Her refusal to accept the rule of the occupier finds expression in her statements regarding terror attacks in Israel or Israel's Independence Day, which for the Palestinian people is known as the *Nakba*, "a day of mourning, not because of Israel's independence but because of other people's grief at whose expense it was achieved." Her participation in Israeli life through both work and her relationship does not mean assimilation, and she does not allow her voice to be mediated by an Israeli point of view. It hardly comes as a surprise that, at the end of the film, Edit and Samina have separated, and that Samira now has a new Israeli girlfriend. If falling in love implies a loss of self, to a certain extent at least, Samira cannot allow herself to do that as this will entail, first and foremost, losing her Palestinian self.

Whereas the film emphasizes the resemblance between Selim and Ezra and suggests that Ezra, through this relationship, can communicate with his repressed roots, it stresses the inevitable distance between Edit and Samira. As an Israeli citizen of Ashkenazi origin, Edit has a privileged status of which she is aware (at one point in the film she says, "Even before I accepted my identity as a Jew who's an occupier, I had to accept that I'm an Ashkenazi who oppresses Mizrahim"). Samira, on the other hand, is a poorly treated minority in what used to be her ancestors' land. Edit's family arrived in Israel from a different continent. In the film, Samira talks about her roots in the land as an indicator of her right to be there. "My existence in this land," she declares, "is very present. I am here—I am not anyone's guest. I'm not apologetic at all about my presence here. [. . .] I'm an indivisible part of this land, this area, this continent. It doesn't exist if I don't exist. If my ancestors don't exist." Samira's words call attention, once again, to the artificial presence of Flanders's grandparents and Edit's parents as representatives of all European-origin Jewish settlers on the land they claim as theirs.

Both Ezra and Edit, as Jewish Israelis, talk about the feelings of disillusionment regarding the state. They both oppose the concept of "enlightened occupation" and attempt to unmask it. Ezra says his education was based on the values of the Labor movement, of socialism, of Judaism, and of humanism. "I believed in it," he says, but as an adult he can see that "theory and practice are completely different. [. . .] It infuriates me. We've lost many of our qualities." Similarly, Edit talks about her ambivalent feelings toward Israel. Being the daughter of Argentinean Jews who fled their country, she sees Israel as the place in which her parents' lives were saved. At the same time, she says, "I have no problem saying that we are to blame. Zionism did not take into account that there was another nation here. It could have been done differently." She jokingly says she does not know which is worse, being an Israeli or an Argentinean. Toward the end of the film, she points to the most significant difference between herself and her parents: "They came to Israel filled with hope. Israel was a dream come true compared to Argentina. The reality in Israel today is very far from the dream that I was brought up on."

Ezra goes further: he uses terminology that has clear associations with the Holocaust when he talks about the occupation. Most of the scenes in which he is present are structured as road movie scenes. Accompanied by Flanders and a camera operator, Ezra goes about his political activity, which, in addition to the actual aid he offers Palestinians, consists of provoking soldiers at checkpoints, roadblocks, and in the occupied territories. Driving along a bypass from Jerusalem to Hebron, the building of which has cut Beitjalla, an Arab village, into two halves and which only Jews are permitted to use, Ezra comments, "If there's a problem they build a bypass, and then another. Of course it's at the taxpayer's expense, and the expense of the Palestinians' lands, and it is usually an 'Aryan' road—for Jews only." Later, referring to Israel's actions toward the Palestinian population, he says, "I call it putting them in ghettos, like in Yatta, like in Hebron. To concentrate them so that they are easier to govern [. . .] no one cares about what happens there, it is far from sight." He confronts an officer and a soldier who hold in their Jeep a blindfolded Palestinian, arrested by them for "looking suspicious," and they justify their actions by saying they are just following orders. To that Ezra responds, "I don't want to be rude, but in Germany they also got orders."

Flanders's decision to follow the stories of the two couples has its roots in a long tradition of exploring the lives of Arab-Jewish mixed couples in Israeli cinema, in feature films such as *Hamsin*, *The Lover* (*HaMehaev*, Michal Bat-Adam, 1986), *On a Narrow Bridge* (*Gesher Tsar Meod*, Nissim Dayan, 1985), and more recently *The Bubble* (see chapter 3). This tradition has derived, as Yosefa Loshitzky observes, from Western culture, in which

Ezra goes about his political activity in Elle Flanders's *Zero Degrees of Separation* (2005).

"European colonizers and their settler descendants have always been terrified by the prospect of miscegenation" (*Identity Politics* 113).

In her analysis of the portrayal of Arab-Jewish relationships in Israeli feature films, Loshitzky referenced Israeli historian Ilan Pappé, who observed how these films often follow the model of Greek tragedy (Loshitzky, *Identity Politics* 112–13). This is, for example, the case in *The Bubble*. Interestingly, *Zero Degrees of Separation*, as a documentary, can be seen to show that real-life experiences are not different from the tragic fictional ones depicted in feature films. *Zero Degrees of Separation* ends on a pessimistic note: Edit and Samira's relationship has ended and Edit left her job in the rape crisis center after Ariel Sharon, then the prime minister, was invited to speak there; Selim, Ezra's boyfriend, was deported after losing his case in court (text appears on the screen informing the viewer that, when last heard of, Selim had gotten married in Ramallah). And the occupation, Flanders informs the viewers in a short text, continues ("It is January 2005. I witness another Israeli bulldozer destroying a Palestinian house and garden").

The brief comment on what may have happened to Selim since his deportation raises questions regarding Flanders's agenda on sexuality.

New Israeli Nonfiction Gay Cinema 175

Flanders's decision to discuss the implications of the occupation through the stories of two interracial gay couples brings homosexuality in Israel back to its original activist roots. The lives that the film's protagonists lead are very different from the commonly accepted notions of gay life in Israel as urban and hedonistic and/or fully adjusted to the heteronormative order, as filmmakers such as Eytan Fox have mostly portrayed. It is not surprising that both Edit and Ezra come from the margins of the gay minority. As a lesbian and as a Mizrahi Jew they do not enjoy the privileges Ashkenazi gay men have. From a gay perspective, the importance of the film is in the representation of different modes of existence within the gay minority, which do not follow the same obvious models, and in the matter-of-fact approach it adopts toward homosexuality and gay identities and relationships.

Having said that, non-Israeli viewers who are not familiar with Israeli gay culture will not necessarily realize this, as Flanders hardly explores homosexuality in Israel or, indeed, Palestine and does not encourage her protagonists to do so. Although it is clearly no accident that the two couples she chose for the film are gay couples, their homosexuality is rendered a marginal, negligible topic. With Selim as an interviewee, the film had the potential to offer an important insight into the ways traditional Palestinian society oppresses its gay members. The fact that Selim is now supposedly a married man could be seen as an indication of an oppressive attitude toward homosexuality. Furthermore, Samira's choice to live in Tel Aviv and the fact she has had mainly (if not solely) Israeli partners, may have some connection to the way homosexuality is perceived in Palestinian society. However, there is no explicit mention of it in the film.

The filmmaker's evasion of discussing the homosexuality of the protagonists clashes with its obvious importance. The film marginalizes the protagonists' homosexuality, discouraging viewers from seeing it as a key factor in their existence. Ezra, for instance, hardly refers to his homosexuality as an issue that requires any consideration. Only once, when telling Flanders about another of Selim's many arrests, does he make a point of discussing the police officers' response to them being a gay couple. The rationale behind the decision to tell a moral story about the effects of the occupation in the private domain through a gay filter remains unexplained.

Gan

Gan follows a year in the lives of two teenage male prostitutes working in the area known as Electricity Garden in Tel Aviv. One of them, Dudu, is an Arab-Israeli. The other, Nino, is a Palestinian. The film explores the impasse the two are at in their attempt to escape their circumstances. *Gan* focuses on two main themes in each of the protagonists' life stories: their religious and racial otherness is one theme; their prostituting themselves is the other. Together these two conditions form a cycle from which Dudu and Nino cannot escape.

Gan is one of several films made in recent years about male prostitution. Two short feature films, *Send Me an Angel* (*Shlach Li Mal'ach*, Nir Ne'eman, 2003) and *Good Boys* (*Yeladim Tovim*, Yair Hochner, 2005) have dealt with similar or related themes. Whereas *Send Me an Angel* is a light-hearted comic drama that tells the love story of a young man and a rent boy (prostitute) he invites to his house on his birthday, *Good Boys*, shot in a documentary style by amateur filmmakers on a meager budget, offers a bleak portrayal of life at the margins of society, without hope of salvation. It is saturated with scenes of extreme violence, including rape and murder, and drug abuse. It has a stereotypically tragic view of male prostitutes as lost and exploited, and as such, it is much closer in spirit to the real-life events of Dudu and Nino in *Gan*.

Both *Good Boys* and *Gan* constitute an alternative to the optimistic, even utopian, gay existence portrayed in Eytan Fox's films. They revisit some of Amos Guttman's major themes, namely the isolation of gay men from the rest of society, a connection between gay life and outlaw existence, and the lack of trust in state institutions to help the individual. Indeed, prostitution as it is depicted in the films becomes a sign of the imperviousness of the authorities to the plight of the individual. The films equate prostitution with social crisis, while making strong references to the corruption in Israeli politics. In *Good Boys*, one of the protagonists meets a man in a club and agrees to go home with him. The man turns out to be a sadistic police officer who also works as a pimp. He rapes the protagonist and then lets one of his clients, a government minister, do the same while the victim is tied to the bed and blindfolded. In *Gan* the protagonists display the scars that long interrogations by both Israeli and Palestinian secret services and violence by family members have inscribed on their bodies. They do not voice their opinions regarding the occupation but merely report its dire consequences to their lives. They mock both Sharon and Arafat and tear election ads off the walls in a rebellious manner.

Life on the street offers Dudu and Nino freedom they cannot have elsewhere. Born into Arab families and raised amid poverty and sexual and physical violence, the two adolescents lose faith in the ability of the authorities to help them. Prostitution is portrayed as their act of survival and resistance. Their insistence that they are the ones who penetrate rather than

Street life: Nino (left) and Dudu in Ruth Shatz and Adi Barash's *Gan* (2003).

being penetrated in gay intercourse has a double meaning: it asserts both their heterosexuality (according to Muslim mores, men who penetrate other men are not considered homosexuals)[22] and their power over their Jewish clients. The streets where they work are the space in which the many restrictions imposed on them in their daily life as Arabs are lifted. "There are no rules on the streets," says Dudu, "you're free."

This freedom, however, changes rapidly into drug abuse and addiction and a series of court appearances. The film illustrates the impasse Dudu and Nino meet and the incompetence of the authorities in offering help. At one point, Nino finds his way to a van of Outreach Teen in Tel Aviv, a service for youth in need, after he has run away (not for the first time) from the juvenile reformatory to which he was sent. Describing his feeling of confinement to a social worker, Nino says, "It's as if I'm in the middle and there's a circle around me. I want to go this way, but it's closed. This way, but it's closed. Everything's closed. Even going back to the family is closed. Completely." Nino then tells about a "childish" dream he has in which he gets a passport, which allows him "to fly away from here."

This wish to run away is expressed several times by Nino and Dudu. The filmmakers, however, underline the impossibility of this dream. Early

The rape scene in Yair Hochner's *Good Boys* (2005): prostitution as a sign of the imperviousness of the authorities to the plight of the individual.

on in the film, Nino is put in Tel Aviv district prison after being arrested for drug dealing and robbery. He is not seen in prison, but the camera pans around the building, which resembles a fortress, while Nino's voice is heard speaking on the telephone with Dudu. The camera then follows an airplane crossing the dark skies above the prison. The contrast between the immobility of imprisoned Nino and the freedom that the movement of the airplane represents intensifies the tragic element of his life. Unlike the fictional protagonists of *Good Boys*, Nino does not represent only those who prostitute themselves. He is also a Palestinian who lives illegally in Israel and whose freedom of movement is restricted by his racial and national identity as much as it is by his profession. Even more than *Zero Degrees of Separation*, *Gan* offers a bleak portrayal of the level of integration of Palestinians and Arab citizens of Israel in Israeli society. It is especially powerful as it is one of the few Israeli-produced films to present the conflict and its implications from the Arab/Palestinian perspective.

The only source of solace is the strong bond between the two boys, who look after each other both emotionally and physically, guiding each other through their frequent encounters with dubious clients and the authorities, both Israeli and Palestinian. Dudu and Nino met in 2002 while fighting on opposing sides. Their similar backgrounds, however, soon led to a remarkably loyal friendship. They both come from families to which they cannot or do not want to return. Nino's family lives in the occupied territories and he has not seen his mother for five years. Dudu, who grew up in a violent

New Israeli Nonfiction Gay Cinema

environment in Hebron, ran away from his family at the age of nine and found shelter at a house in Jerusalem owned by a man who was later arrested "because he raped so many kids." They form an alternative family of their own in which they regularly switch roles: it is Dudu who implores Nino to go back to the reformatory and who comes to meet him after his hearing in court. It is Nino who serves as a father figure when he hears that Dudu has taken heroin.

The filmmakers use their protagonists' youth to great effect. Whereas their life experiences may be those of much older people, their facial expressions, speech, and juvenile antics are a constant reminder of their youth. As teenagers whose view of the world has not been entirely formed, they express "unprocessed" emotions. "Dying is better than living like a stray dog. Or I'll go back to jail. Cool, why not?" says Nino. Their readiness to volunteer as suicide bombers ("They can give me a bomb belt, for all I care. I'm fed up with this life," says Nino) is another expression of nihilism that is at the core of their experience. Cinematically, the filmmakers benefit from the full cooperation they have been granted by the teenagers and the people who populate their world, among them other sex workers and a Jewish client who, for a short time, offers the teenagers a shelter in his house. Their willingness to expose themselves contributes to a highly candid document on a phenomenon that has been, up to this point, underrepresented in mainstream Israeli gay narrative.

Concluding Remarks

More than the previous chapters, this concluding chapter illustrates the diversity of gay, lesbian, and queer experiences in contemporary Israel. By exploring different identities and groups within what is often perceived as a homogenous gay community, it challenges the existence of such a community beyond its discursive, imagined borders, thus responding to one of this project's central objectives as laid out in the introduction.

If in previous chapters the films have all shared a formal, aesthetic, or thematic approach, this chapter is distinctive in that the films discussed in it do not. Indeed, these are all nonfiction films (with the exception of *Good Boys* discussed in relation to *Gan*), yet their filmmakers take very different stances toward principal matters such as gay and lesbian identities and the gay community and its involvement in Israeli society. I have attempted to analyze the films according to some nodal points, namely formal and visual concerns, thematic concerns, and the question of biography/autobiography.

The increasing number of gay documentaries in recent decades is linked to a similar trend in international gay documentary filmmaking, in which new formal means have been tested in order to undermine conventional, fixed categories of sexuality and identity in general. As much as I believe this international movement has inspired many filmmakers in Israel, there are only a very few Israeli films that genuinely achieve this formal subversion. *Last Post* and *Zero Degrees of Separation* are two such films. But even if most of the films are still conventionally scripted and constructed (most probably for commercial reasons, as many of them, as I stated above, were made for TV), they convey, especially when seen and discussed together, the many shapes Israeli gay identity and community have been taking in the past few years, and they hint at future developments.

5

Recent Developments and Future Directions

Some Concluding Notes

The year 2001 will surely be remembered as a turning point in the history of Israeli filmmaking. Due to legislation passed that year to guarantee allocation of government funds to script development production, the local film industry has been able to steadily increase the number of films produced every year, many of which have garnered international critical and commercial acclaim.[1] Several of these films have focused on gay experiences. In this last brief chapter I attend to some recent short, documentary, and feature films that can be examined in relation to an established tradition of cinematic gay representation in Israel but are already expanding and modifying it. The second part of this chapter, which explores the growing interest in the intricate relations between religion and homosexuality in modern-day Israel, is particularly indicative of the many sites of conflicts that are yet to be explored in the area of nonnormative identities and their representations on screen.

This chapter ties up some of the threads that have been woven throughout the book and draws links to the "founding fathers" of Israeli gay cinema, namely Amos Guttman and Eytan Fox. However, as Israeli cinema, gay and other, is still highly fertile with no sign of slowing down, concluding at this

183

point may seem a little premature. Instead, the last section of this chapter suggests ways this project can be used as the basis for future investigations into Israeli cinema and society, both of which will surely keep evolving and changing in the years to come.

A New Queer Horizon: *A Different War* and *Antarctica*

Four years after the second Intifada began in 2000 a student short film chronicling the early days of the conflict toured the international film festival circuit to great acclaim. The film, *A Different War* (*Milchama Acheret*, 2004), directed and written by Nadav Gal, tells the story of Noni (Shimon Amin), a sensitive, "feminine" boy from Gilo, a Jewish neighborhood in East Jerusalem. Suffering under heavy fire out of the Arab village of Beitjalla, the residents of Gilo were expected to put up a bold front in the face of this old-new threat. They became the heroes of the day and the focus of media attention.

Noni's father has been called up to the army, and it is Tzahi (Hillel Kappon), his slightly older brother, who embodies the role of the "man" in the household. He portrays a certain kind of masculine role: every day he and his friends climb up the "defense wall" dividing the Arabs from the Jews and shout "Death to Arabs!" Noni is forced to join them and is encouraged to take part. But Noni has other things on his mind, like putting on makeup and trying on his mother's clothes. The realm of "the feminine" is a site from which Noni can resist the Zionist-Israeli, militaristic mindset. His refusal to play the role of King David in a school play based on the story of David and Goliath further highlights the manner in which his "sissiness" defies both contemporary Israeli machismo and the biblical heroic tales, which, to a certain extent, have fed it.

Noni's sissiness serves as a disruptive force. It breaks away from the Zionist-Israeli narrative in which masculinity, militarism, and heterosexism are intertwined. Noni is a truly subversive figure: in the scene that ends the film, he is forced to climb up the wall once again. Unlike in his previous attempts, however, Noni does not go down immediately and run away. Instead, he remains standing on the wall, his eyes fixed on the Arab village seen in the distance, and then he starts dancing.

With *A Different War* Israeli gay cinema came full circle. As I noted in the introduction, the first films to include homosexual characters, either explicitly gay or merely hinted at, such as *They Call Me Shmil* (*Kor'im Li Shmil*, George Ovadia, 1973) and *Fine Trouble* (*Eize Yofi Shel Tsarot*, Assi Dayan, 1976) singled them out as grotesquely feminine. They were marginal to the

Defying Israeli machismo: Noni (Shimon Amin) dances on the wall in Nadav Gal's *A Different War* (2004).

plot, and their marginality was emblematic of their standing in society. *A Different War* uses similar motifs, but the "feminine" nature of its young male protagonist, which implies his future sexual orientation (although this is not made explicit), is portrayed as a welcome alternative to Israeli masculine and militaristic culture. The ambivalence regarding homosexuality expressed in previous films does not exist in *A Different War*. Rather, the film takes a sympathetic stance toward nonnormative practices and views them as a source of hope for a change.

The relationship between different gay groups, gay men in particular, and Israeli mainstream culture has always been ambiguous. Excluded at first, gay men created an urban culture that dissociated itself from Israeli culture and society. Tel Aviv was the metropolitan center where Israeli gay culture could evolve. The films of Amos Guttman, the majority of which are set in that city, assisted in the creation of a gay "separatist" ethos. The characters in his films show as little interest in the mainstream culture in which they live as the mainstream culture shows in them. Guttman went further, though, by rejecting not only the mainstream ideology but also the prevalent politics of the gay community, which aspired to fit in with the master Zionist-Israeli narrative. His "obsession" with marginality is conveyed not only in the films' bold themes and narratives but also in their visual dimension, namely the "excessive" and artificial mise-en-scène, the use of lighting, and the shooting of interiors. Taken together, these two aspects show how Guttman created some of the most daring films in the history of Israeli cinema.

The films of Eytan Fox, however, present an opposite position: his gay characters command the screen (and the army units in which they serve), but their homosexuality is, for the most part, stripped away, leaving them to act just like their heterosexual counterparts, assimilated and immersed in the mainstream culture to the extent that they pose no, or very little, challenge to the norm. Fox's films draw on commercial cinema and follow Hollywood generic conventions, both thematically and visually. They are an example of the alliance between the liberal-Left bloc and the gay community. The films negate the diversity of gay voices and experiences. It is little wonder that Fox's films have become successful among nongay audiences. By including gay characters the films supposedly highlight Israeli society's liberal stance toward those who are different from the norm. This common perception of Fox's films, however, masks Fox's, and his films', conservative and limited view of homosexuality.

A Different War is one of a growing number of films that attempt to deal with questions of sexual otherness in Israel today without ignoring mainstream culture altogether, on the one hand, or uncritically embracing it, on the other. It represents a wish for "normalization" of a sort, which views gay groups, although different, as an inseparable part of contemporary Israeli society. This is a similar aspiration to that which Fox presents in his films, but whereas Fox assumes gay men are the ones who need to adjust to the dominant culture, namely to become more "virile" and to downplay their gayness, Gal does not. His film celebrates its protagonist's difference, which he sees as an alternative to existing models of masculinity. Unlike Jagger in *Yossi and Jagger* (2002), the protagonists of *The Bubble* (2006), and Ori in *Mary Lou* (2009), Noni is not "punished" for what he is and, unlike the gay characters in *Walk on Water* (2004), his "feminine" side and alleged homosexuality are not pushed outside the frame of Israeli discourse. On the contrary, by remaining true to himself, he is able to stand up to the pressure put on him by society (represented here by his teacher, his brother, and his brother's friends) and to herald a change.

Change is also the driving force in Yair Hochner's second film, *Antarctica* (2008). Moving away from his bleak representation of gay prostitution in *Good Boys* (see chapter 4), Hochner wrote and directed a full-length feature film that celebrates the life of gay men *and* lesbians in contemporary Tel Aviv.[2] The title refers to Shirley's (Lucy Dubinchik) wish to go on a trip to Antarctica before she settles down in Israel with her lesbian partner (and employer), Michal (Liat Akta). Although not seen, a mental image of the remote and icy continent, conjured up by the title as well as several references to it in the film, echoes the snowy landscape in *Yossi and Jagger*. However, the much longed-for Antarctica in Hochner's film is a destination of choice for Shirley, whose sexuality is known to all and a promise of an adventure whose end will symbolically mark her readiness to finally "marry" Michal in Tel Aviv (after calling off the planned wedding once before). Antarctica as it is imagined in the film, therefore, is in sharp contrast to the danger zone in which the closeted Yossi and Jagger consummate their love, seemingly for the last time. Both places offer freedom, but whereas in *Yossi and Jagger* this momentary freedom only leads to a tragic ending, in *Antarctica* the freedom of self-discovery Shirley seeks will eventually facilitate a lasting nonheterosexual bond between her and her partner.

Shirley and Michal's love story is only one thread in a complex narrative structure: opting for a large ensemble of characters who, in the tradition of Robert Altman, cross romantic and social paths, Hochner portrays a close-knit gay world bursting with color and sexual tension. Hochner's vision is bold enough to dedicate the first fifteen minutes of the film to a celebratory introduction of rather graphic gay sex. The viewer follows the daily encounters of Boaz (Ofer Regirer), a young professional who seeks to conceal his feelings of void with quick, anonymous sex. The intensity of his sex life is proficiently portrayed by the use of a split screen in which those encounters are seen simultaneously or back to back. The use of split screen may also suggest a fragmentary and lacking existence, which can only be "repaired" temporarily with the excitement of the sexual act. The film then moves three years forward, when Boaz, still practicing casual sex, is looking for his one "true love." Like him, the rest of the cast are in the process of falling in and out of love while not shying away from celebrating bodily pleasures. *Antarctica* forges a new path for gay Israeli cinema by bringing the worlds of Fox and Guttman together and crossing the assumed chasm between the two. Hochner's characters may seek lasting love in the form of a stable relationship, but casual sex is still unapologetically presented in *Antarctica* as the hallmark of gay culture.

Hochner's emphasis on creating a gay sphere, one that has no or very little contact with the heterosexual world, may suggest an anti-integrationist approach that ties in with Guttman's vision and is in sharp contrast to Fox's tendency to break homo/heterosexual barriers by placing his characters in, for instance, a military environment. This impression is further enhanced by Hochner's decision to bring gay life back to its urban origins: *Antarctica*, like *Good Boys* before it, takes place solely in Tel Aviv. This may suggest an alliance with Guttman's thematic principles and a rejection of Fox's insistence on broadening the cultural and geographical borders of gay experience. But *Antarctica* is not a mere replica of Amos Guttman's films. The city for Hochner is not a symbol of urban, and mental, decay but rather a scintillating sphere where gay sex, love, and courtship are ordinary practices. The moroseness embedded in Guttman's films is supplanted by a favorable, even sanguine, view of gay life in the city.

The comic double act created by the underground drag performer Noam Huberman (better known by his stage name, Miss Laila Carry) lends the film a valuable subversive tone. Huberman shifts between the characters of Shoshana, the mother of a gay son and a lesbian daughter, and Amram, an elderly man who becomes her lover, and in the process comments on unstable identity categories. Huberman's double act disrupts the process of classification and regulation of identities in culture. Shoshana and Amram decide to get married at the end of the film, but their unification has already been accomplished in the decision to cast Huberman to play both characters. Like Ze'ev Revach's dual roles in *The Hairdresser* (*Sapar Nashim*, 1984) and *Double Bouskilla* (*Pa'amayim Buskilla*, 1998, see introduction) before him, and even more so those of Divine (Harris Glenn Milstead) in some of John Waters's films (most notably *Female Trouble* [1974] and *Hairspray* [1988]), Huberman points at the potential of a side-by-side existence of the masculine and the feminine, hetero and homo, in any one of us. Although the rest of the characters stick to the accepted, somewhat restricted categories of gay and lesbian, in this overly theatrical dual performance the film hints at a queer alternative.

Huberman's performance, after Divine and Revach, serves as a mirror to fixed models of gender behavior that more often than not are taken for granted. Huberman's Shoshana, for instance, is a doting mother whose main wish is to see her two children marry their respective gay and lesbian lovers and give her grandchildren. The juxtaposition of normative portrayal of femininity and motherhood by a transgressive drag performer is a source of laughs as much as it is a critical response to our tendencies to see those performed identities as natural and essential. Hochner, therefore, advocates for conceiving gay identities (across gender and sexuality) as ever-changing and evolving, encompassing a wide range of behavioral patterns and preferences—a possibility that was strongly denied by both Guttman and Fox before him.

Normative portrayal of motherhood by a transgressive drag performer: Noam Huberman as Shoshana in Yair Hochner's *Antarctica* (2008).

THE LOVE THAT DARE NOT SPEAK ITS NAME: GAY DESIRE AND RELIGION

Israeli gay men's and lesbians' acquired confidence has brought them in recent years to engage with other, still unresolved, matters within both their own community and in Israeli society in general. Now that homosexuality in itself is not as controversial an issue as it once was, many filmmakers attend to stories, either fictional or nonfictional, in which the protagonists' sexuality is, though important, often just another identity category. In many of those films sexual matters illuminate other modes of oppression, in and outside the gay community, related to ethnicity, gender, and, progressively, religion.

In a recent documentary film, *The Quest for the Missing Piece* (*Be'ikvot HaChaticha HaChasera*, 2007), director Oded Lotan embarks on a journey to discover what happened to his foreskin, removed from his body in the Jewish rite of circumcision (performed on a male child on the eighth day of his life) known as *brith* ("pact" or "covenant" in Hebrew). Lotan explores the reasons for the rite of circumcision and looks into other cultures that perform it. One of his discoveries is its absolute centrality to male Jewish identity, even among secular Jews who may not obey any of the other commandments, and he concludes that this is one of the reasons behind the continuing practice of the ritual. Lotan's investigation into the meaning

Recent Developments and Future Directions

of this ritual is especially poignant because as a gay man he is excluded from the very covenant that the *brith* represents. Thus, although not at the center of it, the film explores the relationship between homosexuality and Judaism and more specifically between the gay community and the State of Israel, which, at the civil level at least, generally follows rabbinical law. The film stresses the importance given to sexuality in creating a sense of belonging to Israeli-Jewish society.

As a secular gay man, Lotan has the freedom to reject those aspects of religion that restrict him or even the Israeli state, whose civil laws are bound with those of the Jewish faith: Lotan's long-term partner is German, and the couple lived for a while in Germany. For others who were born into religious and Orthodox families, however, the choice between following their homosexual desires and practicing religious life is a complicated and painful matter. Gay love within the religious quarters in Israel has been the main concern of several recent local productions, including successful prime-time TV drama *Srugim* (2008–present), which follows a group of young religious men and women in Jerusalem, among them a gay character.

The topic was first explored in Sandi Simcha DuBowski's documentary *Trembling before G-D* (2001), in which a group of Orthodox, mostly American, Jews were interviewed about how they reconcile their sexuality with their beliefs. The film brought to light a phenomenon, which up to that point was hardly addressed, and created a discourse from which the three films to be discussed later in this section have evolved. Essentially, *Trembling before G-D* was not an Israeli film: the majority of the interviewees were not Israelis and the focus was on the clash between homosexuality and the Jewish faith, not the Israeli state. This, however, may also define the three films considered below: all are Israeli by production, language, and location but devoid of any specific mention of Israel's civil, secular values.

The two cities in which the films are set, Jerusalem and Safed, further reinforce their Jewish-rabbinical aspect and, equally, diminish their Israeli-secular-Zionist features. This may attest to the insular character of the Orthodox Jewish community in Israel and in the Diaspora and suggest a stronger affinity between Orthodox communities in different countries than that between a given Orthodox community and the hegemonic national culture within which it is based. Arguably, a similar type of seclusion also characterizes gay communities all over the world. As the Israeli case has shown, however, this perception is flawed: after all, the very basic wish of most Israeli gay activists and filmmakers has been to be accepted by and fully integrated into Israeli life. The adhesion of the Orthodox community in Israel to their traditional ways, as well as the fact that, for the most part, they do not serve in the army, suggests an entirely different approach to that of the secular gay community in its different branches.

Eyes Wide Open (*Einayim Pkuhot*, Haim Tabakman, 2009) is the latest film to explore the inner struggle of Orthodox men with their homosexual desires. It tells the story of Aaron (Zohar Strauss), an introverted butcher, husband, and father of four who takes over the family business after his father dies, and Ezri (Ran Danker), a young religious student, who arrives in Jerusalem from Safed in an attempt to trace his lost love. Ezri enters Aaron's shop to escape the pouring rain outside and asks to make a telephone call. As he has nowhere to go, Aaron suggests he will work for him and live, if only temporarily, in the back room of his shop. The two strike up a close friendship in which each serves as the other's mentor: Aaron teaches Ezri his trade, and Ezri, who has already experienced gay intimacy, initiates the sexual act between them. Throughout the film he remains, despite his apparent confusion, the guiding force in his and Aaron's burgeoning relationship.

Their affair, however, cannot possibly last. It is not long before the rumors about Ezri's past deviance grow, and with them the pressure on Aaron to let Ezri go. Aaron futilely tries to oppose the community's decision to ostracize Ezri, admitting to his rabbi that Ezri's presence "brought him back to life from the dead." There are several references to death at the beginning of the film, among them the notice of the passing away of Aaron's father posted on the butcher shop's door and the delivery of livestock to the shop soon to be slaughtered. Ezri's presence, however, changes the course of Aaron's life as he awakes desires in Aaron he was never fully aware of, having followed the path dictated to him by strict laws and the community's expectations. Realizing that he may destroy his family if he chooses Ezri over them, he returns to his former life. But having experienced a fleeting moment of happiness and fulfillment that defined for him, for the first time, all that was lacking in his life beforehand, he cannot simply make peace with the path chosen for him. In the last scene, Aaron goes back to the spring where Ezri took him shortly after they met and where they made first physical contact. He is seen swimming in the spring by himself and then taking a dive. The final shot shows Aaron with his head underwater, until he cannot be seen. The camera then lingers on the still water, with no trace of Aaron. This may suggest his wish to drown himself, to end the life that feels like death.

The film is important not only in its still unusual portrayal of life in this most segregated community but also in its subversive use of some religious concepts. If religion often describes belief as an enlightening force, in *Eyes*

Awakened desires: Ezri (Ran Danker, left) and Aaron (Zohar Strauss) in Haim Tabakman's *Eyes Wide Open* (2009). Courtesy of Haim Tabakman.

Wide Open, it is anything but. Aaron remains oblivious to his true self for many years, living, even if he does not fully realize it, a lie. His eyes are wide shut to his true desires, and his enlightenment and self-discovery occur only when he finally dares to transgress the oppressive rules imposed on him by his community. To Aaron, these newly experienced sexual urges are not an easy thing to understand: devoid of any other means with which to make sense of his feelings, his immediate reaction is to turn back to religion.

Telling Ezri, after the latter tries to kiss him for the first time on the shop's roof terrace, that their lust for each other is a test from God and that they should not surrender to it is his attempt to frame this new confusing knowledge about himself through the only discursive and conceptual resources he has. He says, "We have an opportunity to rise, to overcome . . . this challenge wouldn't have come to us if we couldn't face it. Why did God create lust? For the catharsis of the soul. The Lord didn't create broken tools." Earlier on, in a meeting with his rabbi, he says, "Worshipping God is an everyday duty. It means loving the difficulties. Being a slave of God means loving the hardship." He soon realizes, however, that the vitality he feels with Ezri is much stronger than his beliefs.

In the end it is the power of the community as a social force rather than Aaron's own faith that makes him turn his back on his relationship with Ezri. When his wife, who quietly observes the two over family dinners (she is never told explicitly of the relationship but guesses it), asks Aaron to decide whether to stay or go, he decides to remain, talking of his homosexuality as an expression of the evil inclination that he is able to overcome. The last scene, however, suggests otherwise.

Rain is used throughout the film as a vigorous symbol: it is normally associated with the ritual baths to which the members of the Orthodox community go to purify themselves. In *Eyes Wide Open*, however, rain is the natural force that summons Ezri to Aaron's shop in his search for shelter. The act of bathing does take place in the film—when Ezri takes Aaron to the spring outside Jerusalem—but it bears a dramatically different meaning from that of the religious ritual. Rain in *Eyes Wide Open* is both an agent of life and of destruction: it washes the Jerusalem neighborhood with gray despair and reinforces a sense of gloom, but it is also a symbol of the new life that surges in Aaron after meeting Ezri. The spring the two go to is stripped of religious connotations. With its location outside the crowded city (it is made clear that this is the first time Aaron has left the city in many years), the experience celebrates the power of nature, including the lust the two protagonists feel for each other. Once the two men take their clothes off they feel freer to finally explore their desires. It may not have been intended as such, but it is indeed an act of purification for Aaron.

Similar in spirit and structure to the classic 1950s melodramas (see chapter 2) in its portrayal of an uneven struggle between the individual and the collective, the film is predominantly critical of the ways of the Orthodox community and its refusal to understand or support those who do not follow its strict rules. Its involvement in its members' lives is total and uncompromising and reaches beyond matters of sexuality. The film is set up to expose not only this totality but also the hypocrisy that accompanies it. The rabbi may preach at one point that "God doesn't want a man to suffer, he shouldn't cause himself trouble. Why has God created the world? To make good for us, to ease our souls," but this has little or no effect when it comes to personal choices of members of the community.

Parallel to the story of Ezri and Aaron, there is another "forbidden" love story in the film, that of Yisrael and Sarah. Considered an outsider and a sinner, Yisrael is warned to leave Sarah, the daughter of a respected member of the community who intends to marry her to a man of his choice. It is an act of aggressive coercion for which Aaron himself is also responsible: he is among those who break into Yisrael's house, search the house for evidence of sin (and find it in the form of a TV set hidden in a cupboard), and order him to leave Sarah alone. Protesting at first, Yisrael says he cannot possibly do that because he loves Sarah, to which Aaron responds angrily and accuses him of humiliating Sarah's father. This happens when Aaron himself is agonizing over his even more transgressive relationship with Ezri, and therefore the encounter can be seen as his barren effort to regulate his own desire. Although giving in to pressure in the end, just like Yisrael, Aaron's attempt at self-discipline fails: once he has realized what his life has lacked, there can be no return to his old self.

The end of the film is inconclusive. Even if Aaron makes it back to his family in Jerusalem it is unknown how his life there, in light of his new knowledge, will unfold. Ezri is forced to leave the community for a similarly unknown future. As the younger character, who is also far more confident about his sexuality and without a family to support, the film allows the viewer to hope for a different destiny for him, one in which he is accepted by the gay community where he belongs. *Eyes Wide Open*, like the two films discussed below, asks why those whose lifestyles do not agree with the principles on which the Orthodox community is based do not simply start their lives over. A fully rationalized answer is not given in any of the films (although they all imply the immense difficulty in doing so), but the character of Ezri may suggest such a choice is not entirely out of reach.

Avi Nesher's *The Secrets* (*HaSodot*, 2006) deals with concerns similar to those explored in *Eyes Wide Open* but from a lesbian perspective. The film is an Israeli-French coproduction with Fanny Ardant in a supporting role as an ailing woman who is seeking absolution for her past crimes. The two young women who help her are Naomi (Ania Bukstein) and Michelle (Michal Shtamler), who study in a nearby seminary for women. Despite the striking differences between the two—Naomi, the daughter of an important rabbi, asks to be sent there in order to postpone and eventually call off her arranged marriage to a man she does not love, whereas Michelle, who lives with her family in France, is sent there against her will—they fall in love. As with Aaron and Ezri in *Eyes Wide Open*, the love affair between the two women takes them by surprise as much as the viewer. But although Naomi is willing to form a committed relationship with Michelle, the latter cannot face the consequences of such a rebellious act and gets married. Although lesbianism is not explicitly forbidden in Jewish law as male homosexuality is, it is still a severe deviation from the norm. Thus, by placing a lesbian love affair within the Orthodox community, Nesher cannot possibly allow it to flourish. The passionate dance between Naomi and Michelle at the latter's

Separated by Jewish law and social taboos: Naomi (Ania Bukstein, left) and Michelle (Michal Shtamler) in Avi Nesher's *The Secrets* (2006).

wedding suggests that the two still love each other but are separated by Jewish law and social taboos.

The dilemmas presented in both *Eyes Wide Open* and *The Secrets* are similar to those discussed in an earlier documentary film, *Et She'ahava Nafshi* (*Keep Not Silent* or *Ortho-Dykes*), directed by Ilil Alexander in 2004. Alexander follows three Orthodox lesbian women, all members of the group Ortho-Dykes, in their attempt to reconcile their faith with their forbidden desires. Two of the interviewees in the film—Miriam-Esther and Ruth—agree to talk only after they are assured that their identity will remain hidden. As members of a small community, they are concerned about the repercussions that the knowledge of their lesbianism might have on those closest to them, their husbands and children. Their exposure, they say, could lead to ostracism.

Of the three, it is only Yehudit who is willing to reveal her identity fully. Alexander follows her in the weeks leading to the alternative wedding ceremony she has organized with her partner, Tal. In the process Yehudit tries to obtain the approval of two important parties: her parents and the rabbi of her community. Her attempts on both fronts fail. The rabbi finds it impossible that "God created people with tendencies they cannot overcome," equates lesbianism with the tendency to steal, rape, and murder, and suggests that Yehudit give up her wish to build a family with the woman she loves and instead dedicate her life to another vocation, such as charity. In the same fashion, her parents refuse to attend her wedding party. Yehudit says that they must put the perceptions of the community before her happiness and that their fear of her difference will also affect their acceptance of her future children. The real-life stories of the three women are just as dramatic as the fictional plotlines of the two feature films discussed above: the drama can be seen in the conversation Yehudit has with the rabbi and in Miriam-Esther's candid talk of her fear of ostracism.

Yehudit's courage to come out to both her parents and her community (as well as to the viewer of the film) stands in contrast to Miriam-Esther's and Ruth's fear of revealing themselves. Of the two, Ruth manages to breach the barriers imposed on her by her community and establish a relationship with a woman while still maintaining her marriage. Her husband, who is also interviewed in the film, appears to have made peace with the arrangement, as long as his marriage is not jeopardized. Their children, however, find it more difficult, and side with their father. Miriam-Esther is confident about her lesbian identity, describing it as much more encompassing than mere physical attraction. It is, she says, the essence of her whole being. Yet, she is the one who cannot consummate her desire, not even partially it seems, out of fear of everything she could lose (it is only later in the film that Miriam-Esther tells of a short relationship that ended due to her partner's decision to get married and have a family).

The real stories of the three women in *Keep Not Silent* echo the main issues that have been dealt with in both *The Secrets* and *Eyes Wide Open*, namely the immense hardship that both lesbians and gay men experience in the Orthodox community, and, perplexingly perhaps to some nonbelievers, their inability to leave that world behind—a world that cannot entirely contain them as they are (this is especially poignant in the case of Ruth in *Keep Not Silent*, who was not born into a religious family but decided to "return to the fold" when she was sixteen). Like the two feature films, *Keep Not Silent* attests to the agony those who deviate from the norm feel on a daily basis and the sacrifice they are required to make. As the rabbi says to Yehudit, "If the Torah prohibits it, the duty of a Torah believer is to obey the Torah, even at a heavy cost." The inevitable question is why they are willing to bear that burden, but this question is not even hinted at, let alone uttered in any of the films discussed above. An important part of what the films try to communicate, it seems, is that for a believer the option of opting out is nonexistent. Rather, they hold the belief that their way of life, and indeed their whole being, has been created by God's desire, and as such, it cannot possibly contradict His commandments.

Interestingly, it is not religion in itself that stops the protagonists of the three films from forming gay relationships but rather social and cultural mores. At one of the Ortho-Dykes meetings, documented in *Keep Not Silent*, one of the members is heard saying, "Why are we religious? For the sake of people or for God? On Judgment Day I'll only stand before God, not before the community. No rabbi will ask me anything. And if they ask, they won't get an answer from me." The scorn for the patriarchal rabbinical system is significant and echoes some of the struggles that characterized the secular branch of the gay community in Israel (fighting against patriarchal systems of their own, such as the army).

None of the three films discussed above provides the viewers or the protagonists with a definitive answer. In all the films, the characters remain in conflict about their standing in relation to two opposite poles: the rabbinical institution at one end and their own credo at the other. Even the happiness of Yehudit, by far the most open character, in marrying her partner is compromised by the absence of her parents from her wedding and the failure to obtain a rabbinical authorization. However, the making of those films, which open up a space from which one can start challenging this sensitive issue, should be seen as an achievement in itself. The religious stance on matters of homosexuality may not change any time soon, but attitudes of closeted religious homosexuals about themselves and their destiny hopefully will. It would be interesting to see if these three powerful films will inspire both filmmakers and gay men and women to further plow through the restrictions imposed by the religious establishment.

Toward Cinema of Marginality

The openness to previously unexplored themes such as religion and ethnicity in recent films, discussed above and in chapter 4, is evidence of the shift in focus that characterizes the more established gay groups in Israel. Gay filmmaking, it seems, can now attend to the "other" within the gay community. The self-reflexive nature and "narcissism" (Shohat 215) of Amos Guttman's *Drifting* (1983), for instance, and Eytan Fox's neocolonial view of Israelis of Mizrahi origin in *Gotta Have Heart* (1997) are replaced by filmmaking that tries to raise awareness of different forms of exclusion and to find solutions for it. This new sensitivity crosses the boundaries of the gay minority itself and links it to other minorities in Israeli society, whose members, like gay men and lesbians, have struggled to achieve recognition and rights while developing their own identity and culture. For, as different as Israeli minorities may be from one another, they all share the narrative of exclusion that has shaped their identity in relation to a discriminating establishment.

Gay men and lesbians constitute only one of many groups that have been formed as cultural, social, and, at times, political entities since the vision of the Israeli melting pot started to fade in the late 1970s. This process accelerated in the late 1980s and 1990s, years in which "the multicultural critique of the melting pot has been at the center of public and scholarly discourse in Israel" (Gutwein 223). Shifting the rigid boundaries between center and periphery, as well as the perceptions of normative and nonnormative practices in Israel, has had significant implications for both dominant and once-marginalized groups in Israel.

This book may open a window on to matters of representation of other minorities in Israel. Drawing on this study, and on similar projects that focus on cinematic representation of certain ethnic, racial, religious, or sexual groups within the new "multicultural" Israeli society, further exploration of its shifting demographic composition might illuminate the broader changes Israel has undergone in recent years. In order to do that, it would be highly significant, I believe, to look at these once-marginalized groups as a single movement that has changed not only the nature of Israeli film but also Israeli society as a whole. Serving as an important means by which to forge a national identity in the early decade of the state, Israeli cinema now functions not only as a reflection of it but also, in part, as a vehicle of its undoing.

In order to comprehend the connections between the many different groups that populate the State of Israel, it is important to explore the way in which they are bound together in relation to the "norm" and national core ideals. Cinema might serve as a means to start looking at these groups and subgroups—sexual, ethnic, and religious. By treating the films about their experiences as constituting a single project, one can come to challenge the very fundamentals of the culturally constructed Israeli identity. Orthodox Jews, members of the Druze community, and gay men and lesbians may not be obvious bedfellows in academic discussion. However, consideration of their combined cinematic representations and misrepresentations should shed new light on the mechanisms of exclusion and inclusion in contemporary Israeli society. In other words, it is by placing the array of voices expressed in Israeli cinema of the past twenty years within a larger and shared context—one that has been defined by a series of drastic changes that rapidly transformed the country and its culture—that one may point to the dramatic directions Israeli society has moved in since the late 1970s.

It would be interesting to see whether the particular case of gay filmmaking, studied in detail in this book, might become the base of a new study, larger in scope, which could further trace the links between an ever-changing Israeli society and its film industry. As more groups are now claiming recognition on the screen and in culture in general, Israeli cinema is becoming a major site where one can examine those shifts. New Israeli films, although they vary in their subject matter, production values, and political aspirations, all point to the fabricated nature of the "normative" Israeli ethos and the instability of the Israeli master narrative, in order to assert other "minor" identities and agendas.

Notes

Introduction

1. *Late Marriage* (*Hatuna Meucheret*, Dover Koshashvili, 2001), *Yossi and Jagger* (Eytan Fox, 2002), *Broken Wings* (*K'nafayim Shvurot*, Nir Bergman, 2003), *Walk on Water* (*Lalechet Al HaMayim*, Eytan Fox, 2004), *Beaufort* (Joseph Cedar, 2007), *Waltz with Bashir* (*Vals Im Bashir*, Ari Folman, 2008), and *Ajami* (Scandar Copti and Yaron Shani, 2009) are just some of the films that have garnered international critical and commercial acclaim in recent years.

2. In *The Will to Knowledge: The History of Sexuality Volume 1*, Michel Foucault claims, "The nineteenth-century homosexual became a personage, a past, a case history, and a childhood, in addition to being a type of life, a life form, and a morphology, with an indiscreet anatomy and possibly a mysterious physiology. [. . .] The sodomite had been a temporary aberration; the homosexual was now a species" (43). Foucault discusses the invention of the homosexual as a noun, and the creation of a homosexual type of human being, fixed in a web of discourses. Focusing on different sexualities as culture-specific practices, David M. Halperin (1990), following Foucault, has emphasized their shifts throughout history. Before the introduction of the term "homosexual," same-sex sexual encounters took place for centuries without the men and women involved defining themselves as such. In his essay on San Francisco's homosexual politics, for instance, Les Wright identifies a moment in which neither the men who had sex with other men nor the nature of their sexual activity was considered "homosexual." Wright says, "The Phallo-centric sexual economy of Gold Rush era San Francisco suggests that we distinguish between penetrative-masculine and receptive-feminine roles in male-male sexual encounters, and that sexual adventurism carried very different meanings to practitioners of the time than they do in American society today" (165).

3. *Stefan Braun* (Itamar Alkalay, 2006) is a recent documentary film based on home movies and archival materials that explores the nature of homosexual liaisons in the time before the gay movement was formed. It tells the story of Braun (1914–90), a Tel Aviv-based, world-renowned furrier, and chronicles his

201

relationship with his lover, Eliezer (Laci) Rath (Rath himself died shortly after the completion of the film and was buried next to his lifelong partner). Braun was married for a short while, but after the disintegration of his marriage he had relationships with men. Despite his employees' and close relatives' knowledge of his homosexuality, and their acceptance of it, some of the interviewees in the film, mostly fellow gay men of Braun's generation, emphasize that at that time homosexuality was considered a felony and that people had to meet in secrecy to avoid clashes with the authorities. Interestingly, the neutral terms with which Braun's relatives described his relationship with Rath did not stop them from challenging Braun's will, in which he bequeathed his fortune to his partner. After four years in the courts the family's appeal was finally rejected, a decision about which Rath declared, "Love won." The family's reaction to Braun's will suggests a refusal on their part to accept the possibility of a strong, lasting bond between two men. The courts' decision, however, made in the 1990s and acknowledging the legitimacy of the gay relationship between Braun and Rath, is further evidence of the changes in legislation and their impact on the standing of gay men and women in Israeli society.

4. It is important to note, though, that in some Western European countries, France, for instance, there was not always an agreement regarding the necessity of forming a gay community. As Michael D. Sibalis claims, "Critics argue that such initiatives are quintessentially American and insist that any talk of a 'gay community' in France smacks of American-style 'identity politics.' They portray the United States as a mosaic of competing minorities, each affirming its own identity and lobbying for its own special interests. [. . .] This runs counter to France's so-called 'republican tradition'" (35).

5. For more on the cultural ties between Israel and America and Israel's process of "Americanization," see Segev, *Elvis in Jerusalem.* For more on the history and future of the American gay movement, see D'Emilio and Freedman, *Intimate Matters* and Hirsch, *The Future of Gay Rights in America.*

6. As G. N. Giladi argues, the Israeli Black Panthers adopted this name "because they believed that there was no fundamental difference between antiblack discrimination in the United States and anti-Sephardi discrimination in Israel" (254).

7. I will discuss changes in legalization in relation to specific films. For an exhaustive discussion of the history of the gay movement in Israel and its legal battles, see the introductions to Fink and Press, and Walzer.

8. This, too, is similar to certain advances in the United States, where the revolutionary aspect of the movement in its early days never fully materialized. Of the American movement, John D'Emilio and Estelle B. Freedman have argued that by the mid-1970s "proponents spoke of fixed sexual orientation rather than polymorphous desires; they campaigned for civil rights legislation rather than a restructuring of family life and sexual socialization. Moreover, though few activists seemed aware of it, the gay movement in important ways was moving in the same direction as mainstream sexual culture" (323). As I will show

in the chapters to follow, the Israeli gay movement has also reoriented itself toward the center of culture, choosing to ally itself with, rather than oppose, national-Zionist values such as the army and the family.

9. In 1998 Revach wrote and directed *Double Bouskilla* (*Pa'amayim Buskilla*), which, with an almost identical plot line, can be read as an updated version of *The Hairdresser*.

10. It is little wonder that Dana International, probably the most famous Israeli transsexual, who won the Eurovision Song Contest for Israel in 1998, is of Yemenite origin, a fact that was stressed in the vast marketing machine formed around her and in her choice of repertoire. As her stage name (Dana was born Yaron Cohen) and life story suggest, Dana has been continuously breaking barriers. She has built her career by boldly crossing gender, ethnic, national, and sexual lines, constantly deconstructing categories and binaries. Although she has identified herself with many of these categories, she has committed herself to none. Shortly after her victory she declared, "I represent gays and lesbians from all over the world. [. . .] I represent the regular Israelis, all the Arabs, the Christians [. . .] everyone who wants to be represented by me" (qtd. in Fink and Press 14).

11. Asulin has since become a successful director of commercials and political broadcasts for election campaigns. In a conversation with me in March 2005, he claimed he did not have a copy of *A Different Shadow.* No copies of the film have been preserved in the state TV archive either.

12. The *Bourekas* films described, in the form of either comedy or melodrama, the conflict between European and Mizrahi Jews in the new state. The genre, which got its name from a local version of a popular Turkish pastry introduced to Israel by Jewish communities from the Balkans, was developed during the 1960s and 1970s following the enormous success of Ephraim Kishon's *Sallah Shabbati* (1964).

13. Featuring a transsexual character, Nadav Levitan's *The Mevorach Brothers* (*HaAchim Mevorach*, 2000) exceeds the "legitimate" gay male experience. It is made in the tradition of the *Bourekas* films of the 1960s and 1970s and focuses on the sexual escapades of three married middle-aged brothers. The transgender character is marginal and associated with the sex industry. Despite this unusual portrayal, the film had a negligible impact on both the gay community and the Israeli film industry.

14. It is interesting to note that the view of Jews as feminine is not the only stereotyped representation that has circulated historically. There is also the legacy of warriors such as Samson, Bar Kochba, and the Maccabees, who inspired Nordau's vision of Jewry of Muscles, or the rabbinic figures in the Middle Ages, who, according to Daniel Boyarin, "were, at the same time, generals in the armies of Spain, and of course they were just as Jewish as the *Yeshiva-Bokhur* 'sissies'" (Boyarin, *Unheroic Conduct* 24). However, these other models were forgotten in the European Diaspora in favor of the model of the *Yeshiva-Bokhur* "sissies." This was the model that the majority of Zionists, most of whom were

Ashkenazim, wished to modify. The production of a new Jewish identity in Palestine was proposed as an alternative to this feminine archetype.

15. It was not only European society that needed the "other" but also European Jews who were looking for ways to differentiate themselves from the gentiles. As Daniel Boyarin has observed, "Jewish society needed an image against which to define itself and produce the 'goy'—the hypermale—as its countertype. [. . .] This form of Jewish stereotyping of the gentile Other had enormous historical tenacity" (*Unheroic Conduct* 4).

16. George L. Mosse argues, "Sexual perversion was thought to be almost as threatening to middle-class life as the restlessness of the lower classes, and much more so than the arrogance of the aristocracy" (*Nationalism* 25).

Chapter 1

1. In her classic essay "Notes on 'Camp'" (1964), Susan Sontag attends to the problem of giving a precise definition to the term "sensibility." She writes, "A sensibility is almost, but not quite, ineffable. Any sensibility which can be crammed into the mold of a system, or handled with the rough tools of proof, is no longer a sensibility at all. It has hardened into an idea" (*Against Interpretation* 276).

2. For a thorough account of the history of Tel Aviv, see Schlör, *Tel Aviv: From Dream to City,* and Azaryahu, *Tel Aviv: The Real City.*

3. Although the gay community has a presence in Jerusalem and Haifa, and the former was also chosen to host World Pride in summer 2006 (cancelled in the end due to the Second Lebanon War), the majority of the community's activities take place in Tel Aviv.

4. Especially in Zohar's Tel Aviv trilogy, *Peeping Toms* (*Metzitzim*, 1972), *Big Eyes* (*Einayim G'dolot,* 1974), and *Save the Lifeguard* (*Hatzilu et HaMatzil*, 1976).

5. See Fink and Press, particularly the interview with Theo Mainz (321–64), and Kama, "From *Terra Incognita* to *Terra Firma*."

6. Although Guttman's films, with the exception of *Amazing Grace* (*Hessed Mufla,* 1992), are not extensively discussed in this chapter, I often refer to them, especially in relation to Ayelet Menahemi's *Crows* (*Orvim,* 1987).

7. Tsukerman's vision of New York City in *Liquid Sky* echoes that of experimental filmmaker Vivienne Dick, who, like Tsukerman, was an immigrant to the United States. The link to *Liquid Sky* is especially apparent in Dick's *Staten Island* (1978), a five-minute-long film in which an androgynous alien wearing a silver suit (Pat Place) is seen emerging from the sea on a beach littered with rubbish. Originally from Ireland, Dick was a prominent figure in the punk scene in New York City in the late 1970s and early 1980s, a scene that introduced a new approach to the arts later known as No Wave. Dick's films of that period were shot on Super 8, and their themes are concerned with sexual politics (featuring mostly women, they are seen from an exclusively female viewpoint), individual

and cultural transgression, and urban life. With their social commentary, commitment to giving voice to the outcast "other," and punk aesthetics—seen in films such as the aforementioned *Staten Island* and *She Had Her Gun Already* (1978)—they resemble and offer a broader context from which to consider Menahemi's outlook in *Crows*.

8. Turjeman's earlier appearances in two of Guttman's films further reinforce the link between Guttman's cinema and *Crows*.

9. The concept of Tel Aviv as a "rootless" city is prevalent in modern Israeli mythology and is captured in numerous novels and films. This myth has been countered in post-Zionist works such as Tamar Berger's *Dionysus at Dizengof Centre*. In her book, Berger tells the story of the deportation of the Palestinian population by the new Israeli state in 1948 through the archaeological history of Dizengof Centre, the first shopping mall in Tel Aviv. In his essay "Re-imagining the 'White City': The Politics of World Heritage Designation in Tel Aviv/Jaffa," Mark LeVine criticizes UNESCO's exclusion of Jaffa from its report on International Style architecture in the city. LeVine sees it as an emblem of the Zionist colonial discourse that portrayed Tel Aviv as a solely Jewish city raised "from the sand" and "erased" Jaffa from "the narrative of the region's modern architecture and planning" (222).

10. As Marianne Hirsch argues, "The novel of formation's concern is both *biographical* and *social*. Society is the novel's *antagonist* and is viewed as a school of life, a locus for experience. The spirit and values of the social order emerge through the fate of one representative individual. Consequently, the novel of formation does not represent a panorama of society and might thus be distinguished from the panoramic or social novel" (297).

11. See *The Economist*'s annual report for 2003.

12. See, for instance, Ofer Shelach's review in *Ma'ariv*, 29 Mar. 1992.

13. Yaron Peleg dedicates a chapter to *Ha'ir*'s innovative style and its cultural importance in his book *Israeli Culture between the Two Intifadas: A Brief Romance*.

14. See the conversation between Amir Kaminer and Rami Rotholtz, *Tel Aviv Magazine*, 25 Sep. 1992: 16–19.

15. Moshe was not the first gay column in Israeli print media. It was preceded by a series of articles in the now defunct *Davar*—a daily newspaper identified with the Labor Party—in 1980. Titled "Pictures from a Married Life" and written by Tuvia Mendelsohn, it documented a gay couple in Amsterdam. Focusing on the life of an Israeli immigrant disillusioned by his own state, Mendelsohn's column was very different from Uchovsky's, which proudly portrayed the life of a gay couple in Tel Aviv.

16. Most of today's senior journalists in Israel's national newspapers started their careers in the local press. They implemented the *mekomonim*'s distinctive writing style and agenda in the more "respectable" and wide-reaching national press.

17. See also my analysis of *Song of the Siren* in this chapter and chapter 3.

18. See, for example, Yehuda Stav's review in *Yediot Achronot,* 5 Apr. 1992.

19. Menahemi wrote and directed *Sharona, Motek,* Yaron wrote and directed *A Cat Operation,* and they collaborated on *Get:* Yaron wrote and Menahemi directed.

20. See Aaron Betsky, *Building Sex* xii, 28.

21. At the time of going to press, Dana International has been chosen to represent Israel—for the second time—in the 2011 Eurovision Song Contest to be held in Düsseldorf, Germany (www.haaretz.com/culture/dana-international-to-represent-israel-at-2011-eurovision-1.348097).

22. The influences of American cinema on Fox's work can be detected in all of his films (see chapter 3). Fox, who was born in the United States, tried in the late 1990s to start a career in Hollywood but eventually returned to direct Hebrew-speaking films in Israel (Karpel 40).

23. Advertising is one of the "creative industries" that are largely associated with both gay populations and urbanity. Linking the three, Richard Florida considers the substantial contribution of gay populations who belong to the "creative class" (a term that describes "the roughly one-third of U.S. and global workers who [. . . are] compensated monetarily for their creative output" [4]) to the economic growth of many US cities: "Gays [. . .] can be thought of as *canaries* of the creative economy, and serve as a strong signal of a diverse, progressive environment. Indeed, gays are frequently cited as harbingers of redevelopment and gentrification in distressed urban neighborhoods. The presence of gays in a metropolitan area also provides a barometer for a broad spectrum of amenities attractive to adults, especially those without children" (131).

24. Amit Kama argues that "AIDS has been scarcely discussed even within the gay community. The strategic ignorance evolved out of the perceived menace of further stigmatization of gay men. [. . .] To be sure, the vast social, economic, political, and moral [. . .] implications and ramifications of the pandemic in other Western countries (especially, the USA) have not been felt in Israel" ("From *Terra Incognita* to *Terra Firma*" 138).

25. The comic reference to the plastic doll is present as well, of course, making a point about the bar's patrons' unwholesomeness, as opposed to the wholesomeness that the American toy comes to represent.

26. The book was published in 1989. Progress in medical research and the way the disease is described in the media have obviously influenced the discourse on AIDS. Yet many of Sontag's observations regarding people's perception of AIDS still seem valid in contemporary Western culture.

27. In *Shuru* (Savi Gabizon, 1990), a film that offers a comic, satiric take on the spreading phenomenon of spiritual cults in 1990s Tel Aviv, the city is a site in which the Zionist movement has literally "lost its way." In one of the key scenes in the film, the members of a communal singing group—mostly identified with the Zionist, and particularly the kibbutz, ethos—are lost in the city asking for the assistance of locals, who are themselves in the midst of some sort of spiritual search, to find their way back to the bus that brought them

there. According to Kronish and Safirman, "The members of the choir, lost in the night, are all dressed in pure white, like angelic messengers of the socialist dream of the 'lost' pioneering generation" (127). The space left by the "disappearance" of the Zionist dream is filled by shady, pseudospiritual, pseudointellectual alternatives (such as the movement that the protagonist, a loser conman [Moshe Ivgi], establishes: a movement whose members believe that acting like "idiots" will bring them salvation).

Chapter 2

1. Guttman directed another film, *Sipurei Badim* (1978), a short documentary about the Israeli fashion industry, for channel 1, Israel's state—and at the time only—TV station. The title of the film means both "cloth tales" and "fabrications." *Badim* can also mean "screens." This is an intentional pun that relies on the multiple meanings of the word *badim* in Hebrew, similar to the etymological link between the words "fabric" and "fabrications" in English. The film, broadcast in June 1978, was poorly received by the critics. As a result Guttman omitted the film from his official filmography, and it was never shown again in his lifetime. It was found in the archives of the Israeli state channel in 2010 and was screened once in the Cinémathèque in Holon, Israel in December of that year.

2. Tal, in 1970, was the first man in Israel to undergo a sex-change operation (http://www.ynet.co.il/articles/0,7340,L-2827233,00.html). It was not only her sexual otherness that made her Guttman's favorite actress. Being a Romanian migrant who had trouble adjusting to life in the Levant, Tal, who spoke in a distinctive heavily accented Hebrew dotted with phrases in English and Romanian, echoed Guttman's own experiences.

Juliano Mer-Khamis, who later in his career was known as a political activist as much as an actor and a director, was shot dead on April 4, 2011, outside a theater that he founded in a refugee camp in the West Bank city of Jenin. At the time of going to press, Israeli security forces were investigating the circumstances of his murder (www.haaretz.com/news/national/israeli-actor-juliano-mer-khamis-shot-dead-in-jenin-1.354044).

3. Maria Laplace defines the "woman's film" as a film "distinguished by its female protagonist, female point of view and its narrative that most often revolves around the traditional realms of women's experience: the familial, the domestic, the romantic—those arenas where love, emotion and relationships take precedence over action and events" (139).

4. Not only by the heterosexual majority but also by gay men themselves. In Richard Dyer's words, "Being a gay man is not the same as being a straight woman, yet when we get together, we often talk as if it were" (*The Culture of Queers* 47).

5. Although the 1950s were characterized by more tolerant attitudes toward sex and a growing media interest in sexual behaviors, existing patriarchal views of sex prevailed. Barbara Klinger argues that "the term 'sexual liberalism' did not connote complete freedom or open-mindedness in this arena of human

affairs. Its liberal dimensions, that is, a greater and more open emphasis on heterosexual pleasures of certain kinds, were constrained by a series of boundaries, including the oft-mentioned double standard and the demarcation of other sexualities, particularly homosexuality and African American sexuality, as deviant" (*Melodrama and Meaning* 52).

6. Susan Sontag suggested camp was "one way of seeing the world as an aesthetic phenomenon. That way, the way of Camp, is not in terms of beauty, but in terms of the degree of artifice, of stylization" (*Against Interpretation* 277). Following Sontag's notes on camp, I would like to argue that as much as Guttman's films, *Bar 51* in particular, make use of camp sensibility in their "love of the exaggerated, the 'off'" (*Against Interpretation* 279) and in that they incarnate "a victory of 'style' over 'content'" (*Against Interpretation* 287), they are not wholly camp. Since "Camp is playful, anti-serious" (*Against Interpretation* 288), it cannot appertain to all of Guttman's work, which was very much engaged with life's tragic aspects. As for the use of the term "camp" in postmodern culture, it is important to note that Sontag's seminal essay was later criticized by queer theorists like Moe Meyer, who argued that in Sontag's version, the term's homosexual connotations are "downplayed, sanitized, and made safe for public consumption" (7) and was part of "the heterosexual/Pop colonization of Camp in the 1960s" (10). For more on this debate, see Meyer (ed.), *The Politics and Poetics of Camp*.

7. Like Guttman, Fassbinder's films challenged the language of national cinema in Germany at the time. Thomas Elsaesser has noted that Fassbinder "is still a most unlikely candidate for pioneering a new national cinema: he was completely outside the traditions of cinematic realism" (*Fassbinder's Germany* 21).

8. The relationship between Apolonia and Thomas echoes that between the aging cleaner and the young Moroccan immigrant in Fassbinder's *Fear Eats the Soul* (1973), a film loosely based on Douglas Sirk's *All That Heaven Allows* (1955). All three films portray the doomed relationship between two parties who are excluded, for different reasons, from mainstream society. In Sirk's it is a bonding between a rich widow and a gardener in class-obsessed 1950s American suburban culture, whereas Fassbinder's film deals with the formation of an impossible relationship between a young Arab and an older lower-class woman against the backdrop of racist German society. According to Thomas Elsaesser, "The plot is similar to Sirk's *All That Heaven Allows* [. . .] but it is obvious that Fassbinder, choosing a much older actress and making his male lead a Moroccan, sharpened the conflict and with it, the unease initially provoked in the spectator when the couple break so many taboos" (*Fassbinder's Germany* 281). Guttman's theme is closer to that of Fassbinder. Like Fassbinder, he emphasizes not only the age and class differences between the two but also their different ethnic origins. Unlike Fassbinder, however, he makes the exploitative element in the relationship between Thomas and Apolonia clear from the outset.

9. Things have long since changed, as exemption from compulsory military service—through a psychiatric diagnosis, for example—became an easier

procedure as well as more common and accepted. In certain circles, it is even considered to have a certain "rebellious" allure. Furthermore, the escalation in the tension between Israelis and Palestinians in Israel and the occupied territories and the growing criticism of Israeli actions have caused a wave of "refuseniks," that is, soldiers in conscript service or reserve soldiers who refuse, for reasons of conscience, to serve in the occupied territories or at all, for which they are usually sent to prison.

10. Fink and Press argue that "according to a 1983 directive, every Israeli soldier known or suspected to be gay had to undergo examination by a mental health officer and the security clearance department" (10). In the teen comedy *Private Popsicle* (*Sapiches*, Boaz Davidson, 1984), the fourth in the popular *Lemon Popsicle* series, two of the protagonists pretend they are a gay couple to get a sick leave in the boot camp where they serve. It was only in June 1993 that a new policy was adopted, and many of the restrictions on the recruitment of gay men and lesbians to the army and their disposition within the forces were lifted (Kama, "From *Terra Incognita* to *Terra Firma*" 147). Since 1998 there have been no official restrictions at all on gay men and lesbians in the army. See Fink and Press, and Walzer.

11. Similarly, love affairs between Israeli-Jewish women and Palestinian men in "forbidden love" Israeli films symbolize, according to Yosefa Loshitzky, "a consolidation of a coalition of minorities against the dominance of the Israeli man" (*Identity Politics* 161).

12. Guttman's *Himmo, King of Jerusalem* and *Amazing Grace* did get government grants.

13. It is also important to note that *Drifting* won two important Israeli awards in 1983, given by the Israeli Film Centre, the Ministry of Industry and Trade, and the Ministry of Education and Culture. The film was awarded a special prize for outstanding achievement in a first feature, and its star, Yonatan Segal, was named best actor (Abileah). The film also garnered favorable reviews outside Israel. The *Village Voice*, for instance, wrote that "Guttman has heroically said to hell with both conformity and traditional masculinity, and made an unprogrammatic film in a country where much of the cinema is propaganda meant to herd the citizenry, to uplift and unify" (Pally).

14. In this respect, Guttman's difficulties in gaining funding and pleasing different subgroups within the gay community were similar to experiences of other non-Israeli filmmakers who struggled to finance their gay films at the time. The British Film Institute Production Board, for instance, refused to assist director Ron Peck with the production of his debut feature *Nighthawks* (1978), which was eventually produced on a meager budget collected from private investors. The film has been billed since its release as the first British gay film. It is likely that the film had some influence over Guttman. Both filmmakers expressed, through aesthetics and narrative, feelings of isolation and loneliness as inherent parts of the gay experience. Like Guttman's films, *Nighthawks* was criticized at the time of its release by gay groups, which protested against what

they perceived as a negative portrayal of gay life (as reported by Peck to Matt Lucas on the DVD edition of *Nighthawks* [2005]).

15. Interestingly, despite a growing interest in Guttman's work after his death, his films were only released on DVD format in 2007.

16. Richard Dyer maintains that "there is nothing about gay people's physiognomy that declares them gay, no equivalents to the biological markers of sex and race. There are signs of gayness, a repertoire of gestures, expressions, stances, clothing, and even environments [. . .] that bespeaks gayness, but these are cultural forms designed to show what the person's person alone does not show: that he or she is gay" (*The Matter of Images* 19). This is best shown in *Far from Heaven* (2002), Todd Haynes's tribute to Douglas Sirk's *All That Heaven Allows* (1955), in which Frank Whitaker (Dennis Quaid), a closeted gay man, is far more accepted by society even after his homosexuality is revealed (he is also the only character who experiences a "happy ending" of a sort, being able to establish a relationship with his young male lover), whereas the other two protagonists—Cathy Whitaker (Julianne Moore), Frank's wife, and Raymond Deagan (Dennis Haysbert), her African American gardener/friend—remain alone and in despair. Frank's unremarkable homosexuality is much less of a threat than Raymond's blackness or the wife's desire for him. In the final scene—at the Hartford railroad station where Raymond and his daughter board a train to leave for Baltimore following the anticipated failure of his and Cathy's budding relationship and the racist attack on his daughter—the two, harboring a forbidden desire for each other, are quite literally made to vanish from the diegesis. Special emphasis is given to their movement (either real, in the case of Raymond, who is on the moving train, or illusory, in the case of Cathy, who seems as if she is moving by the motion of the train's cars) in opposite directions, pulling them apart. Conversely, Frank is seen in the preceding scene securely placed in what seems to be a hotel room with his new male partner. As Mary Ann Doane observes, "In Cathy's point-of-view shot, Raymond is taken farther and farther by the train's movement; in Raymond's point of view, Cathy becomes smaller and smaller. [. . .] It is she who seems to embody movement into the distance rather than the train. [. . .] As Cathy walks away, she parallels the yellow line on the platform and the train tracks, as well as the line of regularized pillars and the lights on the ceiling, all aiming toward the same vanishing point in what is almost a parody of linear perspective. Desire and its denial are subject to the mathematical laws of an infinitely receding distance, the inevitable separation of melodrama becoming the trauma of an expansive space" ("Pathos and Pathology" 11).

17. On the politics of passing in Sirk's *Imitation of Life*, see Mary Ann Doane, chapter 11 in *Femmes Fatales: Feminism, Film Theory, Psychoanalysis*.

18. In the introduction to his collection of interviews with Sirk, conducted in the early 1970s, Jon Halliday writes, "Sirk asked me to hold off writing about the fact that Rock Hudson, who was then still alive, was homosexual, until all concerned were dead" (4).

19. Sirk said about Hudson, "Rock, although homosexual, exerted a powerful influence on women. I don't only mean on the screen, where you can create an illusion. [. . .] But in real life, too" (Halliday 107). The public's "intensely fantasmatic investment in Hudson's particular image of hetero-masculinity," Richard Meyer argues, was reflected in the "tone of betrayal which underwrote many of the commentaries on Hudson's AIDS" in the summer of 1985 (278).

20. Discussing the hostile reaction to the news of Hudson's secret homosexuality and AIDS (see previous note), Richard Meyer suggests that "Hudson's closet was not an effect of individual choice but of homophobia and compulsory heterosexuality, systems of surveillance enforced with particular ferocity in 1950s America" (279).

21. Unlike Sirk's films, in which, according to Fassbinder, "not one of the protagonists realizes that all these things—thoughts, wishes, dreams—grow directly out of their social reality or are manipulated by it" (*The Anarchy of the Imagination* 87).

22. One can find Guttman's interest in portraying this ambiguity tangentially echoing "Sirkean" themes. As Jon Halliday notes, Sirk's preference for complex, incoherent, even split, characters derived from his own experience: his life in Germany at the time of the Nazi party coming to power, his second marriage to a Jewish woman and his subsequent separation from his son, whom he was not allowed to see (the son was later killed on the Russian front), and his escape to America. Halliday writes about how Sirk once told him, "There are two Douglas Sirks" (4). This remark can summarize, to a certain extent, the ambiguous persona that Guttman himself had. In an interview with Halliday, Sirk says, "The type of character I always have been interested in, in the theatre as well as in the movies, and which I also tried to retain in melodrama, is the doubtful, the ambiguous, the uncertain. Uncertainty, and the vagueness of men's aims, are central to many of my films, however hidden these characteristics may be" (46).

23. Developed in the journals *Screen* and *Screen Education,* screen theory, according to Hall, "Though principally relating to film texts and practices [. . .] has far-reaching implications for the analysis of all signifying practices, as well as for the debates on the problem of language/ideology and representation. This body of work [. . .] draws extensively on recent French theoretical writing in a number of different fields: film theory [. . .] the theory of ideology [. . .] the psychoanalytic writings of the Lacan group, and recent theories of language and discourse" ("Recent Developments" 157).

24. The film won the Silver Palm in Valencia (1992), Honorable Mention in Houston (1992) and Turin (1992), the Wolgin award in Jerusalem (1992), and the Critics' Jury Prize in Haifa (1993) (Kronish and Safirman 190).

Chapter 3

1. By Israeli nationalism I refer to that which was defined in 1948. Neo-Zionism may indeed be seen as a typical form of expansive nationalism, one

that identifies a "greater Israel" of the 1948 borders *and* the territories occupied in 1967. However, its "messianic" emphasis on the biblical lands takes it beyond modern forms of nationalism.

2. Daniel Gutwein argues that "despite its decline, Zionism, founded as it is on values of national and social solidarity, is still the hegemonic ethos in Israel, providing legitimacy to its social structure and values" (225).

3. See Daniel Gutwein, "From Melting Pot to Multiculturalism; or, The Privatization of Israeli Identity," *Israeli Identity in Transition* 215–31.

4. It was announced in December 2010 that director Eytan Fox is planning a sequel to *Yossi and Jagger* to begin ten years after the death of Jagger. Ohad Knoller will reprise his role as Yossi (www.haaretz.com/print-edition/news/news-in-brief-1.328488).

5. As Uri Ram states, this war was the first in Israeli history to be declared "a war of choice." The war was deeply contested in Israel. The resistance to it marked "the genesis of an autonomous civil society in Israel, where state and society had usually been intimately meshed" (26).

6. *Yossi and Jagger* is different in its approach not only from *Time Off* but also from another early Fox film, *Song of the Siren.* In his first feature film, Fox voices a fierce critique of both the military and its dominance in Israeli society and of the importance given to matters of national security, often at the expense of civil rights (see chapter 1).

7. In Hebrew, Kings of Israel Square, where Rabin was assassinated. The name of the square was changed shortly after the assassination to Kikar Rabin.

8. Things are changing, of course, and the success of Dana International, both a transsexual and of Mizrahi origin, is one prominent example of a shift in attitude and visibility within the Israeli gay community.

9. Like Merito, Mitzi is a non-Israeli name. The film, however, focuses on the formation of masculine identities. Thus, the male characters' names bear a greater symbolic significance than Mitzi's.

10. In her analysis of *My Michael* (Dan Wolman, 1974), Yosefa Loshitzky observes the eroticization of the "noble savage" in the film, in this case manifested by a fantasized interracial relationship between the Ashkenazi Jew female protagonist and Arab twin brothers. The film is an example of the shifting perception of the Orient by the Ashkenazi, Western-inclined elite in Israel: if at the beginning of Zionist settlement in Palestine, before the establishment of the state, the view of the "other" was a "romantic utopian view," it was gradually replaced by "the fetishization of 'low-class' (both Arabs and Mizrahi Jews) 'objects of desire'" (*Identity Politics* 99).

11. A similar binary regarding black men is delineated by Isaac Julien and Kobena Mercer. They argue that "the gay subculture [. . .] is dominated by the needs and demands of white males. Black men fit into this territory by being confined to a narrow repertoire of types—the supersexual stud and the sexual savage on the one hand, the delicate and exotic 'Mizrahi' on the other. The repetition of these stereotypes betrays the circulation of 'colonial fantasy'" (qtd. in Gove 11).

12. A possible explanation for the less graphic sex scene in *Yossi and Jagger* compared to that in *Gotta Have Heart,* made five years earlier, is Fox's growing desire to reach wider, nongay audiences as well as his more established standing in the Israeli film industry.

13. See chapter 5 of Raz Yosef's *Beyond Flesh* 154–63.

14. Avner Bernheimer, who wrote the script for *Yossi and Jagger,* explored similar themes in his later TV series *Until the Wedding* (*Ad HaHatuna,* two seasons broadcast on Israel's commercial channel 2, 2008–2010, created with Anat Shenhav-Weizman), which centers on several relationships, one of which is gay. The gay couple, Amir (Niv Raz) and Harel (Ofer Shechter), keeps their relationship strong while those of their friends and relatives around them are disintegrating. The planned wedding of Aya (Tal Lifschitz), Harel's sister, and Ran (Ohad Knoller) falls through after she has an affair with Ran's best friend; their roommate is having a secret relationship with a married man; Harel's parents are deciding to get a divorce; and Ran's parents are experiencing problems in their married life around issues of infidelity. Whereas the first season focuses mainly on the heterosexual relationship of Aya and Ran and its (ultimately unfulfilled) realization in marriage, in the second season equal attention is given to each of the relationships, of which Amir and Harel's is one of the strongest. They even reject the option of an "open relationship," which is often associated with gay culture and a more permissive approach to sex and which the couple briefly explores in the first season, in favor of a committed partnership.

15. Describing almost every Hollywood (i.e., commercial) film, Harry Benshoff and Sean Griffin argue that "when queer characters were depicted, they were usually relegated to minor parts and/or were the butt of jokes, by contrast reinforcing the central and socially appropriate nature of the heterosexual love story" (6).

16. The colonel's remark is an allusion to the famous sequence in Francis Ford Coppola's *Apocalypse Now* (1979), in which American helicopters fire missiles and drop mustard yellow smoke bombs while Colonel Kilgore, played by Robert Duvall, announces, "I love the smell of napalm in the morning." This reference suggests that the IDF actions in Lebanon were comparable to the American army's actions in Vietnam, a comment that stands as one of the very few in the film made against war and its implications.

17. In recent years Pick has been mostly known for writing the music for the song "Diva," with which Dana International won the Eurovision Song Contest in 1998 (see the introduction) and for performing as one of the judges on *Kochav Nolad,* the Israeli version of *American Idol.*

Chapter 4

1. See Yosefa Loshitzky, *Identity Politics on the Israeli Screen* 72–89.

2. For more on autobiographical films—or "I Movies"—in Israeli cinema, see Duvdevani, *First Person Camera.*

3. These achievements have recently been summed up in the documentary *Gay Days* (*HaZman HaVarod*, 2009), named after Aguda's (now defunct) magazine. The film was directed by Yair Qedar, who was also the first editor of that publication. The release of the film (it was first screened as part of gay pride events in Israel in June 2009) may suggest that the community can now look outward and that its interests and concerns should expand further.

4. The filmmaker Yair Lev, for instance, whose film *Yakantalisa* (1996) is discussed in this chapter, said in an interview with *Zman Tel Aviv* that his idea of making a documentary came after his attempts to raise money for his fiction feature film fell through (Lev Ari 45).

5. I use the term "performativity" after Judith Butler. Suggesting we perform our identity (gendered or other), rather than express it, Butler argues that "there is no preexisting identity by which an act or attribute might be measured" (*Gender Trouble* 180).

6. It is important to note that although Waugh focuses mainly on the volatile boundaries between fiction and nonfiction and between realism and artifice in gay filmmaking, this blurring of genres and cinematic modes can also be found outside the gay or queer domain. In Israel, as in other places, "hybrid cinema" has also served filmmakers who have explored their ethnic identity, sometimes in conjunction with feminism, such as Hanna Azulay Hasfari, who wrote the script for the film *Shchur* (1994).

7. For a thorough discussion on representations and metaphors of AIDS, see Susan Sontag, *AIDS and Its Metaphors;* Marita Sturken, *Tangled Memories;* and Douglas Crimp (ed.), *AIDS: Cultural Analysis, Cultural Activism.*

8. As Janet Jakobsen and Beverly Seckinger have argued, the low-quality image of the camcorder had, by the late 1980s, become a familiar means for signifying "realness." It has become such an acknowledged signifier that nowadays it is a widely used device on television commercials and reality TV shows to signify "unproduced, raw reality" (150, 156n22).

9. Following Catherine Russell and Alisa S. Lebow, we can also think of these films as "autoethnographic," in that "cultural concerns are explored or displayed through the representation of the self" (Lebow xv). Lebow takes Russell's assertion that "autobiography becomes auto-ethnography at the point where the film or video maker understands his or her personal history to be implicated in larger social formations and historical processes" (qtd. in Lebow xv) and expands it to matters of reception as well, that is, when a film in the first person is read as such by the viewer or the critic.

10. The planned screening of the film in spring 2005 in Doc-Aviv, a documentary film festival held in the Tel Aviv Cinémathèque, was cancelled to comply with the demands of the filmmaker's family. And in July of that year the family members threatened legal action if the special screening of the film to members of the Israeli Film Academy was not cancelled (Pinto).

11. The film is named after the family business, an old-fashioned pension (boardinghouse) established by Goldberg's grandparents, where parts of the film were shot. Literally, the word means either "convalescent" or "salubrious."

12. The mother's central role in the series is further emphasized in Heymann's latest film, *I Shot My Love* (2010), which is largely based on *The Way Home*. The former expands the story of the relationship of Heymann and his German partner (which in the series is told in the last two episodes) and examines it in relation to the German roots of Heymann's mother (both her parents immigrated to Palestine from Germany in the 1930s). She thus becomes a central link in Heymann's own attempt to reconnect with his lost European roots, which is also demonstrated in his most recent relationship.

13. Camatoy was found dead in November 2007 in Al-Wada, Dubai. He had moved there a few weeks earlier to take a job as a hairdresser (http://groups.yahoo.com/group/transgendernews/message/24517; www.khaleejtimes.com/DisplayArticlenew.asp?section=theuae&xfile=data/theuae/2007/november/theuae_november567.xml).

14. Kotzer made other films in a similar fashion: *Gay Games* (*Mis'hakim Alizim*, 1999), which follows the Israeli team to the Gay Olympics in Amsterdam in 1998; *Amos Guttman: Film Director* (*Amos Guttman: Bamay Kolnoa*, 1997) on the late filmmaker (see also chapter 2); and *Death Cause: Homophobia* (*Sibat HaRetzach: Homophobia*, 2003), which deals with the increasing number of murders of closeted older homosexual men by younger hustlers with whom they had established steady relationships.

15. AIDS is also the theme of Dan Wolman's *Tied Hands* (*BeYadayim Kshurot*), released ten years after both *Yakantalisa* and *Positive Story*, in 2006. In the film, the mother of a young man who is dying of the disease goes out in an attempt to find marijuana to ease her son's pain. In her nocturnal journey to the darker corners of Tel Aviv, she reflects on her complex relationship with her son. The film is impressive with its strong performances but, although made in recent years, associates the disease with themes of death, despair, and darkness, rather than the hope for survival that can be found in *Positive Story*, for instance.

16. It is mainly with the death of international pop star Ofra Haza of the disease in 2000 that the discourse on AIDS in Israel has expanded further to also include heterosexual victims.

17. Itamar and Kai's earlier attempt to have a child is revealed at a visit to the grave of a close friend of theirs in an early scene. This attempt ended in a miscarriage that led, according to Itamar, to their friend's death. In this case, Kai was the prospective biological father of the gay couple's child, a fact that suggests that initially no significance was attached to who would donate the sperm.

18. Sara Ahmed, after Lisa Duggan (2003) and Judith Halberstam (2005), refers to this tendency as "homonormativity" (172), "a politics of following the straight line even as a deviant body" (173). The effect of this, according to Ahmed, however, is limited: "It is hardly likely that attempts to follow the straight line as gays and lesbians will get you too many points" as "inhabiting forms that do not extend your shape can produce queer effects, even when you think you are 'lining up.' There is hope in such failure, even if we reject publicly (as we must) this sexual as well as social conservatism" (174).

19. Yosefa Loshitzky has observed the paradoxical image of the bulldozer in the film *Hamsin*, which critiques the confiscation of Arab lands by Jews. Whereas within the Zionist iconography the bulldozer symbolizes the building of a new Jewish homeland, for the Palestinians it "signifies the Zionist passion to expand and demolish traditional, agrarian, rural Palestine" (*Identity Politics* 121).

20. Flanders is not seen in any frame, but her voice is sometimes heard. Furthermore, the texts that appear on the screen often contain information about her. She is, therefore, an active participant in the film, and her provisional presence in Israel, and in the frame, can be read as carrying a symbolic meaning.

21. Their full (and real, in the case of Selim) names, Ezra Nawi and Fuad Musa, have been given in articles in the press. Nawi is also the subject of Nissim Mossek's documentary *Citizen Nawi* (*HaEzrach Nawi*, 2007), which focuses on Nawi's battle against the occupation, homophobia, and the way Israeli authorities treat political activists. It was recently reported that Nawi has been found guilty of assaulting a police officer who was demolishing a Palestinian house in July 2007. He was sentenced to one month's imprisonment in October 2009.

22. As Jeffrey Weeks has argued, Muslim culture allows, or at least condones, male same-sex activity under certain clearly defined limitations, one of which dictates that Muslim men be the penetrators. In this culture, Weeks maintains, there is "no concept of 'the homosexual,' except where it has been imported from the West, no notion of exclusive homosexuality, and no gay way of life" ("Foreword" x).

Chapter 5

1. Israel has landed three consecutive Academy Awards nominations for best foreign language film between 2008 and 2010—*Beaufort* (Joseph Cedar, 2007), *Waltz with Bashir* (Ari Folman, 2008), and *Ajami* (Scandar Copti and Yaron Shani, 2009), and Samuel Maoz's *Lebanon* (2009) won the Golden Lion at the 2009 Venice Film Festival.

2. Hochner also contributed a piece to the anthology of shorts *Fucking Different Tel Aviv* (2008), the third edition of a conceptual series (the first two editions were filmed in Berlin and New York), in which lesbian directors create short films about gay men and vice versa. Varying in genre, the films (whose running times are between three and seven minutes) constitute a mélange of fictional, documentary, and experimental films, a gamut that challenges the quest to define a singular gay and/or lesbian Israeli sensibility.

Filmography

ALL FILMS WERE PRODUCED IN ISRAEL, UNLESS OTHERWISE STATED.

Adama, Helmer Lerski, 1947
Ajami, Scandar Copti and Yaron Shani, Israel/Germany, 2009
All That Heaven Allows, Douglas Sirk, USA, 1955
Almost There [*Kim'at Sham*], Sigal Yehuda and Joelle Alexis, 2004
Amazing Grace [*Hessed Mufla*], Amos Guttman, 1992
Amos Guttman: Film Director [*Amos Guttman: Bamay Kolnoa*], Ran Kotzer, 1997
Antarctica, Yair Hochner, 2008
Apocalypse Now, Francis Ford Coppola, USA, 1979
The Aunt from Argentina [*HaDoda MeArgentina*], George Ovadia, 1983
Bar 51 (also known as *Orphans of the Storm* and *Sister of Love*), Amos Guttman, 1985
Beaufort, Joseph Cedar, 2007
Big Eyes [*Einayim G'dolot*], Uri Zohar, 1974
Big Girl [*Yalda G'dola*], Nirit Yaron, 1987
Blow Job, Andy Warhol, USA, 1964
Blow Up, Michaelangelo Antonioni, UK, 1966
Broken Wings [*K'nafayim Shvurot*], Nir Bergman, 2003
The Bubble [*HaBuah*], Eytan Fox, 2006
Citizen Nawi [*HaEzrach Nawi*], Nissim Mossek, 2007
Cloth Tales [*Sipurei Badim*], Amos Guttman, 1978
Crows [*Orvim*], Ayelet Menahemi, 1987
Death Cause: Homophobia [*Sibat HaRetzach: Homophobia*], Ran Kotzer, 2003
Despair [*Eine Reise ins Licht*], Rainer Werner Fassbinder, West Germany/France, 1977
Desperately Seeking Susan, Susan Seidelman, USA, 1985
A Different Shadow [*Tsel Acher*], Ron Asulin, 1983

A Different War [*Milchama Acheret*], Nadav Gal, 2004
Dizengof 99, Avi Nesher, 1979
Double Bouskilla [*Pa'amayim Buskilla*], Ze'ev Revach, 1998
The Dress (also known as *Boys and Girls*) [*HaSimla*], Judd Ne'eman, 1969
Drifting (also known as *Afflicted*) [*Nagua*] (short), Amos Guttman, 1979
Drifting (also known as *Afflicted*) [*Nagua*] (long), Amos Guttman, 1983
Edinburgh Doesn't Wait for Me (also known as *Don't Cry for Me, Edinburgh*) [*Edinburgh Lo Mechaka Li*], Erez Laufer, 1996
Eyes Wide Open [*Eynayim Pkuhot*], Haim Tabakman, Israel/Germany/France, 2009
Family Matters [*Mishpuche*], David Noy and Yoram Ivry, 2004
Far from Heaven, Todd Haynes, USA, 2002
Fear Eats the Soul [*Angst essen Seele auf*], Rainer Werner Fassbinder, West Germany, 1973
Female Trouble, John Waters, USA, 1974
Fine Trouble (also known as *Beautiful Trouble*) [*Eize Yofi Shel Tsarot*], Assi Dayan, 1976
Fireworks, Kenneth Anger, USA, 1947
Flaming Creatures, Jack Smith, USA, 1963
Florentine (TV series), Eytan Fox, 1997
Fucking Different Tel Aviv, various filmmakers, Israel/Germany, 2008
Gan, Ruth Shatz and Adi Barash, Israel/Canada, 2003
Gay Days [*HaZman HaVarod*], Yair Qedar, 2009
Gay Games [*Mis'hakim Alizim*], Ran Kotzer, 1999
Give Me Ten Desperate Men [*Havu Li Asara Anashim Meyuashim*], Pierre Zimmer, 1964
Good Boys [*Yeladim Tovim*], Yair Hochner, 2005
Gotta Have Heart [*Ba'al Ba'al Lev*], Eytan Fox, 1997
The Hairdresser [*Sapar Nashim*], Ze'ev Revach, 1984
Hairspray, John Waters, USA, 1988
HaMavri, Ayal Goldberg, 2001
Hamsin, Daniel Wachsmann, 1982
He Who Steals from a Thief Is Not Guilty [*Gonev MiGanav Patur*], Ze'ev Revach, 1977
Hide and Seek [*Machbo'im*], Dan Wolman, 1980
Himmo, King of Jerusalem (also known as *Bell Room*) [*Himmo, Melech Yerushalayim*], Amos Guttman, 1987
I Shot My Love, Tomer Heymann, Israel/Germany, 2010
Imitation of Life, Douglas Sirk, USA, 1959
It Kinda Scares Me [*Tomer VeHasrutim*], Tomer Heymann, 2001
Keep Not Silent (also known as *Ortho-Dykes*) [*Et She'ahava Nafshi*], Ilil Alexander, 2004
Kuni Lemel in Tel Aviv, Yoel Zilberg, 1978
Last Post [*Michtav Meuchar*], Anat Dotan, 1997

The Last Winter [*HaChoref HaAcharon*], Riki Shelach Nissimoff, Israel/USA, 1983
Late Marriage [*Hatuna Meucheret*], Dover Koshashvili, 2001
Lebanon, Samuel Maoz, Israel/France/UK, 2009
Life According to Agfa [*HaChayim Al Pi Agfa*], Assi Dayan, 1992
Liquid Sky, Slava Tsukerman, USA, 1982
The Lover [*HaMehaev*], Michal Bat-Adam, 1986
Mamma Mia!, Phyllida Lloyd, UK/USA/Germany, 2008
Mary Lou [*Tamid Oto Halom*] (TV series), Eytan Fox, 2009
The Mevorach Brothers [*HaAchim Mevorach*], Nadav Levitan, 2000
Moments (also known as *Each Other*) [*Rega'im*], Michal Bat-Adam, 1979
My Michael [*Michael Sheli*], Dan Wolman, 1975
New York Stories, Martin Scorsese, Francis Ford Coppola, Woody Allen, USA, 1989
The Night Soldier [*Hayal HaLayla*], Dan Wolman, 1984
Nighthawks, Ron Peck, UK, 1978
Nora Helmer, Rainer Werner Fassbinder, West Germany, 1973
On a Narrow Bridge [*Gesher Tsar Meod*], Nissim Dayan, 1985
Paper Dolls [*Bubot Niyar*], Tomer Heymann, 2006
Past Continuous [*Zichron Dvarim*], Amos Gitai, Israel/France/Italy, 1995
Peeping Toms [*Metzitzim*], Uri Zohar, 1972
Positive Story [*Sipur Chiuvi*], Ran Kotzer, 1996
Private Popsicle [*Sapiches*], Boaz Davidson, 1984
Querelle, Rainer Werner Fassbinder, West Germany/France, 1982
The Quest for the Missing Piece [*Be'ikvot HaChaticha HaChasera*], Oded Lotan, 2007
Repeat Dive [*Tslila Hozeret*], Shimon Dotan, 1982
Repeat Premieres [*Premierot Hozrot*], Amos Guttman, 1976
A Safe Place [*Makom Batuach*], Amos Guttman, 1977
Sallah Shabbati, Ephraim Kishon, 1964
Save the Lifeguard [*Hatzilu et HaMatzil*], Uri Zohar, 1976
Say Amen! [*Tagid Amen!*], David Deri, 2005
The Secrets [*HaSodot*], Avi Nesher, Israel/France, 2006
Send Me an Angel [*Shlach Li Mal'ach*], Nir Ne'eman, 2003
Shchur, Shmuel Hasfari, 1994
She Had Her Gun Already, Vivienne Dick, USA, 1978
Shuru, Savi Gabizon, 1990
Smithereens, Susan Seidelman, USA, 1982
Snoker [*Hagiga BaSnoker*], Boaz Davidson, 1975
Song of the Siren [*Shirat HaSirena*], Eytan Fox, 1994
Srugim (TV series), Eliezer Shapira, 2008–present
Staten Island, Vivienne Dick, USA, 1978
Stefan Braun, Itamar Alkalay, 2006
Superstar: The Karen Carpenter Story, Todd Haynes, USA, 1987

Filmography

Tarnation, Jonathan Caouette, USA, 2004

Tel Aviv Stories (also known as *Three Women* and *Tales of Tel Aviv*) [*Sipurei Tel Aviv*], Nirit Yaron and Ayelet Menahemi, 1992

They Call Me Shmil [*Kor'im Li Shmil*], George Ovadia, 1973

Tied Hands [*BeYadayim Kshurot*], Dan Wolman, 2006

Time Off [*After*], Eytan Fox, 1990

Trembling Before G-D, Sandi Simcha DuBowski, Israel/USA/France, 2001

The Troupe (also known as *Sing Your Heart Out*) [*HaLahaka*], Avi Nesher, 1978

Until the Wedding [*Ad HaHatuna*] (TV series), Oded Lotan, 2008–2010

Walk on Water [*Lalechet Al HaMayim*], Eytan Fox, Israel/Sweden, 2004

Waltz with Bashir [*Vals Im Bashir*], Ari Folman, Israel/Germany/France/USA, 2008

The Way Home [*BaDerech HaBaita*] (TV series), Tomer Heymann, 2009

Weekend Circles [*Ma'agalim Shel Shishi-Shabat*], Idit Shechori, 1980

Yakantalisa, Yair Lev, 1996

Yoman [*Diary*] (six installments), David Perlov, 1973–1983

Yossi and Jagger, Eytan Fox, 2002

Zero Degrees of Separation, Elle Flanders, Canada, 2005

Bibliography

Selected Newspaper Articles, Interviews, and Reviews

Abileah, Rudi. "Awards." *Screen International* 24 Sep. 1983: 10.

Abramov, Eti, Ziv Cohen, and Ogen Shapira. "HaMa'apecha HaVrooda" [The Pink Revolution]. *Tel Aviv Magazine* 18 June 1999.

Avigal, Shosh. "Romantika Rav Minit" [Poly-sexual Romance]. *Koteret Rashit* 17 May 1983.

Bar-Kadma, Imanuel. "Arba Nashim VeOd Isha" [Four Women and Another]. *Yediot Achronot* 23 May 1980.

Bernheimer, Avner. "Sheinkin Higi'a Rachok" [Shienkin Has Gone Far]. *Ma'ariv Magazine* 30 Dec. 1994: 40–45.

Brown, Hannah. "Soldiers Boys Making Love, Not War." *Jerusalem Post* 28 Oct. 2002.

Frid, Yaron. "Eich Ze ShNiv'ateti Hachutza" [Why Was I Pushed Outside?]. *Hadashot Magazine* 26 Apr. 1991: 40–41.

Grant, Linda. "Tel Aviv Tales." *Guardian G2* 19 Nov. 2003: 7.

Green, Eitan. "Kolnoa Yisraeli '83: Amos Guttman, BaDerech HaKasha" [Israeli Cinema '83: Amos Guttman, The Hard Way]. *Monitin* Mar. 1983.

Haimovitz, Gili. "Ezor HaTa'asiya" [Industrial Zone]. *Ha'ir* 23 Aug. 1996: 83.

Halutz, Doron. "HaSachkan Alon Levi Lo Muchan Le'hastir et HaUvda Shehu Homo. Az Ma Im Acherim Choshvim Sheze Mezik Lakaryera" [The Actor Alon Levi Is Refusing to Conceal the Fact That He Is Gay. So What If Everyone Else Thinks It's Bad for Your Career]. *Ha'aretz* 23 Oct. 2009.

Ingber, Nachman. "Noge'a" [Touching]. *Ha'ir* 21 Oct. 1983.

Kaminer, Amir, and Rami Rotholtz. "Tel Aviv Ze Ani" [Tel Aviv Is Me]. *Tel Aviv Magazine* 25 Sep. 1992: 16–19.

Karpel, Dalia. "HaBaby Shelahem" [Their Baby]. *Ha'aretz Magazine* 12 Mar. 2004.

Klein, Uri. "Arba Shanim Acharei" [Four Years Later]. *Ha'aretz* 29 Sep. 1993.

Lazarus, Charles. "Gay-Themed *Nagua* at Montreal Target of Israeli Snubs." *Variety* 31 Aug. 1983.

———. "Israeli Director Receives Little Support for Gay Film." *Canadian Jewish News* 7 Sep. 1983: 25.

Lev Ari, Shiri. "Akum Hu Reicha Shel HaYakantalisa" [The Fragrance of the Yakantalisa Is Bent]. *Zman Tel Aviv* 29 Nov. 1996: 44–45.

Lev, Yair. "Keitzad Osim Seret She'et HaGibor Shelo Ee Efshar LeTsalem?" [How Do You Make a Film with a Protagonist You Can't Film?]. *Camera Obscura Magazine* Oct. 1996.

Lord, Amnon. "Adam Holech VeNe'elam" [A Person Is Disappearing]. *Tel Aviv Magazine* 6 Dec. 1996.

Misgav, Uri. "*Ha'ir:* Gilayon 1,000" [*Ha'ir:* The 1000th Issue]. *Ha'ir* 26 Nov. 1999: 18–37.

"Misrad HaChinuch Lo Eesher Ma'anak Kaspi LaSeret HaHomosexuali, UvaTelevizia Amroo: Lo, Toda" [The Ministry of Education Refused Financial Grant for Gay Film, and at the Television Headquarters They Said: No, Thanks]. *Lahiton* 4 Nov. 1980.

Na'aman, Idit. "Homo Ivry: Mi Yeda Chayecha?" [Hebrew Gay Man: Who Will Know Your Life?]. *Yediot Achronot* 23 Sep. 1983.

Ne'eman, Rachel. "Matzor" [Siege]. *Koteret Rashit* 21 Oct. 1987.

Negev, Ayelet. "HaEmet Tamid Meshachreret" [The Truth Always Liberates]. *Yediot Achronot Magazine* 7 Nov. 1997: 36–39.

Ohad, Michael. "Rutz Al Chayecha, Himalet Al Nafshecha" [Run for Your Life]. *Ha'aretz Magazine* 16 Sep. 1983.

Pally, Marcia. "The Lost Tribe." *Village Voice* 1 May 1984.

Pearl, Moshe. "Kolnoa Aliz" [Gay Cinema]. *Lahiton* 9 Nov. 1983.

Peled, Asafa. "Aba Yesh Rak Echad" [There Is Only One Dad]. *Yediot Achronot Magazine* 25 June 2004: 56.

Perchak, Roni. "*Shchur* ve *Shirat HaSirena:* Lo Tsofim Mitoch Hizdaut" [*Shchur* and *Song of the Siren:* People Do Not Watch Out of Identification]. *Ha'aretz* 2 Mar. 1995.

Pinto, Goel. "Nisayon Limno'a Hakranat *Tagid Amen!* LeChavrei HaAcademia LeKolnoa" [An Attempt to Prevent Screening of *Say Amen!* to Members of the Film Academy]. *Ha'aretz* 11 July 2005.

Qedar, Yair. "Dana Kama" [Dana Rises Up]. *Ha'ir* 15 May 1998.

Raveh, Yair. "Pasim VeKochavim, Degalim U'Mutagim" [Stars and Stripes, Flags and Brand Names]. *Zman Tel Aviv* 11 Nov. 1994.

Reuveni, Yotam. "Gvarim Mukim" [Beaten Men]. *Monitin* Mar. 1983.

Rosenblum, Doron. "Tchum HaShiput HaMitrachev VeHolech Shel HaMekomon" [The Ever-Growing Municipal Area of the Local Newspaper]. *Koteret Rashit* 27 Nov. 1985.

Shaked, Ra'anan. "*Sipurei Tel Aviv:* HaSipur HaMale" [*Tel Aviv Stories:* The Full Story]. *Tel Aviv Magazine* 26 Mar. 1992: 74.

Sharon, Eli. "Gvirotay VeRabotay: Ma'apecha" [Ladies and Gentlemen: A Revolution]. *Ha'ir* 21 June 2001.

Shelach, Ofer. "Tel Aviv Ze Lo New York" [Tel Aviv Is Not New York]. *Ma'ariv* 29 Mar. 1992.

Stav, Yehuda. "Kchu Otan BeKalut" [Take Them Easy]. *Yediot Achronot* 5 Apr. 1992.

Tajima, Renee. "Suffer the Little Children." *Village Voice* 29 Nov. 1988.

Tal-Shir, Anat. "Tirturo Shel Guttman" [Pushing Guttman Around]. *Ha'ir* 11 Mar. 1983.

"Twentieth Century Fox." (Interview with Eytan Fox). *Jerusalem Post Magazine* 11 Nov. 1994: 13.

Wallach, Aliza. "Ein Ahavot Smechot" [There Are No Happy Love Stories]. (Interview with Amos Guttman). *Davar Magazine* 23 Sep. 1983: 16.

Waugh, Thomas. "Dreams, Cruises and Cuddles in Tel Aviv." *The Body Politic* Nov. 1983.

Yosha, Itzik. "Yevavat HaSirena" [The Wail of the Siren]. *Yediot Achronot Magazine* 2 Dec. 1994: 38–39.

Yovel, Ruthie. "Gvarim Lo Yitnashkoo" [Men Will Not Kiss]. *Kol Ha'ir* 1 July 1983.

Zimmerman, Dana. "Chadira El Toch Merchav Prati" [Penetration of a Private Space]. *Ha'aretz* 17 Mar. 1996.

———. "HaSeret *Yakantalisa* Yukran BaShavua HaBa" [The Film *Yakantalisa* to Be Screened Next Week]. *Ha'aretz* 17 May 1999.

Books and Articles

Abel, Elizabeth, Marianne Hirsch, and Elizabeth Langland, eds. *The Voyage In: Fictions of Female Development.* Hanover: UP of New England, 1983.

Adams, Timothy Dow. *Telling Lies in Modern American Autobiography.* Chapel Hill: U of North Carolina P, 1990.

Ahmed, Sara. *Queer Phenomenology: Orientations, Objects, Others.* Durham: Duke UP, 2006.

Almog, Oz. "The Globalization of Israel: Transformations." *Israeli Identity in Transition.* Ed. Anita Shapira. Westport: Praeger, 2004. 233–56.

———. *The Sabra: The Creation of the New Jew.* Trans. Haim Watzman. Berkeley: U of California P, 2000.

Altman, Dennis. "Global Gaze/Global Gays." *Postcolonial and Queer Theories: Intersections and Essays.* Ed. John C. Hawley. Westport: Greenwood, 2001. 1–18.

Anderson, Benedict. *Imagined Communities: Reflections on the Origin and Spread of Nationalism.* London: Verso, 1983.

Avidan, David. *Tel Aviv by Night* (in Hebrew). Tel Aviv: Tirosh, 1983.

Azaryahu, Maoz. *Tel Aviv: The Real City, A Historical Mythography* (in Hebrew). Sede Boqer: Ben-Gurion U of the Negev P, 2005.

Barnard, Ian. "The United States in South Africa: (Post)Colonial Queer Theory?" *Postcolonial and Queer Theories: Intersections and Essays.* Ed. John C. Hawley. Westport: Greenwood, 2001. 129–38.

Barthes, Roland. "Semiology and the Urban." *The City and the Sign: An Introduction to Urban Semiotics.* Ed. M. Gottdiener and Alexandros Ph. Lagopoulos. New York: Columbia UP, 1986. 87–98.

Baudrillard, Jean. *Selected Writings.* Ed. Mark Postner. Stanford: Stanford UP, 1988.

Beattie, Keith. *Documentary Screens: Nonfiction Film and Television.* Basingstoke: Palgrave Macmillan, 2004.

Ben-Ami, Shlomo. "Israel as a Multicultural Society" (in Hebrew). *Israel: From Mobilized to Civil Society?* Ed. Adi Ophir and Yoav Peled. Jerusalem: Van Leer Jerusalem Institute and Hakibbutz Hameuchad, 2001. 18–23.

Ben-Ari, Eyal. "Tests of Soldierhood, Trials of Manhood: Military Service and Male Ideals in Israel." *Military, State, and Society in Israel.* With the assistance of Galeet Dardashti. Ed. Eyal Ben-Ari, Daniel Maman, and Zeev Rosenhek. New Brunswick: Transaction, 2001. 239–67.

Ben-Ari, Eyal, Daniel Maman, and Zeev Rosenhek. "Military, State and Society in Israel: An Introductory Essay." Introd. to *Military, State, and Society in Israel.* Ed. Daniel Maman, Eyal Ben-Ari, and Zeev Rosenhek. New Brunswick: Transaction, 2001. 1–39.

Ben-Shaul, Nitzan S. *Mythical Expressions of Siege in Israeli Films.* Lewiston: Edwin Mellen, 1997.

Benshoff, Harry, and Sean Griffin, eds. *Queer Cinema: The Film Reader.* New York: Routledge, 2004.

Berger, Tamar. *Dionysus at Dizengof Centre* (in Hebrew). Tel Aviv: Hakibbutz Hameuchad, 1998.

Bersani, Leo. *Homos.* Cambridge: Harvard UP, 1995.

———. "Is the Rectum a Grave?" *AIDS: Cultural Analysis, Cultural Activism.* Ed. Douglas Crimp. Cambridge: MIT P, 1988. 197–222.

Betsky, Aaron. *Building Sex: Men, Women, Architecture, and the Creation of Sexuality.* New York: William Morrow, 1995.

———. *Queer Space: Architecture and Same-Sex Desire.* New York: William Morrow, 1997.

Bhabha, Homi K. "DissemiNation: Time, Narrative, and the Margins of the Modern Nation." *Nation and Narration.* Ed. Homi K. Bhabha. London: Routledge, 1990. 291–322.

———. *The Location of Culture.* London: Routledge, 1994.

Biale, David. *Eros and the Jews: From Biblical Israel to Contemporary America.* Berkeley: U of California P, 1997.

Biskind, Peter. *Easy Riders, Raging Bulls: How the Sex-Drugs-Rock 'n' Roll Generation Saved Hollywood.* London: Bloomsbury, 1998.

Bluher, Dominique. "Perlov, Mekas, Morder, Lehman and the Others: In Search of the Unpredictable Quiverings of Daily Life." Trans. Moira Tierney. *David Perlov's Diary.* Ed. Mira Perlov and Pip Chodorov (Book accompanying the first video release of *Diary*). Re:Voir Video, 2006.

Boyarin, Daniel. "Homotopia: The *Fem*inized Jewish Man and the Lives of Women in Late Antiquity." *Differences: A Journal of Feminist Cultural Studies* 7.2 (1995): 41–81.

———. *Unheroic Conduct: The Rise of Heterosexuality and the Invention of the Jewish Man.* Berkeley: U of California P, 1997.

Boyarin, Jonathan. "At Last, All the *Goyim:* Notes on a Greek Word Applied to Jews." *Postmodern Apocalypse: Theory and Cultural Practice at the End.* Ed. Richard Dellamora. Philadelphia: U of Pennsylvania P, 1995. 41–58.

Brennan, Timothy. "The National Longing for Form." *Nation and Narration.* Ed. Homi K. Bhabha. London: Routledge, 1990. 44–70.

Brittan, Arthur. *Masculinity and Power.* Oxford: Basil Blackwell, 1989.

Bronski, Michael. *Culture Clash: The Making of Gay Sensibility.* Boston: South End, 1984.

Burgin, Victor. *Some Cities.* London: Reaktion, 1996.

Bursztyn, Igal. *Face as Battlefield* (in Hebrew). Tel Aviv: Hakibbutz Hameuchad, 1990.

———. Introduction. *Scripts 1* (in Hebrew). Ed. Orly Lubin and Rennen Schorr. Tel Aviv: Jerusalem Film and Television School/Kinneret Publishing House, 1996.

Butler, Judith. *Gender Trouble: Feminism and the Subversion of Identity.* 1990. New York: Routledge, 1999.

———. "Restaging the Universal: Hegemony and the Limits of Formalism." *Contingency, Hegemony, Universality: Contemporary Dialogues on the Left.* Ed. Judith Butler, Ernesto Laclau, and Slavoj Žižek. London: Verso, 2000. 11–43.

Byars, Jackie. *All That Hollywood Allows: Re-reading Gender in 1950s Melodrama.* London: Routledge, 1991.

Camper, Fred. "The Films of Douglas Sirk." *Imitation of Life: Douglas Sirk, Director.* Ed. Lucy Fischer. New Brunswick: Rutgers UP, 1991. 251–67.

Certeau, Michel de. *The Practice of Everyday Life.* Trans. Steven Rendall. Berkeley: U of California P, 1988.

Chasin, Alexandra. *Selling Out: The Gay and Lesbian Movement Goes to Market.* New York: Palgrave, 2000.

Chetrit, Sami Shalom. *The Mizrahi Struggle in Israel: Between Oppression and Liberation, Identification and Alternative 1948–2003* (in Hebrew). Tel Aviv: Am Oved, 2004.

Cohen, Ed. "Who Are 'We'? Gay 'Identity' as Political (E)motion (A Theoretical Rumination)." *Inside/Out: Lesbian Theories, Gay Theories.* Ed. Diana Fuss. New York: Routledge, 1991. 71–92.

Crimp, Douglas, ed. *AIDS: Cultural Analysis, Cultural Activism.* Cambridge: MIT P, 1988.

D'Emilio, John, and Estelle B. Freedman. *Intimate Matters: A History of Sexuality in America.* New York: Harper & Row, 1988.

Dickinson, Peter. "'Go-Go Dancing on the Brink of the Apocalypse': Representing AIDS." *Postmodern Apocalypse: Theory and Cultural Practice at the End.* Ed. Richard Dellamora. Philadelphia: U of Pennsylvania P, 1995. 219–40.

Doane, Mary Ann. *Femmes Fatales: Feminism, Film Theory, Psychoanalysis.* New York: Routledge, 1991.

———. "Pathos and Pathology: The Cinema of Todd Haynes." *Camera Obscura* 57 (2004): 1–20.

Donner, Batya. "From Gymnasium to Tower." *Ariel* 77–78 (1989): 93–98.

Duggan, Lisa. *The Twilight of Equality: Neoliberalism, Cultural Politics, and the Attack on Democracy.* Boston: Beacon, 2003.

Duvdevani, Shmulik. *First Person Camera* (in Hebrew). Jerusalem: Keter Books, 2010.

Dyer, Richard. *The Culture of Queers.* London: Routledge, 2002.

———. *The Matter of Images: Essays on Representation.* 1993. London: Routledge, 2002.

———. *Now You See It: Studies on Lesbian and Gay Film.* London: Routledge, 1990.

———. *White.* London: Routledge, 1997.

The Economist Pocket World in Figures. London: Profile, 2003.

Edelman, Lee. *Homographesis: Essays in Gay Literary and Cultural Theory.* New York: Routledge, 1994.

———. *No Future: Queer Theory and the Death Drive.* Durham: Duke UP, 2004.

Elizur, Yuval. "Israeli Television and the National Agenda." *Ariel* 99–100 (1995): 114–27.

Ellenzweig, Allen. "Picturing the Homoerotic." *Queer Representations: Reading Lives, Reading Cultures, A Center for Lesbian and Gay Studies Book.* Ed. Martin Duberman. New York: New York UP, 1997. 57–68.

Elon, Amos. *Jerusalem: City of Mirrors.* 1990. London: Flamingo, 1996.

Elsaesser, Thomas. *Fassbinder's Germany: History, Identity, Subject.* Amsterdam: Amsterdam UP, 1996.

———. "Tales of Sound and Fury: Observations on the Family Melodrama." *Home Is Where the Heart Is: Studies in Melodrama and the Woman's Film.* Ed. Christine Gledhill. London: BFI, 1987. 43–69.

Ezrahi, Yaron. *Rubber Bullets: Power and Conscience in Modern Israel.* New York: Farrar, 1997.

Fanon, Frantz. *Black Skin, White Masks.* London: Pluto, 1968.

Fassbinder, Rainer Werner. *The Anarchy of the Imagination: Interviews, Essays, Notes.* Ed. Michael Töteberg and Leo A. Lensing. Trans. Krishna Winston. Baltimore: Johns Hopkins UP, 1992.

Ferncase, Richard K. *Outsider Features: American Independent Films of the 1980s.* Westport: Greenwood, 1996.

Fink, Amir Sumaka'i, and Jacob Press. *Independence Park: The Lives of Gay Men in Israel.* Stanford: Stanford UP, 1999.

Florida, Richard. *Cities and the Creative Class.* New York: Routledge, 2005.

Forrest, David. "'We're Here, We're Queer, and We're Not Going Shopping': Changing Gay Male Identities in Contemporary Britain." *Dislocating Masculinity: Comparative Ethnographies.* Ed. Andrea Cornwall and Nancy Lindisfarne. London: Routledge, 1994. 97–110.

Foucault, Michel. *The Use of Pleasure: Volume 2 of The History of Sexuality.* Trans. Robert Hurley. London: Viking, 1986.

———. *The Will to Knowledge: The History of Sexuality Volume 1.* 1976. Trans. Robert Hurley. London: Penguin, 1998.

Frankel, Jonathan. "The 'Yizkor' Book of 1911: A Note on National Myths in the Second Aliya." *Essential Papers on Zionism.* Ed. Jehuda Reinharz and Anita Shapira. London: Cassell, 1996. 422–53.

Freeman, Mark. *Rewriting the Self: History, Memory, Narrative.* London: Routledge, 1993.

Frye, Marilyn. *The Politics of Reality: Essays in Feminist Theory.* Trumansburg: Crossing, 1983.

Fuchs, Esther, ed. *Israeli Women's Studies: A Reader.* New Brunswick: Rutgers UP, 2005.

Garber, Marjorie. *Vested Interests: Cross-Dressing & Cultural Anxiety.* New York: Routledge, 1992.

Gertz, Nurith. *Holocaust Survivors, Aliens and Others in Israeli Cinema and Literature* (in Hebrew). Tel Aviv: Am Oved and the Open U of Israel, 2004.

———. *Myths in Israeli Culture: Captives of a Dream.* London: Vallentine Mitchell, 2000.

Gertz, Nurith, Orly Lubin, and Judd Ne'eman, eds. *Fictive Looks: On Israeli Cinema* (in Hebrew). Tel Aviv: Open U of Israel P, 1998.

Giladi, G. N. *Discord in Zion: Conflict between Ashkenazi & Sephardi Jews in Israel.* London: Scorpion, 1990.

Gilman, Sander L. *Freud, Race, and Gender.* Princeton: Princeton UP, 1993.

———. *Sexuality, An Illustrated History: Representing the Sexual in Medicine and Culture from the Middle Ages to the Age of AIDS.* New York: John Wiley, 1989.

Gledhill, Christine. "The Melodramatic Field: An Investigation." *Home Is Where the Heart Is: Studies in Melodrama and the Woman's Film.* Ed. Christine Gledhill. London: BFI, 1987. 5–39.

Gluzman, Michael. "Longing for Heterosexuality: Zionism and Sexuality in Herzl's *Altneuland*" (in Hebrew). *Theory and Criticism* 11 (1997): 145–62, 217–18.

———. *The Politics of Canonicity: Lines of Resistance in Modernist Hebrew Poetry.* Stanford: Stanford UP, 2003.

Golomb-Hoffman, Anne. "Bodies and Borders: The Politics of Gender in Contemporary Israeli Fiction." *The Boom in Contemporary Israeli Fiction.* Ed. Alan Mintz. Hanover: Brandeis UP/UP of New England, 1997. 35–70.

Gottdiener, M., and Alexandros Ph. Lagopoulos, eds. *The City and the Sign: An Introduction to Urban Semiotics.* New York: Columbia UP, 1986.

Gove, Ben. *Cruising Culture: Promiscuity, Desire and American Gay Literature.* Edinburgh: Edinburgh UP, 2000.

Gramsci, Antonio. *Selections from Prison Notebooks.* Ed. Quintin Hoare and Geoffrey Nowell-Smith. London: Lawrence and Wishart, 1971.

Gross, Aeyal M. "Challenges to Compulsory Heterosexuality: Recognition and Non-recognition of Same-Sex Couples in Israeli Law." *Legal Recognition of*

Same-Sex Partnerships: A Study of National, European and International Law. Ed. Robert Wintemute and Mads Andenæs. Oxford: Hart, 2001. 391–414.

Grundmann, Roy. *Andy Warhol's Blow Job.* Philadelphia: Temple UP, 2003.

Gutwein, Daniel. "From Melting Pot to Multiculturalism; or, The Privatization of Israeli Identity." *Israeli Identity in Transition.* Ed. Anita Shapira. Westport: Praeger, 2004. 215–31.

Halberstam, Judith. *In a Queer Time and Place: Transgender Bodies, Subcultural Lives.* New York: New York UP, 2005.

Hall, Stuart. "Cultural Studies and the Centre. Some Problematics and Problems." *Culture, Media, Language.* 1980. Ed. Stuart Hall, Dorothy Hobson, Andrew Lowe, and Paul Willis. London: Routledge, 1992. 15–47.

———. "Recent Developments in Theories of Language and Ideology: A Critical Note." *Culture, Media, Language.* 1980. Ed. Stuart Hall, Dorothy Hobson, Andrew Lowe, and Paul Willis. London: Routledge, 1992. 157–62.

Halliday, Jon. *Sirk on Sirk: Conversations with Jon Halliday.* 1971. London: Faber and Faber, 1997.

Halperin, David M. *One Hundred Years of Homosexuality and Other Essays on Greek Love.* New York: Routledge, 1990.

Halpern, Ben, and Jehuda Reinharz. *Zionism and the Creation of a New Society.* Hanover: Brandeis UP, 2000.

Hammond, Mike. "The Historical and the Hysterical: Melodrama, War and Masculinity in *Dead Poets Society.*" *You Tarzan: Masculinity, Movies and Men.* Ed. Pat Kirkham and Janet Thumim. London: Lawrence and Wishart, 1993. 52–64.

Handelman, Don. *Nationalism and the Israeli State: Bureaucratic Logic in Public Events.* Oxford: Berg, 2004.

Hanson, Ellis, ed. *Out Takes: Essays on Queer Theory and Film.* Durham: Duke UP, 1999.

Harel, Alon. "The Rise and Fall of the Israeli Gay Legal Revolution." *Columbia Human Rights Law Review* 31 (2000): 443–71.

Higgs, David, ed. *Queer Sites: Gay Urban Histories since 1600.* London: Routledge, 1999.

Hirsch, H. N., ed. *The Future of Gay Rights in America.* London: Routledge, 2005.

Hirsch, Marianne. "The Novel of Formation as Genre: Between Great Expectations and Lost Illusions." *Genre* 12 (1979): 293–311.

Hjort, Mette, and Scott MacKenzie, eds. *Cinema & Nation.* London: Routledge, 2000.

Horrigan, Bill. "Notes on AIDS and Its Combatants: An Appreciation." *Theorizing Documentary.* Ed. Michael Renov. New York: Routledge, 1993. 164–73.

Jakobsen, Janet, and Beverly Seckinger. "Love, Death, and Videotape: *Silverlake Life.*" *Between the Sheets, in the Streets: Queer, Lesbian, Gay Documentary.*

Ed. Chris Holmlund and Cynthia Fuchs. Minneapolis: U of Minnesota P, 1997. 144–57.

Kabbani, Rana. *Europe's Myths of Orient.* London: Macmillan, 1986.

Kama, Amit. "From *Terra Incognita* to *Terra Firma:* The Logbook of the Voyage of Gay Men's Community into the Israeli Public Sphere." *Journal of Homosexuality* 38.4 (2000): 133–62.

———. *The Newspaper and the Closet: Israeli Gay Men's Communication Patterns* (in Hebrew). Tel Aviv: Hakibbutz Hameuchad, 2003.

Kaniuk, Yoram. *Himmo, King of Jerusalem.* Trans. Yosef Shachter. London: Chatto & Windus, 1969.

Kaplan, Danny. *David, Jonathan and Other Soldiers: Identity, Masculinity and Sexuality in Combat Units in the Israeli Army* (in Hebrew). Tel Aviv: Hakibbutz Hameuchad, 1999.

Katz, Jonathan Ned. *The Invention of Heterosexuality.* New York: Dutton, 1995.

Kimmerling, Baruch. *The End of Ashkenazi Hegemony* (in Hebrew). Jerusalem: Keter, 2001.

———. "Militarism in Israeli Society" (in Hebrew). *Theory and Criticism* 4 (1993): 123–40.

Klinger, Barbara. "'Cinema/Ideology/Criticism' Revisited: The Progressive Genre." *Film Genre Reader.* Ed. Barry Keith Grant. Austin: U of Texas P, 1986. 74–90.

———. *Melodrama and Meaning: History, Culture, and the Films of Douglas Sirk.* Bloomington: Indiana UP, 1994.

Knopp, Lawrence, and Mickey Lauria. "Toward an Analysis of the Role of Gay Communities in the Urban Renaissance." *Urban Geography* 6 (1985): 152–69.

Kronish, Amy, and Costel Safirman. *Israeli Film: A Reference Guide.* Westport: Praeger, 2003.

Laplace, Maria. "Producing and Consuming the Woman's Film: Discursive Struggle in *Now, Voyager.*" *Home Is Where the Heart Is: Studies in Melodrama and the Woman's Film.* Ed. Christine Gledhill. London: BFI, 1987. 138–66.

Lapsley, Rob. "Mainly in Cities and at Night: Some Notes on Cities and Film." *The Cinematic City.* Ed. David B. Clarke. London: Routledge, 1997. 186–208.

Lebow, Alisa L. *First Person Jewish.* Minneapolis: U of Minnesota P, 2008.

Levin, Michael. "When Tel Aviv Was White." *Ariel* 77–78 (1989): 55–68.

LeVine, Mark. "Re-imagining the 'White City': The Politics of World Heritage Designation in Tel Aviv/Jaffa." *City: Analysis of Urban Trends, Culture, Theory, Policy, Action* 8 (2004): 221–28.

Levi, Emanuel. *Cinema of Outsiders: The Rise of American Independent Film.* New York: New York UP, 1999.

Loshitzky, Yosefa. "The Bride of the Dead: Phallocentrism and War in *Himmo, King of Jerusalem.*" *Film/Literature Quarterly* 21 (1993): 218–29.

———. *Identity Politics on the Israeli Screen.* Austin: U of Texas P, 2001.

———. "A Tale of Three Cities: Amos Gitai's Urban Trilogy." *Framework* 43 (2002): 134–51.

Lubin, Orly. "The Woman as Other in Israeli Cinema." *Israeli Women's Studies: A Reader.* Ed. Esther Fuchs. New Brunswick: Rutgers UP, 2005. 301–16.

———. *Women Reading Women* (in Hebrew). Haifa: Haifa UP and Zmora Bitan, 2003.

Massad, Joseph. "The 'Post-colonial' Colony: Time, Space, and Bodies in Palestine/Israel." *The Pre-occupation of Postcolonial Studies.* Ed. Fawzia Afzal-Khan and Kalpana Seshadri-Crooks. Durham: Duke UP, 2000. 311–46.

McHugh, Kathleen. "Irony and Dissembling: Queer Tactics for Experimental Documentary." *Between the Sheets, in the Streets: Queer, Lesbian, Gay Documentary.* Ed. Chris Holmlund and Cynthia Fuchs. Minneapolis: U of Minnesota P, 1997. 224–40.

Medhurst, Andy. "That Special Thrill: *Brief Encounter,* Homosexuality and Authorship." *Screen* 32 (1991): 197–208.

Melman, Billie. "The Legend of Sarah: Gender, Memory and National Identities (*Eretz Yisrael*/Israel, 1917–90)." *Gender and Israeli Society: Women's Time.* Ed. Hannah Naveh. London: Vallentine Mitchell, 2003. 55–92.

Menahemi, Ayelet. "Script for *Crows*" (in Hebrew). *Scripts 1.* Ed. Orly Lubin and Rennen Schorr. Tel Aviv: Jerusalem Film and Television School/Kinneret Publishing House, 1996. 115–60.

Meyer, Moe, ed. *The Politics and Poetics of Camp.* London: Routledge, 1994.

Meyer, Richard. "Rock Hudson's Body." *Inside/Out: Lesbian Theories, Gay Theories.* Ed. Diana Fuss. New York: Routledge, 1991. 259–88.

Moore, Tracy, ed. *Lesbiōt: Israeli Lesbians Talk about Sexuality, Feminism, Judaism and Their Lives.* London: Cassell, 1995.

Mort, Frank. *Cultures of Consumption: Masculinities and Social Space in Late Twentieth-Century Britain.* London: Routledge, 1996.

Mosse, George L. *Confronting the Nation: Jewish and Western Nationalism.* Hanover: Brandeis UP/UP of New England, 1993.

———. *The Image of Man: The Creation of Modern Masculinity.* Oxford: Oxford UP, 1996.

———. *Nationalism and Sexuality: Respectability and Abnormal Sexuality in Modern Europe.* New York: Howard Fertig, 1985.

Mulvey, Laura. "Notes on Sirk and Melodrama." *Home Is Where the Heart Is: Studies in Melodrama and the Woman's Film.* Ed. Christine Gledhill. London: BFI, 1987. 75–79.

Neale, Steve. "Prologue: Masculinity as Spectacle, Reflections on Men and Mainstream Cinema." *Screening the Male: Exploring Masculinities in Hollywood Cinema.* Ed. Steven Cohan and Ina Rae Hark. London: Routledge, 1993. 9–20.

Ne'eman, Judd. "The Empty Tomb in the Postmodern Pyramid: Israeli Cinema in the 1980s and 1990s." *Documenting Israel.* Ed. Charles Berlin. Cambridge: Harvard College Library, 1995. 117–51.

Nichols, Bill. *Blurred Boundaries: Questions of Meaning in Contemporary Culture.* Bloomington: Indiana UP, 1994.

Nordau, Max. "Jewry of Muscles." *The Jew in the Modern World: A Documentary History.* Ed. Paul Mendes-Flohr and Jehuda Reinharz. Oxford: Oxford UP, 1980. 434–35.

Nowell-Smith, Geoffrey. "Cities: Real and Imagined." *Cinema and the City: Film and Urban Societies in a Global Context.* Ed. Mark Shiel and Tony Fitzmaurice. Oxford: Blackwell, 2001. 99–108.

Ophir, Adi, and Yoav Peled. Preface. *Israel: From Mobilized to Civil Society?* (in Hebrew). Ed. Adi Ophir and Yoav Peled. Jerusalem: Van Leer Jerusalem Institute and Hakibbutz Hameuchad, 2001. 9–17.

Pappé, Ilan. "The Square Circle: The Struggle for Survival of Traditional Zionism." *The Challenge of Post-Zionism: Alternatives to Israeli Fundamentalist Politics.* Ed. Ephraim Nimni. London: Zed, 2003. 42–62.

Pearl, Monica B. "AIDS and New Queer Cinema." *New Queer Cinema: A Critical Reader.* Ed. Michele Aaron. Edinburgh: Edinburgh UP, 2004. 23–35.

Peled, Rina. *'The New Man' of the Zionist Revolution: Hashomer Haza'ir and His European Roots* (in Hebrew). Tel Aviv: Am Oved, 2002.

Peleg, Yaron. *Israeli Culture between the Two Intifadas: A Brief Romance.* Austin: U of Texas P, 2008.

Pellegrini, Ann. "Whiteface Performances: 'Race,' Gender, and Jewish Bodies." *Jews and Other Differences: The New Jewish Cultural Studies.* Ed. Jonathan Boyarin and Daniel Boyarin. Minneapolis: U of Minnesota P, 1997. 108–49.

Peres, Shimon. *The New Middle East: A Framework and Processes toward an Era of Peace* (in Hebrew). Bnei Brak: Steimatzky, 1993. Translated as *The New Middle East* (Dorset, UK: Element, 1993).

Plummer, Ken. *Telling Sexual Stories: Power, Change and Social Worlds.* London: Routledge, 1995.

Preston, Peter, and Paul Simpson-Housley. "Writing the City." Introd. to *Writing the City: Eden, Babylon and the New Jerusalem.* Ed. Peter Preston and Paul Simpson-Housley. London: Routledge, 1994. 1–14.

Ram, Uri. "From Nation-State to Nation - - - - State: Nation, History and Identity Struggles in Jewish Israel." *The Challenge of Post-Zionism: Alternatives to Israeli Fundamentalist Politics.* Ed. Ephraim Nimni. London: Zed, 2003. 20–41.

Renov, Michael. "Introduction: The Truth about Non-fiction." Introd. to *Theorizing Documentary.* Ed. Michael Renov. New York: Routledge, 1993. 1–11.

———. *The Subject of Documentary.* Minneapolis: U of Minnesota P, 2004.

Rosenberg, Robert. "Snapshots 1989." *Ariel* 77–78 (1989): 172–83.

Said, Edward W. *Orientalism.* 1978. London: Penguin, 2003.

Savoy, Eric. "'That Ain't *All* She Ain't': Doris Day and Queer Performativity." *Out Takes: Essays on Queer Theory and Film.* Ed. Ellis Hanson. Durham: Duke UP, 1999. 151–82.

Saxey, Esther. *Homoplot: The Coming-Out Story and Gay, Lesbian and Bisexual Identity.* New York: Peter Lang, 2008.

Schlör, Joachim. *Tel Aviv: From Dream to City.* Trans. Helen Atkins. London: Reaktion, 1999.

Schnitzer, Meir. *Israeli Cinema: Facts/Plots/Directors/Opinions* (in Hebrew). Tel Aviv: Kinneret, 1994.

Schweitzer, Ariel. *The New Sensitivity: Modern Israeli Cinema of the 1960s and 1970s* (in Hebrew). Tel Aviv: Babel and Third Ear, 2003.

Sedgwick, Eve Kosofsky. *Epistemology of the Closet.* Hertfordshire: Harvester Wheatsheaf, 1991.

Segev, Tom. *Elvis in Jerusalem: Post-Zionism and the Americanization of Israel.* Trans. Haim Watzman. New York: Metropolitan, Henry Holt, 2002.

Shohat, Ella. *Israeli Cinema: East/West and the Politics of Representation.* Austin: U of Texas P, 1989.

Sibalis, Michael D. "Paris." *Queer Sites: Gay Urban Histories since 1600.* Ed. David Higgs. London: Routledge, 1999. 10–37.

Siegel, Marc. "Documentary That Dare/Not Speak Its Name: Jack Smith's *Flaming Creatures.*" *Between the Sheets, in the Streets: Queer, Lesbian, Gay Documentary.* Ed. Chris Holmlund and Cynthia Fuchs. Minneapolis: U of Minnesota P, 1997. 91–106.

Silverman, Kaja. *Male Subjectivity at the Margins.* New York: Routledge, 1992.

Simon, Roger. *Gramsci's Political Thought: An Introduction.* 1982. London: Lawrence & Wishart, 1991.

Sinfield, Alan. *Gay and After.* London: Serpent's Tail, 1998.

Sion, Liora. *Images of Manhood among Combat Soldiers: Military Service in the Israeli Infantry as a Rite of Initiation from Youthood to Adulthood.* Jerusalem: Hebrew University of Jerusalem, Shaine Center for Research in Social Sciences, 1997.

Smith, Paul Julian. *Desire Unlimited: The Cinema of Pedro Almodóvar.* 1994. London: Verso, 2000.

———. *Vision Machines: Cinema, Literature and Sexuality in Spain and Cuba, 1983–93.* London: Verso, 1996.

Solomon, Alisa. "Viva la Diva Citizenship: Post-Zionism and Gay Rights." *Queer Theory and the Jewish Question.* Ed. Daniel Boyarin, Daniel Itzkovitz, and Ann Pellegrini. New York: Columbia UP, 2003. 149–65.

Sontag, Susan. *Against Interpretation and Other Essays.* New York: Anchor Doubleday, 1990.

———. *AIDS and Its Metaphors.* New York: Penguin, 1989.

Sturken, Marita. *Tangled Memories: The Vietnam War, the AIDS Epidemic, and the Politics of Remembering.* Berkeley: U of California P, 1997.

Suárez, Juan A. *Bike Boys, Drag Queens, and Superstars: Avant-Garde, Mass Culture, and Gay Identities in the 1960s Underground Cinema.* Bloomington: Indiana UP, 1996.

Taubin, Amy. "Beyond the Sons of Scorsese." *American Independent Cinema: A Sight and Sound Reader.* Ed. Jim Hillier. London: BFI, 2001. 89–92.

———. "'Nowhere to Hide' (interview with Todd Haynes: *Safe*)." *American Independent Cinema: A Sight and Sound Reader*. Ed. Jim Hillier. London: BFI, 2001. 100–07.

Thomsen, Christian Braad. *Fassbinder: The Life and Work of a Provocative Genius*. 1991. Trans. Martin Chalmers. London: Faber and Faber, 1997.

———. "Five Interviews with Fassbinder." *Fassbinder*. Ed. Tony Rayns. London: BFI, 1980. 82–101.

Troen, Ilan S. *Imagining Zion: Dreams, Designs, and Realities in a Century of Jewish Settlement*. New Haven: Yale UP, 2003.

Turner, Mark W. *Backward Glances: Cruising the Queer Streets of New York and London*. London: Reaktion, 2003.

Utin, Pablo. *The New Israeli Cinema: Conversations with Filmmakers* (in Hebrew). Tel Aviv: Resling, 2008.

Walzer, Lee. *Between Sodom and Eden: A Gay Journey through Today's Changing Israel*. New York: Columbia UP, 2000.

Warner, Michael, ed. *Fear of a Queer Planet: Queer Politics and Social Theory*. Minneapolis: U of Minnesota P, 1993.

Waugh, Thomas. "The Third Body: Patterns in the Construction of the Subject in Gay Male Narrative Film." *Queer Looks: Perspectives on Lesbian and Gay Film and Video*. Ed. Martha Gever, Pratibha Parmar, and John Greyson. New York: Routledge, 1993. 141–61.

———. "Walking on Tippy Toes: Lesbian and Gay Liberation Documentary of the Post-Stonewall Period 1969–84." *Between the Sheets, in the Streets: Queer, Lesbian, Gay Documentary*. Ed. Chris Holmlund and Cynthia Fuchs. Minneapolis: U of Minnesota P, 1997. 107–24.

Weeks, Jeffrey. "Against Nature." *Homosexuality, Which Homosexuality? Essays from the International Scientific Conference on Lesbian and Gay Studies*. Ed. D. Altman et al. London: Gay Men's Press, 1989. 199–213.

———. Foreword. *Sexuality and Eroticism among Males in Moslem Societies*. Ed. Arno Schmitt and Jehoeda Sofer. New York: Harrington Park, 1992. ix–xi.

White, Armond. "On the Waterfront." *Sight & Sound* 13.8 (2003): 22–24.

Whittle, Stephen. "Consuming Differences: The Collaboration of the Gay Body with the Cultural State." *The Margins of the City: Gay Men's Urban Lives*. Ed. Stephen Whittle. Hants: Arena, 1994. 27–41.

Wilton, Tamsin, ed. *Immortal, Invisible: Lesbians and the Moving Image*. London: Routledge, 1995.

Wirth-Nesher, Hana. *City Codes: Reading the Modern Urban Novel*. Cambridge: Cambridge UP, 1996.

Wright, Les. "San Francisco." *Queer Sites: Gay Urban Histories Since 1600*. Ed. David Higgs. London: Routledge, 1999. 164–89.

Yosef, Raz. *Beyond Flesh: Queer Masculinities and Nationalism in Israeli Cinema*. New Brunswick: Rutgers UP, 2004.

———. "The Military Body: Male Masochism and Homoerotic Relationships in Israeli Cinema" (in Hebrew). *Theory and Criticism* 18 (2001): 11–46, 262.

Zimerman, Moshe. *Hole in the Camera: Gazes of Israeli Cinema* (in Hebrew). Tel Aviv: Resling, 2003.

———. *Tel Aviv Was Never Small* (in Hebrew). Tel Aviv: Ministry of Defense Press, 2001.

Žižek, Slavoj. *For They Know Not What They Do: Enjoyment as a Political Factor*. 1991. London: Verso, 2002.

Index

Abecassis, Yael, 38
Aboutboul, Alon, 63
Activism/activist(s), gay, 79, 85, 90, 91, 115, 190, 202n8; and *Zero Degrees of Separation* (Flanders), 170, 176, 216n21. *See also* Aguda
Adama (Lerski), 97
advertising, 42, 43, 45, 47, 206n23
African Americans, 210n16; and sexuality, 208n5. *See also* Black Panthers (United States); Blacks
African man, 100. *See also* "Savage Man"
Aguda, 37, 57, 58, 75, 78, 79; changes of titles and agendas, 6; and magazine, 214n3
Ahmed, Sara, 7, 215n18
AIDS, 10, 116, 130, 131, 206n24, 206n26, 214n7, 215n15; and *Amazing Grace* (Guttman) 50, 54, 59, 65; and documentaries/memoirs, 134, 137; as a "gay disease", 166; and Guttman, 15, 57, 58, 137; and Ofra Haza, 215n16; and Rock Hudson, 81, 211n19, 211n20; and *Positive Story* (Kotzer) and *Yakantalisa* (Lev), 162–66, 215n15
Ajami (Copti and Shani), 201n1, 216n1
Akta, Liat, 187
Alexander, Ilil, 195
Alexander, Sharon, 52, 54, 58
Alexis, Joelle, 17, 138, 143, 144, 145, 149

Alkalay, Itamar, 201n3
All That Heaven Allows (Sirk), 66, 83, 208n8, 210n16
Allen, Woody, 35
Almagor, Gila, 52, 118
Almost There (Yehuda and Alexis), 17, 138, 143–46, 147, 148, 149, 150, 151
alternative/gay parenthood, 130, 166–69
Altman, Dennis, 8–9
Altman, Robert, 187
Amar, Daniel, 15
Amazing Grace (Guttman), 22, 38, 57, 60, 67, 70, 83, 164, 204n6, 209n12; critical acclaim of, 86; and death, 58–59; and dystopian representations of Tel Aviv, 49, 50, 54–56; and family, 64–66; and gay bar, 59; and Israeli "personal" cinema, 61–62, 63; and *Last Post* (Dotan), 135
American symbols/cultural tokens, 9, 36, 46, 99, 131, 136, 206n25
Americanization, 25, 36, 202n5
Amin, Shimon, 184
Amos Guttman: Film Director (Kotzer), 60, 75, 80, 86, 215n14
Anderson, Benedict, 5
Anger, Kenneth, 69, 136
Antarctica (Hochner), 186–88
antisodomy law, 6, 92
Antonioni, Michelangelo, 35
apocalypse, 50, 53
Apocalypse Now (Coppola), 213n16

235

Arab Jew(s), 98, 100, 172. *See also* Mizrahi Jew(s)
Arab/Muslim culture, homosexuality in, 176, 178, 216n22
Arabic Language, 172
Arab(s), 65, 102, 203n10, 208n8, 212n10; and assimilation to Israeli society, 173; and *A Different War*, 184; and *Drifting* (Guttman, long), 23, 76–77, 82; and *Fear Eats the Soul* (Fassbinder), 208n8; and Fox's cinema, 98, 100, 102, 105, 121; and *Hamsin* (Wachsmann), 14; and *Hide and Seek* (Wolman), 14, 28; and *Life According to Agfa* (Dayan), 49, 50, 51, 52, 53; and Juliano Mer-Khamis, 60; and *My Michael* (Wolman), 212n10; and self, 173; and *Zero Degrees of Separation* (Flanders) and *Gan* (Shatz and Barash), 169–80. *See also* Palestinians
Arafat, Yasser, 177
architecture, 69, 98, 102, 103; and the city, 27. *See also* Tel Aviv: International Style
Ardant, Fanny, 194
Ariel, Meir, 110, 111
army, 11, 91–92, 165, 184; and Fox's cinema, 23, 46, 94, 95, 96, 98, 102, 103, 108, 115, 119, 120, 121, 122, 123, 126, 186; and Guttman's cinema, 75, 76; and Tomer Heymann, 148; as an Israeli cultural signifier, 105; and *It Kinda Scares Me* (Heymann), 152, 155; and *Life According to Agfa* (Dayan), 50, 52, 56; as a male dominated institution/hypermasculine nature of, 20, 21, 197; and Orthodox Jews, 191; and restrictions imposed on gay men, 20, 76, 104, 155, 209n10; and right to serve in, 168, 197, 203n8, 209n10. *See also* IDF (Israel Defense Forces); military
Artzi, Shiri, 123, 125
Ashkenazi Jew(s)/Ashkenazim (Jews of European origin), 171, 204n14; and actors, 118; and *Bourekas* films, 118, 129, 203n12; and elite/dominant ideology, 10, 16, 19, 91, 94, 97, 127, 154, 155, 172, 212n10; and family/ies, 142, 146, 148; and filmmakers, 129; and the gay community/men, 16, 46, 93, 94, 97, 119, 139, 169, 176; and Guttman, 62; and hegemonic culture, 13; and immigrants, 19; and masculinity, 13, 14; and narrative of "coming out", 101; and oppression of Mizrahi Jews, 173; representation of in Fox's cinema, 91, 97, 98, 99, 101, 103, 117, 119; as Sabra, 53; and soldier, 23; and urban man, 10, 94; and values, 172. *See also* white/whiteness
Ashkenazi, Lior, 115
Assimilation/adjustment to Israeli heteronormative norms, 8, 139, 159, 168; and Fox's cinema, 94, 113, 116–17, 156–57, 176, 186; and Guttman's cinema, 73, 81
Asulin, Ron, 15, 131, 203n11
Aunt from Argentina, The (Ovadia), 11
auteur/auteur culture, 43, 61
authorities (state), 41, 56, 68, 154, 155, 177, 178, 179, 202n3, 216n21. *See also* government
authorship, 43
autobiographical films, 16, 17, 46, 87, 130, 132, 180, 213n2; and "autoethnographic" (Russell, Lebow), 214n9; and "domestic ethnography" (Renov), 138–51; and formal concerns, 24, 130; and found footage, 132, 133; and Guttman, 57, 60, 64, 71, 80, 82, 133, 164; and reenactment, 133, 137; and society, 132
avant-garde cinema: and Guttman's cinema, 66–71; and *Last Post* (Dotan), 136
Avidan, David, 27,
Avni, Aki, 65
Avoda (labor party/movement), 89, 174, 205n15; and 1977 general elections, 149
Ayad, Hagai, 160, 161, 162

Bannay, Uri, 96
Bar 51 (Guttman), 57, 83; and camp, 208n6; and death, 58; and family, 64; and influences of Sirk and Fassbinder, 208n8; and Israeli "personal" cinema, 61, 62, 63; and realism, 67; and Tel Aviv, 55, 135; and Zionist master narrative, 73, 74
Bar Kochba, 203n14
Barash, Adi, 169
Barbi, Doron, 31
Barkan, Yehuda, 118
Barnard, Ian, 101
bar(s), 37, 39; and Guttman's cinema, 51, 54, 59, 62, 70, 135–36; and *Life According to Agfa* (Dayan), 49, 50, 51, 52, 53
Baruch, Zion, 123
Bat-Adam, Michal, 16, 174
Bat Shalom, 42
Beaufort (Cedar), 201n1, 216n1
Beit Tzvi film school, 30, 61
Ben-Gurion, David, 72
Ben-Shaul, Nitzan S., 35
Benousilio, Gili, 31
Berger, Knut, 115, 118
Berger, Tamar, 205n9
Bergman, Nir, 201n1
Berkman, Tsak, 98
Berlin, 115, 117, 118, 148, 216n2
Bernheimer, Avner, 104, 213n14
Bersani, Leo, 7, 59, 94–95, 97
Betsky, Aaron, 69
Beyond Flesh (Yosef), 2–3
Bezalel Academy of Arts and Design, 98, 146
Biale, David, 8, 18, 20
Big Eyes (Zohar), 13, 204n4
Big Girl (Yaron), 15
bildungsroman, 32. *See also* novel of formation
Bin-Noun, Rivka, 165
biography, 134, 180
biracial sexual relationships, 14; and *The Bubble* (Fox), 119–23. *See also* forbidden love; interracial couples; miscegenation
bisexual(s), 6, 17, 30, 98, 169

Black Laundry (*Kvisa Shchora*), 169–70
Black Panthers (Israel), 9, 97, 202n6
Black Panthers (United States), 9, 202n6
Black(s)/blackness, 116; and *Far From Heaven* (Haynes), 210n16; and Fassbinder's cinema, 79; and gay subculture, 212n11; and *Imitation of Life* (Sirk), 81
Blow Job (Warhol), 106–07
Blow Up (Antonioni), 35
B'not Pesya (The Pesya Girls), 162
Bonanni, Angel, 124
borders, 33, 101, 104, 106, 107, 118; of the frame, 107, 118; of gay community/experience, 180, 188; and 1948 "green line", 90, 212n1; sexual and racial, 172; of Zionist-Israeli discourse, 22
Bourekas films, 17, 21, 60, 67, 118, 129, 203n12, 203n13. *See also* Israeli cinema
Boyarin, Daniel, 8, 19, 203n14, 204n15
Boyarin, Jonathan, 53
brith, 19, 189, 190
British Mandate, 14
Broken Wings (Bergman), 201n1
Bubble, The (Fox), 16, 94, 95, 98, 119–23, 125, 126, 186; and Arab-Jewish mixed couples, 174, 175; and fantasy, 124; and Israeli-Palestinian conflict, 169; and political protest, 122
Bukstein, Ania, 194
bulldozer(s), 170, 171, 175, 216n19
Burton, Richard, 100
Butler, Judith, 133, 214n5

Camatoy, Salvador (Sally), 157, 215n13
camcorder, 137, 167, 214n8
Camp, 38, 67, 102, 208n6
Camper, Fred, 68, 71
Caouette, Jonathan, 132, 139
Carlisle, Ann, 31
castration, 19
Cedar Joseph, 201n1, 216n1
censorship, 4; of *A Different Shadow* (Asulin), 15, 131; external 2; and Guttman, 15; self-, 2, 107

Index   237

channel 2 (Israeli TV), 126, 213n14. *See also* Israeli TV
checkpoint(s): and *The Bubble* (Fox), 120, 121, 122; and *Zero Degrees of Separation* (Flanders), 174. *See also* roadblocks
Chetrit, Sami Shalom, 9
childhood/children, 12, 55, 165, 172, 201n2, 206n23; and adoption, 168; and *Antarctica* (Hochner), 188; and *brith,* 189; and "domestic ethnography" (Renov) films, 138, 140, 144, 145, 148, 149, 150; and *Family Matters* (Noy and Ivry), 166–69, 215n17; and Fox's cinema, 102, 103, 117, 118, 119, 123; and *Gan* (Shatz and Barash), 178; and Guttman's cinema, 64, 66; and *Keep Not Silent* (Alexander), 195, 196; and *Tel Aviv Stories* (Yaron and Menahemi), 39, 41
Cinguetti, Gigliola, 118
circumcision, 19, 189
city(ies), 26, 27, 29, 35, 42; and the "creative industries" (Florida), 206n23. *See also* Tel Aviv
Citizen Nawi (Mossek), 216n21
civil partnerships, 168
class, 34, 62, 90, 101, 144, 146, 204n16; and cities, 27; and "creative", 206n23; and gay men/lesbians, 10, 26, 46, 93, 94, 98, 139, 151; and hegemony, 93; and melodrama, 208n8; and Orientalism, 212n10; and plurality of Israeli gay experiences, 133
Clinton, Chelsea, 99
Cloth Tales (Sipurei Badim, Guttman), 207n1
club(s), 33, 35, 37, 103, 116, 124, 154, 177; and Guttman's cinema, 59, 68, 75; and *Paper Dolls* (Heymann), 157, 159; and S&M, 165
Cohen, Itzik, 160, 161, 162
colonial fantasy, 212n10, 212n11; of Mizrahi men in *Gotta Have Heart* (Fox), 98–104
colonialism, 100, 101, 175; and Fox's cinema, 23, 197; Zionist movement as an extension of European, 3, 171, 205n9
coming out, 4, 79, 82, 97, 101, 108, 110, 124; and *Almost There* (Yehuda and Alexis), 144; and Heymann, 148, 152, 153, 154, 155; and *Keep Not Silent* (Alexander), 196; and *Say Amen!* (Deri), 139–42
consumerism, 25, 36, 43–49, 90
Coppola, Francis Ford, 35, 213n16
Copti, Scandar, 201n1, 216n1
creative industries, the, 206n23
Crows (Menahemi), 30–35, 37, 40, 49, 94, 204n6, 205n7, 205n8
cruising, 37, 51, 64, 68, 70, 73, 80, 96. *See also* Independence Park

Dana International, 42, 203n10, 206n21, 212n8, 213n17
Danker, Ran, 191
Davar (newspaper), 77, 205n15
Dayan, Assi, 5, 10, 49, 52, 53, 54, 184
Dayan, Moshe, 53
Dayan, Nissim, 174
death/dying, 95; and *The Bubble* (Fox), 121, 122; and *Crows* (Menahemi), 32, 33; and *Death Cause: Homophobia* (Kotzer), 215n14; and *Eyes Wide Open* (Tabakman), 191; of Guttman, 15, 23, 58, 60, 86, 134, 165, 210n15; and Guttman's cinema, 52, 54, 58, 59, 63, 64, 65, 71, 73, 86; of Ofra Haza, 215n16; and *Last Post* (Dotan), 137, 138; of Hezi Leskly, 163, 164, 165; and *Life According to Agfa* (Dayan), 52, 54; and *Mary Lou* (Fox), 124; of Yitzhak Rabin, 96, 97, 126; and *Repeat Dive* (Dotan), 14; and *Tied Hands* (Wolman), 215n15; and *Walk on Water* (Fox), 117; and *Yakantalisa* (Lev), 162–66; and *Yossi and Jagger* (Fox), 95, 104, 105, 106, 109, 112–15, 123, 212n4
Death Cause: Homophobia (Kotzer), 215n14
degaying (Bersani), 94–95, 97
D'Emilio, John, 202n5, 202n8

Department of Film and Television at Tel Aviv University, 94, 163
Deri, David, 138, 139–43, 151
desire: and colonial, 99, 100, 103, 212n10; and "forbidden", 102, 115, 191–97, 210n16; and Fox's cinema, 98, 99, 100, 102, 104, 105, 106, 107, 108, 115, 116; and gay/homosexual, 4, 14, 148, 169, 191, 192, 194; and Guttman's cinema, 59, 66, 70, 75; and lesbian, 145, 194–97; men as objects of, 75, 107; and polymorphous, 202n8; to rear children, 169; and women, 66, 67
Despair (Fassbinder), 67
Desperately Seeking Susan (Seidelman), 30
Diary (Perlov), 149–50
Diaspora, 33, 190
Diaspora Jews, 13, 108; and feminine/effeminate/sissy, 19, 90, 97, 203n14; and homosexuality, 19, 21; and rabbinic figures, 203n14
Dick, Vivienne, 204n7
difference: and age, 208n8; and class, 208n8; and ethnic, 170, 208n8; and gay life, 150; among gay men, 97, 159; and Guttman, 57, 80; and Jews in Christian Europe, 20; and racial, 13, 170, 177; and religious, 177; and sexual, 13, 139, 156, 164, 186, 196; and sex between men, 107. *See also* otherness
Different Shadow, A (Asulin), 15, 131, 203n11
Different War, A (Gal), 184–86
Diker, Avital, 52
Dionysus at Dizengof Centre (Berger), 205n9
discourse, 85, 190, 198, 201n2, 211n23; and AIDS, 206n26, 215n16; and the city, 26, 27, 37; and dominant, 3, 77, 116; and gay/queer, 5, 17, 24, 26, 49, 92, 93, 116, 130, 141, 168; and gender 5, 29; and heterosexual, 116; and ideology, 84; and Israeli/national, 3, 5, 11, 15, 22, 29, 52, 77, 86–87, 98, 108, 165, 186; and militarist, 101; and minority, 23, 60, 67; and Orientalist/colonial, 102, 103, 205n9; and political, 92; and queer 7, 168; and sexuality 5, 29; and Tel Aviv, 37; and "Third World films" (Shohat), 44; and Zionist, 17, 22, 23, 205n9
Divine (Harris Glenn Milstead), 188
Dizengof 99 (Nesher), 15, 16
Doane, Mary Ann, 210n16, 210n17
documentaries, 16; and *Amos Guttman, Film Director* (Kotzer), 60, 80; and Direct Cinema, 131; and "domestic ethnographies" (Renov), 138–51; and fantasy elements, 136–37; and fictional elements, 151; and gay themes, 23, 87, 127, 129–81, 183; and international, 181; and Israeli cinema, 20; and *Keep Not Silent* (Alexander), 195–97; and lesbianism, 15, 130, 143–46, 195–97; and *The Quest for the Missing Piece* (Lotan), 189–90; and technology advances, 130–31; and *Trembling before G-D* (DuBowski), 190
Dotan, Anat, 133–38
Dotan, Shimon, 14
Double Bouskilla (Revach), 188, 203n9
drag, 156; and *Antarctica* (Hochner), 188; and *Edinburgh Doesn't Wait for Me* (Laufer), 162; and *Fine Trouble* (Dayan), 11; and *Mary Lou* (Fox), 118, 124, 125; and *Paper Dolls* (Heymann), 152, 157, 159; and *Positive Story* (Kotzer), 164; and *Snuker* (Davidson), 11
Dress, The (Ne'eman), 35–36, 51
Drifting (*Nagua*, Guttman, long), 8, 10, 15, 57, 58, 62, 67, 68, 73, 74, 75, 133, 197; and awards, 209n13; and family, 64; and funding, 77–78; and Guttman's conflicting selves, 81, 83; and Israeli-Palestinian conflict, 169; and notion of "abroad", 61; and reception, 79–80; and sex scene, 23, 76–77; and Tel Aviv, 55
Drifting (*Nagua*, Guttman, short), 15, 57, 80, 81

Index 239

Druze, 198
Dubinchik, Lucy, 187
DuBowski, Sandi Simcha, 190
Duggan, Lisa, 215n18
Duvall, Robert, 213n16
Dyer, Richard, 81, 107, 108, 207n4, 210n16
dystopia: and Guttman's cinema, 73; and Tel Aviv, 29, 50, 51

Edelman, Lee 7, 108, 168–69
Edinburgh Doesn't Wait for Me (Laufer), 151, 152, 159–62
Einy, Menachem, 11
Elian, Yona, 11, 16
Elizur, Yuval, 131
Elsaesser, Thomas, 208n7, 208n8
Eretz Yisrael, 18, 73. *See also* Land of Israel; Palestine (pre-state Israel)
essentialism: and difference of Jews, 20; and identities, 26, 79, 151, 188; and sexualities, 7, 19, 137, 151
Ethiopian immigrants, 91
ethnicity/ethnic identities, 46, 91, 94, 97, 133, 203n10; and discrimination/oppression, 13, 64, 142, 170, 189; representations of in Israeli cinema, 2, 23, 41, 46, 61, 98, 101, 103, 122, 139, 157, 197, 198, 208n7, 214n6
ethnography, 138, 156, 157; and "domestic" (Renov), 138–51
Eurovision Song Contest, 99, 102, 103, 111, 203n10, 206n21, 213n17
excess, stylistic: and Fox's cinema, 43, 111; and Guttman's cinema, 15, 68, 186; and Sirk's cinema, 67, 68;
exoticism, 99, 101, 159, 212n11
Eyes Wide Open (Tabakman), 28, 191–94, 195, 196

family, 15, 23, 45, 96, 118, 177, 178, 179, 202n3, 202n8; and alternate/alternative, 31, 130, 166–69, 180; and autobiographical films, 24, 138–51, 214n10, 214n11; and Guttman's cinema, 60, 63–66, 70, 83; and Orthodox Jews, 191, 193, 194, 195, 196

Family Matters (Noy and Ivri), 166–69
Fanon, Frantz, 65
Far from Heaven (Haynes), 210n16
fashion industry, 47, 207n1
Fassbinder, Werner-Rainer, 59, 69, 70, 79, 108; and *Fear Eats the Soul*, 208n8; and national cinema, 208n7; and 1950s melodrama, 22, 66; and realism, 67; on Sirk's films, 81, 82, 83, 211n21
fathers, absence of, 55, 64, 65
Fear Eats the Soul (Fassbinder), 208n8
Feigenboim, Miri, 111
female singers/voices, 110, 111, 118
Female Trouble (Waters), 188
feminine: Jew, 19, 20, 97, 203n14; order/activities/realm, 41, 173, 184
femininity, 17, 18, 118, 188, 214n6; and gayness/homosexuality, 11, 47, 48, 66, 74, 108, 110, 112, 114, 124, 159, 162, 184, 185, 186, 201n2, 207n4; and Israeli/Zionist society, 21
feminism, 4; and Israel 9, 97; and *Shchur* (Hasafri), 214n6; and *Song of the Siren* (Fox), 45; and *Tel Aviv Stories* (Yaron and Menahemi), 41
Filipino workers in Israel, 152, 157–59. See also *Paper Dolls* (Heymann)
film: formal and visual elements, 4, 21, 22, 24, 62, 132, 133, 136, 165, 171, 180, 181, 186; and narrative/theme, 4, 21, 22, 43, 61, 62, 111, 132, 136, 180, 186, 209n14; textual analysis of, 4
film festivals, 2, 104, 148, 184; Doc Aviv, Tel Aviv, 214n10; Jerusalem International, 162; London Lesbian and Gay, 144; Montreal World, 78; Venice, 216n1
Fine Trouble (Assi Dayan), 10, 184
Fireworks (Anger), 69
Flaming Creatures (Smith), 136
Flanders, Elle, 133, 170–76, 216n20
Florentine (Fox), 49, 94, 95–97, 126
Florida, Richard, 206n23
Folk, 34; dancing, 75, 102, 103, 117, 124–25, 126; and imagery, 171; and

songs/music, 55–56, 68, 74, 99, 102, 103, 111, 126
Folman, Ari, 201n1, 216n1
forbidden love, 14, 121–22, 193, 209n11. *See also under* desire
foreign workers in Israel, 157. *See also* Filipino workers in Israel; *Paper Dolls* (Heymann),
Foucault, Michel, 1, 201n2
Four Mothers, 42
Fox, Eytan, 17, 23, 28, 37, 87, 89–127, 169, 177, 188, 201n1, 212n4, 213n12; and the army, 23, 95, 96, 186, 212n6; and Ashkenazi hegemonic elite, 16, 23; and fantasy/dreamlike reality, 98, 99, 123, 124, 125; and heteronormativity, 91, 92, 114, 115, 117, 176, 186; and Hollywood, 206n22; and homophobia, 94, 105, 111; and influence, 130, 154, 156, 183, 187; and music, 111–12, 117, 118, 121; and neocolonial view, 197; and public/private or political/personal barrier, 95–98, 112, 122; and *Song of the Siren*, 5, 22, 38, 42–49; and stereotypes, 116, 124, 160–62; and Tel Aviv, 22, 28
frame, cinematic, 32, 38, 141, 148, 163, 216n20; and Fox's cinema, 46, 107, 112, 118; and Guttman's cinema, 62, 67, 68. *See also under* borders
France, 194, 202n4
Frank, Gil, 96
free-market economy, 33, 43
Freedman, Estelle B., 202n5, 202n8
French New Wave Cinema, 61
Freud, Sigmund, 134–35
Friedman, Alon, 120
Frumer, Avinof, 163–66
Fucking Different Tel Aviv, 216n2
Furstenberg, Hani, 113
fututrism, 52, 168, 169

Gabizon, Savi, 206n27
Gal, Nadav, 184
Gan (Shatz and Barash), 169, 176–80
Ganor, Bella, 64

gay: and active/passive or top/bottom binary, 101, 107, 108; approaches 7; and bar, 54, 59, 62, 70; and consciousness, 1, 9, 26, 43, 67; and the "creative industries", 206n23; and discourse, 5, 17, 24, 26, 49, 93, 141, 168, 169; and districts, 28–29
gay-straight dichotomy 7, 12, 21; and icon, 110; and liberal European, 116; linguistic term 6; and macho "clone" look, 107; and marriage/wedding, 167, 187, 195, 197; and narrative, 23, 43, 47, 112, 139, 180; stereotypical/archetypal image of, 10, 12, 14, 48, 66, 106, 107, 108, 110, 114, 124, 212n11; and visibility, 10, 92, 93, 95, 155, 156, 212n8
gay community, 5, 7, 43, 169, 202n4; and global, 9; "imagined community", 46; and oppressive practices, 168, 169
gay community in Israel, 2, 5, 6, 7, 9, 18, 24, 43, 189, 190, 194, 197, 203n13; and AIDS, 206n24; and alliance with liberal-Left bloc, 23, 186; aspiration for 5, 24; challenging of 6, 151, 180; construction/emergence of, 21, 24; diversity of, 5, 133, 180, 181, 186; and endorsement of/subordination to oppressive practices, 10; and Fox's cinema, 16, 23, 28, 89–127; and Guttman's cinema, 23, 57–87, 185; and homogenous, 180; and integrationist approach, 10, 16, 28, 31, 33, 48, 91, 156, 185–86, 190, 202–03n8; and internalization of heterosexist norms 10, 102, 108, 115; and mainstream ideology, 22; and nonfiction cinema, 129–81; and "positive" self images, 23, 75, 79, 80; and practices of inclusion and exclusion, 23, 46, 80, 139, 157; and presence, 26, 28; and separatist ethos, 185; social acceptance of 10, 91, 130, 155; and urbanism/Tel Aviv, 21, 22, 25–56, 21, 94, 119, 140, 176, 185, 188; and violent, 54, 59; and *Yakantalisa* (Lev), 163, 164

Index 241

gay culture, 187, 213n14; and Israel, 4, 15, 22, 28, 36, 176; and Israeli cinema 10; and Tel Aviv, 25–56, 37, 38, 49, 185

Gay Days (Qedar), 214n3

gay/lesbian/same sex experience, 17, 45, 209n14; and Fox's cinema, 23, 111, 186; in Israel, 5, 10, 18, 24, 139, 160, 180, 183, 188, 203n13; and plurality, 133, 150; and Tel Aviv, 15

Gay Games (Kotzer), 215n14

gay identity/selfhood, 1–2, 4, 6, 8, 17, 130, 170, 180, 181; and autobiographical films, 24, 132; construction of in Israel, 15; and consumerism, 43–49; destabilization of, 4, 188; emergence of in Israel 9; and Fox, 16, 89–127; and Guttman 8, 15, 22, 57–87; in opposition to queer 7; and performance/performativity, 151–59; and "sissiness", 98, 104–15, 184; and the United States, 28

gay men in Israel, 18; exclusion from the army, 20, 104, 209n10; and representations in Israel media, 9; and Tel Aviv, 25–56

gay movement (international), 9; and United States/North America, 7, 8, 9, 202n5, 202n8

gay movement (Israel), 130, 201n3, 202n7; and Ashkenazi elite/hegemonic culture, 91, 92, 93, 97, 203n8; emergence/shaping of 2, 4, 7, 8, 9, 10, 20; and Guttman's cinema, 57; and "leftist" views, 123; and Tel Aviv, 24, 28, 29; visibility of, 9, 10, 93

gay revolution: in Israel 8, 91, 93; legal aspects of 9, 20, 86, 92, 104, 126, 130, 202n3

gay sensibility, 25–26; and Israel, 216n2; and *Song of the Siren* (Fox), 43–49. *See also* sensibility

gayness, 3, 8, 12, 18, 21, 26, 38, 159; and autobiographical/nonfiction films, 133, 142, 146, 148, 159; and Fox's cinema, 16, 37, 97, 98, 101, 102, 105, 106, 108, 110, 118, 127, 186; and Guttman, 62, 81; and Rock Hudson, 81; signs of, 210n16

gaze, 74, 81, 107–08, 138, 141; and penetrative, 41, 74

gender; 118; and Dana International, 203n10; essentialist/fixed model of, 137, 188, 214n5; and gay community/life, 2, 46, 94, 188, 189; and gay relations, 107, 108, 111; and Israeli collective memory, 73; and Israeli discourse 5, 29; and Tel Aviv/urbanity, 30, 31, 41, 47; and Zionism, 18, 20

Genet, Jean, 165

gentiles, 161, 204n15

German Jews, 27

Germans, 125. *See also under* Nazism/Nazis

Germany, 116, 174, 190, 206n21; and *Drifting* (Guttman, long), 61, 64; and *Family Matters* (Noy and Ivry), 166, 167, 168; and Fassbinder, 208n7, 208n8; and Heymann, 215n12; and Sirk, 211n22

Gertz, Nurith, 2, 3, 22

Gilman, Sander L., 8

Gitai, Amos, 54

Give Me Ten Desperate Men (Zimmer), 105

Gledhill, Christine, 67

Gluzman, Michael, 8

Goldberg, Ayal, 138, 146–47, 214n11

Goldberg, Ruthie, 38

Good Boys (Hochner), 177, 179, 180, 186, 188

Gordon, Maya, 164, 165

Gotta Have Heart (Fox), 94, 98–104, 107, 124, 125, 126, 197, 213n12

Gove, Ben, 116

government: and financial aid to cinema, 77, 78, 183, 209n12; and *Good Boys* (Hochner), 177; and indifference to people with HIV/AIDS, 164

Grad, Tzahi, 160, 161

Gramsci, Antonio, 93

Grundmann, Roy, 106–07

Gulf War, 29, 50; and *Song of the Siren* (Fox/Linur), 45–49, 95
Guttman, Amos, 57–87, 8, 10, 15, 16, 22, 37, 38, 44, 94, 95, 97, 164, 165, 197, 207n1, 208n7, 208n8, 211n22, 215n14; and awards, 209n13, 211n24; and camp, 208n6; and casting, 118, 205n8, 207n2; and censorship, 15, 78; and conflicting selves, 80–85, 211n22; and *Crows*, 31, 204n6, 205n8; and dance, 75; and expressionism, 57; and funding, 77–78, 209n12, 209n14; and gay community, 23, 54; and hyperrealism, 15; and influence, 17, 21, 30, 31, 127, 130, 177, 183, 187, 188, 204n6; and *Last Post* (Dotan), 133–38; and *Nighthawks* (Peck), 209–10n14; and Palestinian-Israeli conflict, 169; and reception of his films, 77–81, 86, 210n15; and self-oppression/internal homophobia, 79; and Tel Aviv, 22, 28, 40, 50, 51, 52, 55, 185; and Zionist-Israeli society, 54, 56, 126, 129, 177, 185
Gutwein, Daniel, 212n2, 212n3

Haganah, 14
Ha'ir (newspaper), 36, 37, 205n13. See also local press; *mekomonim*
Hairdresser, The (Revach), 11, 188, 203n9
Hairspray (Waters), 188
Hakim, Osnat, 98
Halberstam, Judith, 215n18
Hall, Stuart, 84
Halliday, Jon, 210n18, 211n22
Halperin, David M., 112, 201n2
HaMavri (Goldberg), 138, 146–47, 148, 150, 214n11
Hammas, 117
Hammond, Mike, 68
Hamsin (Wachsmann), 14, 169, 174, 216n19
Hanson, Ellis, 115
Harel, Alon, 92–93
Hasafri, Hannah Azulay, 214n6
Hasafri, Shmuel, 130

Haynes, Todd, 58
He Who Steals from a Thief Is Not Guilty (Revach), 11
Hebrew literature, 1, 2, 42; and Tel Aviv, 38
hegemonic culture/values, 93, 97, 105, 168; and Fox's cinema, 111, 118, 126; and Guttman's cinema, 58, 62, 73
Heroic-nationalist genre, 20, 60, 62, 63, 67, 73, 75, 105, 161, 162. See also Israeli cinema
Herzl, Theodor, 69
heteronormative values/order/domain, 9, 23, 28, 29, 43, 117, 167, 169
heterosexist values/establishment/norms in Israel, 10, 47, 74, 85, 91, 92, 114, 115, 117, 126, 184
heterosexual: actors in gay roles, 118, 160; AIDS victims, 215n16; arena, 166; becoming, 64; blueprint/code/model/status, 102, 106, 108, 115; characters in *Song of the Siren* (Fox), 43, 45, 47, 48; colonization of camp (Meyer), 208n6; culture, 18, 95; discourses, 116; filmmakers, 4, 132; hegemony, 23, 112; homosexual-dichotomy, 12; identity, 21; Israeli society, 20, 75, 80; Jew, 19, 20, 108; majority, 80, 81, 97, 207n4; militaristic morals, 114; norms, 167; passing for, 12, 82; patriarchy, 18; pleasures, 208n5; relations/love stories, 11, 14, 101, 113–14, 117, 122, 132, 154, 213n14, 213n15; Sabra masculinity, 112; sex, 82; world, 74, 187
heterosexuality, 97, 120, 123; as compulsory, 7, 42, 211n20; and *Edinburgh Doesn't Wait for Me* (Laufer), 161; and *Fine Trouble* (Dayan), 11; and Guttman's cinema, 83; and Rock Hudson, 81, 211n20; and *It Kinda Scares Me* (Heymann), 154; and male prostitution, 178; and stereotypes, 114, 129; and *Yossi and Jagger* (Fox), 114; and Zionism, 17, 18, 19, 42

Index   243

heterosexual(s), 12, 13, 16, 30, 161, 168; and Fox's cinema, 23, 89, 95, 107, 120, 123, 186
Heymann, Tomer, 139, 146, 147–59, 215n12
Hide and Seek (Wolman), 14, 28, 169
Himmo, King of Jerusalem (Guttman), 57, 58, 60, 67, 71–73, 80, 83, 85, 86
Himmo, King of Jerusalem (Kaniuk), 71, 73
Hirschfeld, Ariel, 165
HIV virus/status, 54, 57, 65, 116; and documentaries, 134, 137; and *Positive Story* (Kotzer), 162–66
Hochner, Yair, 177, 186–88, 216n2
Hollywood, 81, 110; and Fox's cinema, 44, 46, 99, 114, 186, 206n22; and Guttman's cinema, 66–71, 75; and musical, 75; and queer characters, 213n15
Holocaust, 50, 165; memory of, 115, 125; and second generation of survivors in *Walk on Water* (Fox), 115–19; and terminology in relation to Israeli occupation, 174
home movies: and *Say Amen!* (Deri), 139; and *Stefan Braun* (Alkalay), 201–02n3; and *Tarnation* (Caouette), 132; and *The Way Home* (Heymann), 150; and *Zero Degrees of Separation* (Flanders), 170, 171
homoeroticism: and Fox, 104; and *Hamsin* (Wachsmann), 14; and *Himmo, King of Jerusalem* (Guttman), 73; and *Repeat Dive* (Dotan), 14
homonormativity (Ahmed), 215n18
homophobia, 42, 154, 167, 211n20, 216n21; and Fox's cinema, 23, 94, 105, 109, 111, 114, 116; and Guttman/Guttman's cinema, 57, 58, 79
homosexual: ambivalence, 73; body, 108, 112, 114; camp connotations, 208n6; characters, 184; desire(s), 14, 104, 116, 190, 191; experiences, 18; heterosexual-dichotomy, 12; identity(ies), 169; Jew, 19, 21; life/practices in Israel, 9, 10, 97; as linguistic term, 6, 201n2; politics,

201n2; practices, 169; self, 69, 109; trait, 79
homosexuality, 6, 18, 165, 170, 176; and "domestic ethnography" (Renov) films, 138, 139, 140, 141, 142, 143, 144, 146, 148, 151; and *Edinburgh Doesn't Wait for Me* (Laufer), 159, 161; and Fox's cinema, 43, 89, 94, 102, 109, 110, 113, 114, 115, 116, 118, 121, 124, 125, 186; and Guttman's cinema, 15, 57, 64, 65, 69, 81, 82, 86; and Heymann, 152, 153, 154, 155, 158; and Rock Hudson, 81, 210n18, 211n19, 211n20; and Israel, 9, 10, 18, 38, 92, 183, 189, 202n3; and Judaism, 32, 190, 193, 194, 197; and Mizrahi Jews, 13, 101; and Muslim culture, 216n22; and 1950s American culture, 208n5, 210n16; representations of in Israeli cinema, 4, 7–8, 10, 11, 14, 15, 112, 185, 189; and urbanity, 26
homosexual(s): 7, 11, 142; and Meir Ariel, 110; and the army, 155, 165; and Christian Europe, 20; and *Crows*, 30, 31; and Fox's films, 16, 114; and Guttman's cinema, 75; and Mizrahi, 101; murder of, 215n14; and Muslim mores, 178; and religion, 197; as species, 201n2
Hoyberger, Gal, 54, 59
Huberman, Noam, 188
Hudson, Rock, 81, 82, 210n18, 211n19, 211n20
humanism, 174
Huri, Sami, 98
Huyssen, Andreas, 134
hybrid cinema, 17, 130, 214n6
hybridity, 103
hypermasculinity, 125, 204n15
hypersexuality, 13, 212n11

I Shot My Love (Heymann), 215n12
identity politics in Israel, 60, 67, 87; and gay, 4. *See also* pluralism
ideology: and national, 151–62; and patriarchy, 84–85; "struggle" in, 84, 85

244　　　　　　　　　　　　　　　　　　　　　　　　　　　　　　　　　　　　Index

IDF (Israel Defense Forces), 32, 213n16; dominance of, 91–92; and *It Kinda Scares Me,* 152; and *Life According to Agfa* (Dayan), 49, 50, 52, 54; and *Yossi and Jagger* (Fox), 104, 105, 106
Imitation of Life (Sirk), 66, 82, 84; and passing, 210n17; and whiteness, 81
immigration, 145, 157, 167, 171. *See also* foreign workers in Israel; Israel; *Paper Dolls* (Heymann)
Independence Park, 37, 73, 82
Ingber, Nachman, 86
interfemale intimacy, 16
interracial couples: and gay 8, 98; and *Zero Degrees of Separation* (Flanders), 170–76. *See also* biracial sexual relationships; forbidden love; miscegenation
intertextuality, 4
Intifada: first, 172; second, 52, 184
Ish Kassit, Moshe, 11
Israel: archenemies of, 116, 118; and civic values, 190, 212n5, 212n6; cultural and political history of, 4; emigration from, 143–46, 151, 171, 205n15; establishment of (1948), 89, 170; and female perspective, 40; and flag, 46; immigration to, 144, 215n12; and Jews, 149; and law, 190; liberal image of/disposition, 1, 9; liberalization of, 91, 92; and peace agreement with Jordan, 91; and politics, 2, 177; and public sphere, 2
Israeli-Arab conflict/struggle, 105, 119. *See also* Israeli-Palestinian conflict
Israeli cinema/filmmaking, 2, 3; books on 2; and *Bourekas* films, 21, 60, 67; and censorship 2, 4, 15; and the Committee to Encourage Film Production, 77; and critical apparatuses, 61; and distribution apparatuses, 2; and funding, 4, 77, 183, 214n4; and governmental discrimination against, 77; and heroic-nationalist genre, 20, 60, 62, 63, 67, 73, 75, 105, 161, 162; history of, 183, 186; and industry, 4, 199, 203n13; and institutional apparatuses, 4, 183; and Israeli society, 129; and marginality, 197–99; and military films, 3, 98; and nation, 2; and nonfiction, 129–81; and "personal" cinema, 20, 60–63, 68; and pre-state Israel, 3, 20; and production, 2; and queer films/filmmaking, 3, 132, 142; and reception in Israel and abroad, 2, 201n1; and representations of Israeli manhood, 20; revival of 2, 183; scholarly interest in 2; and television broadcasting, 4, 131; and "universal" films, 61–62, 63
Israeli collective: and identity, 3, 36, 90, 97, 139, 198; and individual concerns, 36; and memory, 73
Israeli culture, 3, 89, 92; and dominant, 32; and Guttman, 62; and mainstream, 166; and national-masculine discourse 3, 108
Israeli film academy awards, 42–43, 60
Israeli national narrative, 129, 184; and Guttman's cinema, 73, 75; and *Yossi and Jagger* (Fox), 106
Israeli "New Wave" cinema, 35–36, 44, 51. *See also* Israeli "personal" cinema
Israeli "personal" cinema, 20, 129; and Guttman, 60–63, 68, 83
Israeli-Palestinian conflict, 44, 115, 122, 123, 126, 169–80, 209n9; and the wall, 170. *See also* Arab-Israeli conflict/struggle
Israeli TV: and cable, 126, 131; and channel 2, 126, 213n14; and commercial, 131; and *A Different Shadow* (Asulin) 15, 131, 203n11; and gay-themed films, 131, 181; and Guttman, 15, 207n1; and reality and talk shows, 131, 214n8; and satellite, 131; and state channel, 15, 131, 203n11, 207n1; and *Yakantalisa* (Lev), 131, 133
It Kinda Scares Me (Heymann), 151–57, 159
Ivgi, Moshe, 207n27
Ivry, Yoram, 166

Index   245

Jaffa, 26, 205n9
Jagger, Mick, 108
jazz, 35
Jerusalem 48, 49, 95, 96, 120, 166, 174, 180, 184, 190, 204n3; and *Eyes Wide Open* (Tabakman), 191–94; and gay pride, 149; and *Himmo, King of Jerusalem* (Guttman), 71–73; and Tel Aviv, 27–28, 56
Jewish body, 19, 20, 118. See also Muscle Jew
Jewish male, 3; and "effeminate", 18, 19. See also Muscle Jew
Jewishness/Jewish identity, 132, 143, 189
Jordan, peace agreement with, 91
jouissance, 68, 169
Judaism, 174; and homosexuality, 32, 189–97; and lesbianism, 194–97; and sexuality 8
Jules and Jim (Truffaut), 35
Julien, Issac, 212n11

Kabbani, Rana, 100
Kahn, Dalit, 43
Kalchinsky, Smadar, 51, 58
Kama, Amit, 79, 89, 206n24
Kaminer, Amir, 38, 80, 205n14
Kapon, Hillel, 184
Karlin, Sean, 135
Kaspi, Natan, 131
kibbutz/kibbutzim, 17, 33, 34, 72, 118, 206n27; breakdown of, 36
Kikar Malchei Yisrael, 96, 97, 212n7
Kimchi, Alona, 58
Kimmerling, Baruch, 90, 105
Kishon, Ephraim, 203n12
Klinger, Barbara, 207–08n5
Knoller, Ohad, 104, 120, 212n4, 213n14
Kohner, Susan, 81
Kol Ha'ir (newspaper), 36. See also local press; *mekomonim*
Koshashvili, Dover, 201n1
Kotzer, Ran, 60, 162–66, 215n14
Kronish, Amy, 130
Kuni Lemel in Tel Aviv (Zilberg), 11

Lacan group, 211n23
Lacan, Jacques, 135

land, 171, 173; and Arab, 216n19
Land of Israel/ancient, Biblical land of Israel, 20, 55, 68, 90, 94, 102, 108. See also *Eretz Yisrael*; Palestine (pre-state Israel)
language, 84–85
Lapid, Yair, 47
Last Post (Dotan), 133–38, 181
Last Winter, The (Riki Shelach Nissimoff), 15, 16
Late Marriage (Koshashvili), 130, 201n1
Laufer, Erez, 151, 159, 160
Lebanon, 42, 95, 96, 104–15, 125, 213n16
Lebanon (Maoz), 216n1
Lebanon War (first), 32, 95, 127, 149, 212n5
Lebow, Alisa L., 132, 214n9
left camp, 122, 123, 170. See also Avodah (Labor) party; liberal-left bloc in Israel
legal: restriction on gay citizens in Israel, 9; revolution/change in Israel 9, 20, 86, 92; rights for LGBT 1, 91, 104. See also gay revolution
Lerski, Helmer, 97
lesbian: experience, 180; identity, 17, 132, 180. See also interfemale intimacy
lesbians, 6, 10, 17, 24, 41, 58, 86, 90, 91, 92, 93, 103, 126, 139, 151, 169, 189, 197, 198; and *Almost There* (Yehuda and Alexis), 17, 138, 143–46; and filmmaking, 18, 130, 216n2; and Israeli cinema, 15, 17, 187; and *Keep Not Silent* (Alexander), 195–97; and representations in Israel media, 9; and *The Secrets* (Nesher), 194–95; and *Zero Degrees of Separation* (Flanders), 170–76
Leskly, Hezi, 131, 163–66
Lev, Yair, 131, 162–66, 214n4
Levi, Alon, 118, 124
Levi, Hemda, 14
Levi, Yehuda, 104
LeVine, Mark, 205n9
Levitan, Nadav, 203n13
Liba, Zohar, 122

liberal-left bloc in Israel, 23, 186. *See also* Avodah (Labor) party; left camp
Lider, Ivri, 111
Life According to Agfa (Dayan), 5, 49–56
lifestyle magazines, 48, 49
Lifschitz, Tal, 213n14
lighting in film, 4, 67, 186
Likud political party, 90
Linur, Irit, 42
Liquid Sky (Tsukerman), 30–31, 204n7
Lloyd, Phyllida, 123
local press, 26, 27, 36, 37, 38. See also *mekomonim*
London, 37, 62, 164; and Lesbian and Gay Film Festival, 144; and Swinging, 35
Loshitzky, Yosefa, 2, 3, 27, 53, 54, 100, 121, 174–75, 209n11, 212n10, 216n19
Lover, The (Bat-Adam), 174
Lubin, Orly, 2, 41, 43, 74
Lucas, Matt, 210n14

Maccabees, 203n14
Macht, Stephen, 16
madness, 52. *See also* mental illnesses
Mainz, Theo, 204n5
male body, 17, 59, 108, 109. *See also* Muscle Jew
male dominance/norms, 39–40, 114
male experience in Israel, 18
male prostitution, 8, 130, 176–80
Mamma Mia! (Lloyd), 123
Manhattan, 27
Manhood, 19; and Israeli cinema, 20, 184
Maoz, Samuel, 216n1
marginality, 4, 90, 157, 161, 185, 186
Marx, Karl, 1
Mary Lou (Fox), 94, 98, 118, 123–26, 186
masculinity, 17, 18, 19, 81, 109, 110, 111, 186; crisis of, 64; and European Jewish, 18; and hegemonic Ashkenazi, 14; and Tomer Heymann, 148, 152, 155, 159; and identity, 69; and Israeli society, 3, 8, 21, 66, 85, 96, 102, 184, 185; and Mizrahi Jews, 13; and performativity, 110, 184; and Zionist-Israeli, 13

Mazia, Edna, 77, 80
McHugh, Kathleen, 82
media in Israel 5, 184; and AIDS, 165; and authority, 41; and Guttman, 135; and representation of gay men and lesbians 9; and *Song of the Siren* (Fox), 47
Meiri, Noam, 160, 161
mekomonim, 36, 37, 45, 205n16
melodrama, 125, 207n3; and Fassbinder, 67; and Guttman's cinema, 44, 66–71; and *Mary Lou* (Fox), 124, 125; and 1950s Hollywood, 22, 66, 73, 193; and Sirk, 211n22
melting pot, 109, 198
memory, 134; and authenticity, 134, 135; and cultural, 134
Menahemi, Ayelet, 5, 30–42, 94, 204n6, 205n7
mental illnesses, 132. *See also* madness
Mercer, Kobena, 212n11
Mer (Mer-Khamis), Juliano, 58, 60, 207n2
Mevorach Brothers, The (Levitan), 203n13
Meyer, Moe, 208n6
Meyer, Richard, 81, 211n19, 211n20
Michaeli, Rivka, 65
Middle East: and Fox, 99, 120; and Israeli "personal cinema", 61, 62; and Mizrahi Jews/Mizrahim, 6, 129; and "new," 87, 91
migration, 145. *See also* immigration; Israel
military, 3, 9, 52, 65, 71, 164, 212n6; and "Biblical Land of Israel", 90; and exemption from service, 76, 208n9; and Fox's cinema, 23, 96, 98, 102, 103, 104–15, 188, 212n6; and *It Kinda Scares Me* (Heymann), 156; and *Repeat Dive* (Dotan), 14. *See also* army; IDF (Israel Defense Forces)
minority groups in Israel, 89, 197–99, 209n11; fear of, 10
mirrors, in Guttman's cinema, 69; in *Say Amen!* (Deri), 141

Index 247

mise-en-scène 4, 111; and Guttman's cinema, 66, 68, 186; and the Hollywood melodrama, 66; 67; and *Song of the Siren* (Fox), 43

miscegenation, 175. *See also* biracial sexual relationships; forbidden love; interracial couples

Mizrahi Jew(s)/Mizrahim, 44, 91, 171, 176; and *Bourekas* films, 118, 129, 203n12; and Dana International, 203n10; and family, 142; and Fox's cinema, 23, 98–104, 197; and gay men/community 6, 10, 97, 139, 212n8; as homosexuals, 13; as hypersexual, 13; inherent inequality of 3; and Israeli cinema, 129; and *It Kinda Scares Me* (Heymann), 155; and *Life According to Agfa* (Dayan), 49, 53; and the "Muscle Jew", 13; and oppression by Ashkenazim, 173; and *Tel Aviv Stories* (Yaron and Menahemi), 41

Modernism, 56

Moments (Bat-Adam), 15, 16

Moore, Juanita, 82

Mort, Frank, 47, 48

moshav/moshavim: and *Crows* (Menahemi), 33–35; and *The Way Home* (Heymann), 148

"Moshe" (Uchovsky), 37–38, 205n15

Mossad, 44, 115, 116, 117

Mosse, George L. 8, 204n16

Mossek, Nissim, 216n21

motherhood, 114, 188

mothers, 17

Mulvey, Laura, 73

Muscle Jew/Muscular Jew/Jewry of Muscle, 1, 3, 8, 13, 19, 20, 48, 108, 203–04n14

music, 1, 63, 110, 213n17; and documentaries, 151; and *The Dress* (Ne'eman), 35; and film 4; and Fox's cinema, 99, 102, 103, 111–12, 117, 118, 121, 126; and Guttman's cinema, 66, 68; and the Hollywood melodrama, 66; and *Tarnation* (Caouette), 132; and Tel Aviv, 37, 38; and *The Way Home* (Heymann), 150

musical (genre): and Fox, 44, 123–26; and Guttman, 75

My Michael (Wolman), 212n10

myths, national, 53, 66, 73, 74, 117; and *Edinburgh Doesn't Wait for Me* (Laufer), 161, 162; of the Sabra, 3, 23, 72; and Tel Aviv, 31, 164, 205n9

Nachträglichkeit, 134–35

Nakba, 90, 170, 173

narcissism, 69, 197

national (Israeli) agenda/cause, 39, 45, 48, 49, 92, 96, 126, 131

national cinema, 67, 208n7

national identity(ies), 35, 73, 129, 130, 151, 157–59, 179, 198

national (Israeli) press, 27, 37, 205n16

nationalism, 34

Nazism/Nazis, 115; and the Final Solution, 117; and third generation, 115, 117

Ne'eman, Judd 2, 35, 51, 76

Ne'eman, Nir, 177

negation of exile/diaspora, 20, 203–04n14

neo-Zionism, 90, 91, 211–12n1

Nesher, Avi, 11, 15, 194

Nesher, Doron, 14, 70

New Jew, 18, 20, 33; and Ezer Weizman, 90. *See also* Muscle Jew

new journalism, 36. *See also* local press; *mekomonim*

New York City, 27, 30, 35, 37, 59, 61, 63, 68, 216n2; and Punk scene, 204n7

New York Stories (Scorsese, Coppola, Allen), 35, 39

Nichols, Bill, 137

Night Soldier, The (Wolman), 76

Nighthawks (Peck), 209–10n14

nihilism/nihilistic approach, 30, 50, 180

1948 War (Independence War), 72, 73, 85, 86, 90. See also *Nakba*

1973 War (Yom Kippur War), 16, 149

1967 War (Six Day War), 9, 11, 20

Nini, Itzik, 32
Nirgad, Liron, 14
No Wave, 204n7
Nora Helmer (Fassbinder), 67
Nordau, Max, 19, 108, 203n14
novel of formation, 32, 205n10. *See also* bildungsroman
Noy, David, 166

occupation, Israeli 8, 95, 105, 106, 120, 122, 125, 177, 216n21; and *Zero Degrees of Separation* (Flanders), 170–76
occupied territories, 90, 174, 179, 209n9, 212n1; and settlements, 170; and the wall, 170, 184
Omanuti, Uri, 98
On a Narrow Bridge (Dayan), 174
Ophir, Karin, 65
oppression, 59, 67, 68, 79, 80, 82, 170, 173, 189; and ethnic, 170, 189; and gender, 189; and Jerusalem, 28; and racial, 170, 189; and religion, 189, 192; and self-, 109, 114; and sexual/sexuality 6, 18, 82, 108, 116, 170. *See also* Guttman, Amos
oppressive: hegemonic culture/system/society/mechanism/social order, 32, 35, 66, 69, 79, 169; "military phallic laws" (Yosef), 112; practices/values/attitude/rules, 6, 10, 23, 168, 176, 192; sexual mores, 116
Orient and Orientalism, 99, 159, 212n10, 212n11
Orthodox/ultra-Orthodox Jews, 10, 32, 33, 90, 190, 191–97, 198; and community/ies, 190, 191, 193, 194, 196, 197
Oscars (Academy Awards), 83, 216n1
Oslo Peace Accord, 87, 91
otherness: and dominant culture, 92; ethnic, 103, 207n2; and the gay community, 23, 157; and Guttman, 80, 85; and Jews, 20; and Juliano Mer, 60; and non-Western, 101; racial, 177; religious, 177; and sexual, 11, 23, 101, 109, 116, 161, 186, 207n2; and Tel Aviv, 28. *See also* difference
Ovadia, George, 10, 184
overreproduction, 13

Palestine (pre-state Israel), 19, 33, 102, 146, 170, 203–04n14. See also *Eretz Yisrael*
Palestine (modern day), 216n19; and gay culture, 176
Palestinian Authority, 91
Palestinians, 52, 90, 91, 116, 120, 121, 124, 216n19; and gay men 6; and self, 173; and *Zero Degrees of Separation* (Flanders) and *Gan* (Shatz and Barash), 169–80. *See also* Arabs/Arabness
Paper Dolls (Heymann), 151–59
Pappe, Ilan, 90, 91, 175
Paris, 62, 68; and student riots, 9
parody, 67
passing, 81, 82, 110, 114–15, 210n16
Past Continuous (Gitai), 54
patriarchy, 18, 85, 168; and cinema, 112; and domain, 114; and ideology, 84–85; and rabbinical system, 197
Peace Now movement, 95
Pearl, Monica B., 54
Pearl-Beker, Yael, 114
Peck, Ron, 209–10n14
Peeping Toms (Zohar), 13, 51, 204n4
Peres, Shimon, 91
performance, 136; and documentaries, 151–62
performativity, 110, 214n5; and documentaries, 136, 137, 151–62; and *Last Post* (Dotan), 134. *See also* performance
periphery, 90, 142, 156, 198
Perlov, David, 149–50
Peters, Caroline, 115
Pick, Tsvika, 123, 124, 213n17
"Pictures from a Married Life" (Mendelson), 205n15
pioneers, 102, 171, 207n27
Place, Pat, 204n7

Index   249

pluralism, 87, 92; and cultural, 90
Polak, Avshalom, 96
politics of casting, 118, 126
Positive Story (Kotzer), 162–66, 215n15
postcolonial theory 4
poststructuralism, 133–34
post-Zionism, 90, 91; and *Crows* (Menahemi), 30; and Tel Aviv, 205n9
postpunk music scene, 37. See also rock music
pride parade, 149, 156
private domain/sphere, 129, 145, 176
Private Popsicle (Davidson), 210n10
privatization, 36
procreation, 18
promiscuity, 116–17, 119, 160
prostitution, 33
psychoanalysis, 135
punk aesthetics, 205n7. See also Dick, Vivienne

Qedar, Yair, 214n3
queer, 21, 115; alternative, 168, 188; approaches, 7; call, 168; characters, 213n15; critique, 42; culture, 7, 169; discourse, 168; domain, 214n6; effects, 7, 215n18; experience, 5, 82, 180; filmmaking, 142; flaws of, 7; and heterosexual men, 47; identification, 112; identity/selfhood, 17, 24, 132, 138–51; ideology, 7; linguistic term, 6, 7, 115; politics, 7, 107; and "repressed" Jews, 3; resistance, 10, 91; sensibilities, 140; theory/theorists, 4, 9, 208n6; thought, 161
queerness, 7, 54, 132, 168, 169; and Israeli society 3, 82
Querelle (Fassbinder), 59, 108
Quest for the Missing Piece, The (Lotan), 189
Quinlan, Kathleen, 16

rabbinical law, 190
Rabin, Yitzhak, 91, 96, 126; assassination of, 95; funeral, 96, 97
race, 85, 94, 97, 100, 101, 122, 210n16; and discrimination, 169; and family, 142; and *Paper Dolls* (Heymann), 157–59. See also Black(s)/blackness; passing
Raginiano, Sharon, 104
Ram, Uri, 90, 212n5
Rath, Eliezer (Laci), 202n3
Raz, Niv, 213n14
realism, 67, 208n7; and documentaries, 132, 133, 136–37, 138, 150, 151, 214n8; and Israeli cinema, 53, 67. See also *vraisemblance*
Regirer, Ofer, 187
Re'im, Hanoch, 95
religion: and fundamentalism, 50; and gayness in Israeli cinema, 24, 183, 189–97; and political parties, 92; representation of in Israeli cinema 2; and *Say Amen!* (Deri), 139–43
Renov, Michael, 131, 134–35, 138–39
Repeat Dive (Dotan), 14
Repeat Premiers (Guttman), 57, 68–69, 71
resistance, 85; to Israeli heteronormative norms 8; to Israeli occupation, 173, 212n5; and *Positive Story* (Kotzer), 165; and prostitution, 177
Reuveni, Yotam, 79
Revach, Ze'ev, 11–14, 188, 203n9
Rita, 110, 111
roadblocks, 174. See also checkpoints
road movie (genre): and *Almost There* (Yehuda and Alexis), 143; and *Last Post* (Dotan), 136; and Zero *Degrees of Separation* (Flanders), 174
rock music, 35
Roitman-Gil, Galit, 15
romantic comedy (genre), 44
Romeo and Juliet (Shakespeare), 123
Rosenberg, Ido, 124
Rosenblum, Doron, 37
Rot, Danny, 15
Rozovska, Hina, 58
ruralism, 1
Russell, Catherine, 214n9
Russian immigrants to Israel, 10, 91

Sabra, 21, 53, 91, 100, 110, 112; and Fox's cinema, 23, 100; myth of 3, 23, 72

Safe Place, A (Guttman), 57, 64, 70
Safed, 190, 191
Safirman, Costel, 130
Said, Edward, 27, 100, 102
Sallah Shabati (Kishon), 203n12
Sam Spiegel Film School, 133
Samson, 203n14
San Francisco, 201n2
"Savage Man," 100, 212n10, 212n11. *See also* African man; Arab man; savagery
Savagery, 101
Save the Lifeguard (Zohar), 204n4
Saxey, Esther, 142
Say Amen! (Deri), 138, 139–43, 147, 148, 149, 150, 151; and cancellation of planned screenings, 214n10
Scorsese, Martin, 35, 39
screen theory, 85, 211n23
Secrets, The (Nesher), 194–95, 196
secularism, 18, 139, 140, 146, 189, 190; and Tel Aviv, 27, 48, 50, 56
Sedgwick, Eve Kosofsky, 6
Segal, Yonatan, 64, 209n13
Segev, Tom, 36, 202n5
Seidelman, Susan, 30
self, 173; and concealing, 82, 108, 111, 192, 194; and family, 138, 142, 143; and female bildungsroman, 32; homosexual, 69, 109; inconsistency of, 83, 84; and performing/rewriting in documentary/autobiographical films, 132, 134, 135, 138, 214n9; racial/cultural sense of, 142; singularity of, 140; Zionist, 21
self-authored films, 23. *See also* autobiographical films
selfhood, 24, 130, 134
Send Me an Angel (Ne'eman), 177
sensibility, 204n1
settlers (in the occupied territories), 90. *See also* occupied territories, the
sex, 55, 160, 161; anal, 23, 77, 82, 101, 107–08, 216n22; anonymous, 121, 187; between men, without being considered gay/homosexual, 169, 201n2, 216n22; casual, 64, 80, 81, 165, 187; and cinema, 34; and drive, 100,
102, 110; and Fox's cinema, 98, 100, 101, 106, 107, 213n12; and Guttman's cinema, 23, 31, 59, 64, 74, 75, 77, 78, 80, 81, 82, 83; and heterosexual, 13, 40, 53, 82, 83, 113, 114, 123; and industry, 6, 176–80, 203n13; and *Last Post* (Dotan), 136; and 1950s American culture, 207n5; and permissive approach to, 213n14; and power, 75, 101, 108; and preconceived ideas about gay, 154; and promiscuity, 116–17; as self-destructive, 53, 54, 55, 59; and Tel Aviv, 188; and workers, 180; and Zionism, 18. *See also* sexual intercourse
Sex and Character (Weininger),19
sexual: categories, 160, 181; mores, 60, 116; norms, 36, 106; perversion, 204n16; politics, 47, 49, 204n7; preference(s), 5, 6, 99, 141, 154
sexual intercourse, 16, 101, 107, 108, 136, 178
sexuality, 6, 140, 144, 149, 158, 167, 169, 175, 187, 188, 189; and African American, 208n5; and diversity, 86; as essential/fixed 7, 137, 181; and female/interfemale, 16, 41; and Fox/Fox's cinema, 23, 43, 100, 101, 103, 107, 108, 109, 110, 114, 115; and gay districts, 29; and Guttman/Guttman's cinema, 79, 83; and Rock Hudson, 81; and Israeli culture/discourse/society 3, 5, 29, 190; and Judaism 8, 190, 193, 194; and Mizrahi men, 13; and queer discourse/politics 7, 107; and race, 101; and *Song of the Siren* (Fox), 47; and Tel Aviv, 28, 49
Shalom Tower, 36, 39
Shani, Yaron, 201n1, 216n1
Sharon, Ariel, 175, 177
Sharon plan, 33
Sharon, Sarah'le, 74–75
Shatz, Ruth, 169
Shavit, Yael, 131
Shchur (Hasfari), 130, 214n6
She Had Her Gun Already (Dick), 205n7
Shechter, Ofer, 213n14

Index   251

Sheleg, Irit, 63
Shenhav-Weizman, Anat, 213n14
Shikartzi, Ofer, 58
Shimshoni, Ze'ev, 81
Shoaf, Yassin, 14
Shohat, Ella, 2, 3, 20, 35, 44, 60, 62, 63, 77, 105, 118, 197
Shtamler, Michal, 194
Shuru (Gabizon), 206–07n27
Silverman, Kaja, 67, 69
Sirk, Douglas, 59, 66, 67, 70, 71, 83, 84, 208n8, 210n17, 210n18, 211n19, 211n21; and "falseness" (Camper), 68; and split characters, 211n22; and stylistic excess, 67, 68, 111
Six Day War. *See* 1967 War
skyscrapers, 36, 40
Smith, Jack, 136
Smithereens (Seidelman), 30
Snuker (Davidson), 11
socialism, 174
sodomy, 89
soldiers, 11, 14, 23, 74, 75, 76, 96, 103, 209n9; and *The Bubble* (Fox), 120, 121, 122; and *Florentine* (Fox), 96; and gay, army attitude toward, 209n10; and *Himmo, King of Jerusalem* (Guttman), 71–73, 86; and *Life According to Agfa* (Dayan), 49, 50, 52; and *Mary Lou* (Fox), 124, 125; and "refusinks", 209n9; and *Time Off* (Fox), 95–96, 112, 122; and *Yossi and Jagger* (Fox), 95, 104–15, 117; and *Zero Degrees of Separation* (Flanders), 171, 174
Solomon, Alisa, 21,
Song of the Siren (Fox) 5, 22, 38, 42–49, 92, 94, 95, 116, 120, 205n17, 212n6
Song of the Siren (Linur), 42
Sontag, Susan, 54, 204n1, 208n6
split screen, 187
Springsteen, Bruce, 118
Srugim (TV series), 190
Staten Island (Dick), 204–05n7
Stefan Braun (Alkalay), 201–02n3
Steinovitz, Aya, 113
stereotypes, 212n11

Straight, 99, 103, 114, 123, 155, 160, 170; acting, 97, 104, 110, 155, 159; gay-dichotomy 7, 99, 114; line, 7, 215n8; passing for, 81, 110, 114; and women, 41, 42, 207n4. *See also* Heterosexual
Strauss, Zohar, 191
Sturken, Marita, 134
Suarez, Juan A., 69
subject. *See* self
suicide bombings/bombers, 50, 122, 150, 180
Superstar: The Karen Carpenter Story (Haynes), 58
Sweid, Yousef "Joe", 116, 120
symbolic law, 168
symbolic order (Lacan), 84, 135, 168

Tabakman, Haim, 28
Tabwi, Akram, 51
Tal, Ada Valerie, 60, 65, 118, 207n3
Tarnation (Caouette), 132, 139
Tarshish, Shlomo, 14
Tavori, Doron, 14
Tel Aviv, 22, 25–56, 116, 129, 160, 166, 173, 176, 178, 179, 201n3, 204n2, 204n4, 205n15; and *Antarctica* (Hochner), 187, 188; and art scene, 39; and *The Bubble* (Fox), 119–23; in contrast to Jerusalem, 27–28, 119; in contrast to kibbutzim and moshavim: city-country dichotomy, 33–35; and *Crows* (Menahemi), 30–35; and *Diary* (Perlov), 149; and dystopian/apocalyptic visions, 50–56; as a "fortress city", 52; and the gay community/gay culture, 25–56, 185, 204n3; and gay district, 28–29; and *Gotta Have Heart* (Fox), 98, 100, 102, 103; and Guttman, 62, 63, 64, 68, 73, 80, 86, 135; and *Himmo, King of Jerusalem* (Guttman), 71, 72, 86; and internal migrants, 26, 36; and International Style, 27, 51, 205n9; and *It Kinda Scares Me* (Heymann), 152, 153, 154, 155, 156; and jargon and style of writing, 37; and *Life According to Agfa* (Dayan) and

Amazing Grace (Guttman), 49–56; and *Mary Lou* (Fox), 124; and the modernist White City, 51, 56, 205n9; and modernity, 27, 52; and *Paper Dolls* (Heymann), 157; and progress, 27; and "real/fantasized" debate, 26–29, 36–37, 38; as a "rootless" city, 31, 205n9; and *Say Amen!* (Deri), 140, 141, 142, 151; Scud missile attacks on, 45, 50, 95; as a site where identifications with the state are contested 5, 40; and *Shuru* (Gabizon), 206n27; and *Song of the Siren* (Fox), 42–49; and suicide bombers/terrorism, 50, 52, 120, 122; and *Tel Aviv Stories* (Yaron and Menahemi), 35–42; and *Tied Hands* (Wolman), 215n15; and *Weekend Circles* (Shechori), 15; and *Yakantalisa* (Lev), 163, 164; as a Zionist project, 29, 34, 45, 72, 119

Tel Aviv Magazine (newspaper), 36, 38. See also local press; *mekomonim*

Tel Aviv Stories (Yaron and Menahemi), 5, 35–42

terrorism, 50, 52, 95, 115, 117, 120, 122, 173

terrorists, 76, 107

testimony, 134

They Call Me Shmil (Ovadia), 10, 184

Tied Hands (Wolman), 215n15

Time Off (Fox), 95–98, 23, 43, 94, 111–12, 117, 121, 126, 212n6

Topol, Haim, 118

transgenders, 170

transsexuals 10, 41, 60, 92, 126, 132, 139, 203n10; and films, 18, 203n13

transvestites: and *Crows* (Menahemi), 30–35; and *Paper Dolls* (Heymann), 152, 157–59

Traub, Ami, 73

Trembling before G-D (DuBowski), 190

Troupe, The (Nesher), 11

Tsukerman, Slava, 30, 204n7

Tulin, Tina, 65

Turjeman, Boaz, 31, 80, 118, 205n8

Tzuk, Sigal, 133

Uchovsky, Gal, 37–38, 94, 205n15

UNESCO, 56, 205n9

United States, 30, 36, 46, 47, 148, 150, 202n5, 204n7, 206n23, 206n24, 208n8; and antiblack discrimination, 202n6; and civil rights movement, 9; as a desired destination, 52, 61, 63; and Fox, 99, 206n22; and gay documentary filmmakers, 136; and gay identity, 28; and gay movement/community, 8, 202n4, 202n8; and identity politics, 202n4; and nonnormative sexualities in the 1950s, 82, 207n5, 211n20

universalism, 43; and Guttman's cinema, 61–62, 63; and Israeli "personal" cinema, 61

Until the Wedding (TV series), 213n14

urban migration story/narrative, 26, 28, 30, 124, 142

urbanity, 204n7, 206n23

utopian Zionism, 25, 29, 52, 54

victims, Jews as, 117

Vietnam War, 9, 213n16

Village Voice, The, 36, 209n13

violence, 120, 122, 177; and the gay community, 54

Vital, Yedidya, 124

voice-over: and *Almost There* (Yehuda and Alexis), 144, 149; and *Crows* (Menahemi), 31, 32, 33; and *Diary* (Perlov), 149; and *Last Post* (Dotan), 133, 135, 136; and *The Way Home* (Heymann), 149

vraisemblance, 67

Wachsmann, Daniel, 14. See also *Hamsin*

Wachsmann, Iggy, 62

Wagner, Richard, 69

Walk on Water (Fox), 16, 44, 94, 98, 115–19, 120, 123, 126, 186, 201n1

Waltz with Bashir (Folman), 201n1, 216n1

Walzer, Lee, 202n7

War of Independence (1948). See 1948 War

Index 253

Warhol, Andy, 106, 136; and Factory, 135
warriors, Jewish, 18, 19, 20, 108, 117, 203n14
Waters, John, 188
Waugh, Thomas, 112, 214n6
Waxman, Anat, 39
Way Home, The (Heymann), 139, 146, 147–51, 215n12
Weekend Circles (Shechori), 15
Weeks, Jeffrey, 216n22
Weininger, Otto, 19
Weiss-Berkowitz, Ronit, 165
Weizman, Ezer, 89–90
West, the, 103, 168, 174, 202n4; and gay identity, 8–9, 99, 100, 101, 102; and Guttman's cinema, 61–62, 63; and *Song of the Siren* (Fox/Linur), 45, 48; and Tel Aviv, 27, 35
West Bank, 120
white/whiteness, 10, 81, 82, 101, 142, 151; and documentary, 131; and Fox, 94, 100, 101; and gay male, 212n11; and Guttman, 23, 77
Wircer, Daniela, 120
Wolman, Dan, 76, 212n10, 215n15
woman's film. *See* melodrama
women: and discrimination of in Israeli society, 42; and Fassbinder's cinema, 79; and gay community, 97; and *Himmo, King of Jerusalem* (Guttman), 73; and Israel, 17, 18; and Victorian culture, 19; and Ezer Weizman, 89
Words of His Own (play), 160
Wright, Les, 201n2

Yakantalisa (Lev), 131, 214n4, 215n15
Yakobson, Yankale, 96
Yardbirds, The (band), 35
Yaron, Nirit, 15, 35–42
Yehuda, Sigal, 17, 138, 143–46, 147, 149

Yom Kippur War (1973). *See* 1973 War
Yosef, Raz 2, 3, 21, 59, 101, 111–12, 142, 213n13
Yossi and Jagger (Fox), 16, 23, 94, 95, 98, 104–15, 120, 122, 123, 125, 126, 186, 187, 201n1, 212n6, 213n12, 213n14; and sequel, 212n4
youth, 180; and culture, 119; and *It Kinda Scares Me* (Heymann), 151–57

Zero Degrees of Separation (Flanders), 133, 169–76, 179, 181, 216n20, 216n21
Zionism/Zionist movement, 1, 17, 19, 21, 86, 93, 174; and agrarian, 33; decline of, 50–56, 91, 212n2; and dream, 170; and erotic revolution, 18; and ethos, 92, 206n27; as an extension of European colonialism 3, 171, 173, 205n9; and ideology, 53, 89, 99, 170; and imagery/iconography, 171, 216n19; and messianic dimensions, 90, 212n1; and movement, 19; and nation building, 18; in relation to neo-Zionism and post-Zionism, 90, 91, 93; and postnationalism, 90; and pre-state cinema/films, 3, 20; and progress, 55; and symbols, 74; and terminology, 161; and ultra-Orthodox Jews, 32; and utopia, 25, 29, 50, 54, 56; and values, 101, 202–03n8
Zionist body, the, 13. *See also* Muscle Jew
Zionist Congress (Basel), 69
Zionist/Israeli narrative, 23, 85, 92, 186, 199; and biblical heroic tales, 184
Zizek, Slavoj, 135
Zohar, Uri, 13, 28, 51, 60, 129
Zurer, Ayelet, 96